THE IMPULSE OF FANTASY LITERATURE

The Impulse of
Fantasy Literature

C. N. Manlove

The Kent State University Press

Published in the United States by
THE KENT STATE UNIVERSITY PRESS
Kent, Ohio 44242

Printed in Hong Kong

Library of Congress Catalog Card No. 82–15335
ISBN 0–87338–273–0

Library of Congress Cataloging in Publication Data

Manlove, C. N. (Colin Nicholas), 1942–
  The impulse of fantasy literature.

  Includes bibliographical references and index.
  1. Fantastic fiction, English–History and
criticism.   2. Fantastic fiction, American–History
and criticism.   I. Title.
PR830.F3M28 1983   823′.0876′09   82–15335
ISBN 0–87338–273–0   AACR2

For John and David

Contents

Preface

Fantasy,* particularly in its modern form, exhibits a central and recurrent theme. This theme is its insistence on and celebration of the separate identities of created things. Other modern writers in other genres – John Ruskin, Gerard Manley Hopkins, Virginia Woolf or Alain Robbe-Grillet, for example – show a similar interest in the individual, but it is peculiarly pervasive in fantasy. And the concern of fantasy is not with the minutely faithful record for the sake of fidelity to fact, but with the sense of individuality that comes from making things strange and luminous with independent life in a fantastic setting. At the core of the genre is a delight in being, whether it be Charles Kingsley's sense of the miraculous in all physical nature in his *The Water-Babies*; George MacDonald's expression in his *Phantastes* and *Lilith* of the wonder of the reality seen by the unconscious mind; C. S. Lewis's transformation of the solar system into something rich and strange in his trilogy *Out of the Silent Planet*, *Perelandra* and *That Hideous Strength*; J. R. R. Tolkien's love of 'tree and grass; house and fire; bread and wine'[2] as portrayed in *The Lord of the Rings*; T. H. White's love of the image of the Middle Ages he creates in *The Once and Future King*; the search for lost wonder in Peter Beagle's *The Last Unicorn*; or the theme of the restoration of true being in Ursula Le Guin's *A Wizard of Earthsea*, *The Tombs of Atuan* and *The Farthest Shore*.

With this interest of fantasy in the uniqueness of things, it is perhaps understandable that the genre has flourished particularly in Britain and America, which are still generally distinguished among other countries for the scope they give to the individual, the personal and the local. But there are other more general

---

* Defined here as 'A fiction evoking wonder and containing a substantial and irreducible element of supernatural or impossible worlds, beings or objects with which the mortal characters in the story or the readers become on at least partly familiar terms.'[1]

factors behind the concern of fantasy with 'being', and particularly with the growth of the genre over the past two hundred years. Nineteenth-century fantasy can to some extent be seen as part of the larger tradition of Romanticism and late Romanticism, represented by such figures as Keats, Scott, Ruskin, Rossetti, Morris, Swinburne, Pater and Wilde. Many of these writers were, variously, in reaction against the effects of the Industrial Revolution, the advance of science, urbanisation and the general decline of religious certainty: they saw the consequence as a loss of individuality in men and their products, alienation of man from other men, nature and God, and, not least, an increasing inability to see phenomena for themselves rather than as means to an (usually utilitarian) end. They looked to the past, and particularly to an imagined medieval past, for an alternative society. Increasingly in the twentieth century, however, fantasy has become the main vehicle of this tradition and feeling, fuelled now by a perhaps even greater repugnance at the developments of science. But fantasy is always distinguished by its extensive use of the supernatural (which adds strangeness to the object); by the fact that since some of its worlds are the creations of Christians they are the product not merely of wish-fulfilment but of partial belief; and by its existence as a fictional narrative, rather than as direct instruction or isolated poetic intuition.

The celebrations of 'things as they are' in fantasy do not always originate from the same world-view, nor do they refer to the same 'things'. T. H. White's praise in his *The Once and Future King* is of an imaginary medieval world in which things are on the whole more beautiful, more idealistic and more poignant than his own. A similar nostalgia or escapist urge for greater beauty, wonder, excitement, or even for a supposed medieval order itself governs much fantasy, from the German Romantic writers of fairy tale to C. S. Lewis. And within such fantasies, 'common' things are enlivened by the exotic, as they in turn give credibility to the wonder: dragons and rain-showers in Ursula Le Guin, Lothlórien and Longbottom Leaf in Tolkien, afternoon tea and Ritual in Mervyn Peake. Indeed, such a fusion of the mundane and the marvellous is essential, for without it fantasy lacks any felt grip on reality and being. Other fantasies, however, celebrate this world, without going into a fantastic realm – for example, those of Charles Kingsley, T. F. Powys or

Charles Williams: instead they bring the 'supernatural' into this world.

For some fantasy writers existence is praiseworthy for itself. Their worlds and the beings in them, whether near to or remote from this world, are a source of delight to them without the need of any religious sanction. For them, 'being' is simply a good – though it is always a being enlivened by fantasy. Sometimes their enthusiasm is explicit and even alienating, as with E. R. Eddison or Anne McCaffrey; sometimes it is muted, implicit in the variety of the created world itself, as in Mervyn Peake's *Titus Groan*.

With other writers of fantasy, being is seen as a good within a Christian world-view. For George MacDonald the world is only seen aright when each flower, tree or creature is seen with the unconscious mind as a thought in the mind of God. Other writers of Christian fantasy allow 'nature' more independence from the divine. C. S. Lewis portrays this nature as one among a number of different natures, each with its own individuality and character:[3] this is the basis of his fantastic realm of Narnia, and in his *Perelandra* he makes the theme of proper independence from the creator, Maleldil, central. Charles Williams goes still further, seeing that 'Natural life produces a vision of beauties, energies, and glories about which the comments of the officers of the supernatural life seem anxiously inadequate.'[4] While for Williams, 'Nature and grace are categories of one Identity',[5] he does not expect that his readers should refer the glories of this world continuously back to a creator, but rather asks attention to the nature of the world itself as revealed by the 'supernatural' events of his novels. Charles Kingsley, in *The Water-Babies*, perhaps goes furthest of all here, for he in effect asks his readers simply to delight in the 'real' world of nature in the book, and only thereafter to look to a creator of it.[6]

Celebration of 'things as they are' in fantasy also refers to 'things as they were meant to be'. Many fantasies describe a spiritual development on the part of the hero at the same time as delighting in the constant nature of the world to which he belongs. The hero Anodos of George MacDonald's *Phantastes* is not so praiseworthy at the beginning as he is at the end: the story describes how he becomes more fully himself through a process of spiritual evolution. And the same can be said, in varying degrees and modes, of Thackeray's Giglio, Kingsley's Tom, the

Lady in Lewis's *Perelandra*, Tolkien's Frodo or Ursula Le Guin's Ged. But such change is only the dynamic aspect of 'things as they are': the self that is finally produced is the true self, the-self-as-it-ought-to-be; Cinderella's true beauty and worth come to be revealed.

Again, what is delighted in in fantasy is often not only the worlds themselves and what they contain, but the creation, the making of them. The concern is not only with being as product but with being in the making, and being which, when made, comes alive. Of course, this is a delight that is not restricted to writers of fantasy. But it has peculiar poignancy for the writer of fantasy, for he is, in making a fantasy at all, making a new nature, a new world: he has perhaps a special right to the term 'creator', however much the world he makes may partake of the one in which he lives. Indeed several writers of fantasy, such as Tolkien or Williams, see the worlds of fantasy as no less real than their own or any other. For Tolkien the joy of successful 'sub-creation' is at least as great as the recovery of a sense of the richness of being which is also the object of his fantasy:

> To the elvish craft, Enchantment, Fantasy aspires, and when it is successful of all forms of human art most nearly approaches. At the heart of many man-made stories of the elves lies, open or concealed, pure or alloyed, the desire for a living, realized sub-creative art.[7]

But overall, under whatever dispensation, and in whatever direction, the essence of fantasy is delight in the independent life of created things. Fantasy is fundamentally a panegyric genre. If it does not always operate on the assumption that this world is a good place, or that (as for MacDonald's Anodos) a great good is coming to all men, it certainly is full of the feeling that creation itself is of value; the great enemy of fantasy is nonentity. The object of the present book is to show some of the modes in which this interest manifests itself, and some of the problems to which it is subject.

The bulk of chapters 2, 4 and 6 originally appeared in *Mosaic* (1977 and 1979); much of chapter 3 in *Extrapolation* (1980); much of chapter 5 in *Studies in Scottish Literature* (1982); and much of chapter 7 in *The Mervyn Peake Review* (1980). I am grateful to the editors of these journals for permission to reprint. I am also grateful to William Collins Sons and Co. Ltd for permission to quote copyright material from *The Once and Future King* by T. H. White. I should like to thank Macmillan's reader for several helpful suggestions. And once again I am indebted to Mrs Sheila Campbell for the prodigious accuracy and speed of her typing.

The wonder-working done by good people, saints and friends of man, is almost always represented in the form of restoring things or people to their proper shapes . . . I do not say there are no exceptions; but this is the general tone of the tales about good magic. But, on the other hand, the popular tales about bad magic are specially full of the idea that evil alters and destroys the personality. The black witch turns a child into a cat or a dog; the bad magician keeps the Prince captive in the form of a parrot, or the Princess in the form of a hind; in the gardens of the evil spirits human beings are frozen into statues or tied to the earth as trees. In all such instinctive literature the denial of identity is the very signature of Satan. In that sense it is true that the true God is the God of things as they are – or, at least, as they were meant to be.

G. K. Chesterton, 'Wishes',
The Uses of Diversity

1 Introduction: Traditional and Modern Fantasy

Modern fantasy owes its existence in large part to the traditional fairy tale. The German Romantics at the turn of the eighteenth century – Goethe, Novalis, W. H. Wackenroder, Ludwig Tieck, E. T. A. Hoffmann, Clemens Brentano, F. de la Motte Fouqué – all looked to the traditional tale in their creation of their own 'Märchen' or fairy tales; and they themselves had a considerable influence on the interest in fairy tales throughout the nineteenth century. For many of them the fairy tale, based as it was on chance, frequent absence of causal connection and strange images and events, was the product of the unconscious imagination; and since that faculty was seen as the source of true vision into the nature of life, the fairy tale became a picture of the actual condition of existence. Thus Novalis could declare, 'Alles ist ein Mahrchen'; 'Im Mahrchen ist achte Naturanarchie'; 'Ein Mahrchen ist wie ein Traumbild ohne Zusammenhang. Ein Ensemble wunderbarer Dinge und Begebenheiten ... die Natur selbst' ('Everything is a fairy tale'; 'The genuine anarchy of nature is in the fairy tale'; 'A fairy tale is like a dream-picture without coherence, a collection of wonderful things and occurrences ... nature itself').[1] Hoffmann's *The Golden Pot* (1814) illustrates the point: the student Anselmus can only pierce beyond the monotony of his life to the real wonder of existence by seeing aright, with his imagination; whereupon the strange Archivarius Lindhorst and his magical house and daughter Serpentina become present to him in their true natures. Similarly with the later Scottish writer George MacDonald (who owes much to the German Romantics), the existence of fairy tale depends on true 'unconscious' seeing – as for example the magical old lady in *The Princess and the Goblin* (1872) brings the sceptical miner's son Curdie to realise.

Interest in the fairy tale was not wholly new: the views of the Romantics were partly the culmination of a growing, if reticent, fascination for things faërian and marvellous during the eighteenth century. Nor were the preoccupations of the German Romantic writers the sole source of the revival. At the same time a fresh sense of national identity was producing research by scholars into the folk-heritage of their lands. Perhaps the best known example of this is the work of the brothers J. and W. Grimm in the production of their two-volume *Kinder- und Hausmärchen* (Berlin, 1812–15; first English translation by Edgar Taylor, 2 vols, London, 1823–6). The work of the Grimms and of J. Musaeus earlier (translated into English by W. Beckford in 1791) with German folk literature stimulated scholars all over Europe to similar endeavours. In England, Weber, Jamieson and Scott's *Illustrations of Northern Antiquities, from the Earlier Teutonic and Scandinavian Romances* was published in 1814; T. Crofton Croker's *Fairy Legends and Traditions of the South of Ireland* came out in three volumes from 1825 to 1828; Thomas Keightley's *The Fairy Mythology: Illustrative of the Romance and Superstition of Various Countries*, in two volumes, in 1828; Joseph Ritson's *Fairy Tales* appeared in 1831; and the Rev. H. G. Keene's *Persian Fables for Young and Old* in 1833. Thereafter collections were increasingly directed at children, for example E. W. Lane's three-volume translation of the *Arabian Nights* (1839–41), which moralised the tales; Mary Howitt's translation of Hans Andersen's fairy tales, *Wonderful Stories for Children* (1846); Anthony Montalba's *Fairy Tales from all Nations* (1849); Ludwig Bechstein's *The Old Story Teller* (1854); Annie and Eliza Keary's retelling of Norse myths in *The Heroes of Asgard* (1857); or Sir George Webbe Dasent's *Popular Tales from the Norse* (1859).

Although the German Romantics and the scholar helped to give new status to the fairy tale, it was children and what was thought suitable reading matter for them that in England at least caused the explosion of its popularity. During the eighteenth century and the early part of the nineteenth, the fairy tale was repeatedly attacked as a corrupter of childhood by such moralists as Sarah Fielding or Mrs Laetitia Barbauld who, expressing a rationalist and empiricist outlook which had made itself felt in all save Christian contexts since Bacon, Hobbes and Locke in the seventeenth century, deplored the divergence of fairy tale from matters of fact and its violations of natural laws, its seemingly unlicensed imaginativeness and its relatively random attention to improving lessons for the benefit of the little men and women whom they saw as its potential readership. In 1831 a reviewer in *The Ladies Museum*, vol. 2 (1831) claimed: 'The days of Jack the Giant killer, Little Red Riding Hood, and such trashy productions, are gone by, and the infant mind is now nourished by more able and efficient food.'[2] Such denunciations of the fairy tale were stimulated by the fact that throughout the eighteenth century, from the time of Comtesse d'Aulnoy's *Contes de Fées* (trans. into English 1699), there had been frequent editions, originally intended for sophisticated adult taste, of fairy tale collections, such as Charles Perrault's *Histoires ou Contes de Tems Passé, avec des Moralités* (Paris, 1697; first English trans. 1729); Antoine Galland's translation of the *Arabian Nights* (Paris, 1704–7; trans. into English 1705–8); or the vast French fairy library, the *Cabinet des Fées*, 41 vols (Amsterdam, Paris and Geneva, 1785–9; quickly translated in chapbook selections). Many of these soon found their way through parental defences to children, if often only in crude chapbook versions; Coleridge has described his singular good fortune as a child in having an aunt who had a general store which sold books, so that the *Arabian Nights* and other fairy tales were more readily accessible to him than to his contemporaries.[3] But with the Romantics new value was put on the imagination and on the child as a child. There began a series of assaults on the opponents of the fairy tale by such figures as Coleridge, Lamb, Scott and Dickens to the point where the fairy tale began to be more accepted as the rightful property of the child – though the impulse to moralise through the tales endured long.[4] When this change had made itself felt, the first original fairy tales in English began to be written, starting with Catherine Sinclair's 'Uncle David's Nonsensical Story of Giants and Fairies' in her *Holiday House* (1839). Already by 1841 Ruskin had written *The King of the Golden River*, though significantly publication was delayed until 1851. Mark Lemon's *The Enchanted Doll* appeared in 1849.

Throughout the nineteenth century most fantasy tended to be written in the form of fairy tale for a child – Thackeray's *The Rose and the Ring* (1855); Frances Browne's *Granny's Wonderful Chair* (1857); Charles Kingsley's *The Water-Babies* (1863); C. L. Dodgson's *Alice's Adventures in Wonderland* (1865) and *Through the Looking-Glass* (1872); George MacDonald's *Dealings with the*

Fairies (1867), *At the Back of the North Wind* (1871), *The Princess and the Goblin* (1872), and *The Princess and Curdie* (1883) (though not his *Phantastes* (1858)); Jean Ingelow's *Mopsa the Fairy* (1869); the stories of Mrs J. H. Ewing and Mrs M. L. Molesworth; Andrew Lang's *Prince Prigio* (1889) and *Prince Ricardo of Pantouflia* (1893). Adult fantasy tended to be a modification of the Gothic novel into ghost and horror story, as in the writings of Edgar Allan Poe or J. Sheridan Le Fanu. By the 1880s adult fantasy proper and 'alternative world' or 'science' fiction began increasingly to be written, whether in the form of the comic fantasies of F. Anstey (Thomas Anstey Guthrie), Oscar Wilde's *The Picture of Dorian Gray* (1891), the late romances of William Morris, or H. G. Wells's science fiction novels.

The main writers of fantasy in the nineteenth century all look back very markedly to the traditional fairy tale: twentieth-century fantasy does so also, though not so much to the traditional tale directly as to writers already indebted to it, such as George MacDonald or Edith Nesbit. Whenever modern authors discuss fairy tales, they do so with profound admiration tinged with a longing to imitate the simplicity of the form. Describing the stages in the creation of his 'Narnia' books, C. S. Lewis writes how after the mental images or pictures from which he always began,

> came the Form. As these images sorted themselves into events (i.e., became a story) they seemed to demand no love interest and no close psychology. But the Form which excludes these things is the fairy tale. And the moment I thought of that I fell in love with the Form itself: its brevity, its severe restraints on description, its flexible traditionalism, its inflexible hostility to all analysis, digression, reflections and 'gas'. I was now enamoured of it. Its very limitations of vocabulary became an attraction; as the hardness of the stone pleases the sculptor or the difficulty of the sonnet delights the sonneteer.[5]

Tolkien, too, greatly admired the traditional tale, even if, like that of Lewis, his work does not always succeed in recapturing its character. But such tales are now part of the furniture of almost any writer's mind. There are now collections of the folk and fairy tales of every country in the world. And there have been and continue to be numerous translations, imitations and parodies of fairy tale, from the stories of Hans Andersen to Andrew Lang's *The Princess Nobody* (1884), Oscar Wilde's *The Happy Prince and Other Tales* (1888), E. Nesbit's *The Old Nursery Stories* (1908), Walter De La Mare's *Told Again* (1927), Wanda Gág's *Tales From Grimm* (1936), Barbara Leonie Picard's *The Mermaid and the Simpleton* (1949), James Thurber's *The 13 Clocks* (1951), the 'anti-'fairy tales of the American writers Robert Coover and Donald Barthelme, or Angela Carter's violent *The Bloody Chamber and Other Stories* (1979).

A simple comparison of a passage from Grimms' 'The Shoes that were Danced to Pieces' with the version of it in Walter De La Mare's *Told Again* will serve to show some of the basic differences between modern fairy story or fantasy and the traditional fairy tale. The story describes a king who has twelve beautiful daughters who, though their room is locked and barred at night, always appear in the morning with their shoes worn out from dancing. The king offers the hand of any one of his daughters to whoever can discover within three days where they go at night. Many princes try and fail because, unknown to them, they are given a sleeping draught by the daughters each night. Meanwhile an old soldier travelling home from the wars meets an aged woman who tells him of the drugged drink and offers him a cloak of invisibility, upon which he resolves to make the attempt himself. When the princesses give him the drink, he secretly disposes of it and then pretends to be asleep. At midnight, while he is apparently snoring, the princesses rise from their beds, dress themselves in rich clothes, open a concealed trapdoor in the floor, and set off down it; but the soldier is following. Eventually they come to a lake with a castle on the opposite side of it, and twelve boats and twelve handsome princes waiting on the near shore. Each princess gets into a boat, but the soldier goes into the boat with the youngest princess, and all set off. Grimms' version continues thus:

> Then her [the youngest princess's] prince said, 'I can't tell why the boat is so much heavier to-day; I shall have to row with all my strength, if I am to get it across.' 'What should cause that,' said the youngest, 'but the warm weather? I feel very warm too.'[6]

This is De La Mare's rendering:

Then the Princes rowed away softly across the water towards an island that was in the midst of the lake, where was a Palace, its windows shining like crystal in the wan light that bathed sky and water.

Only the last of the boats lagged far behind the others, for the old soldier sitting there invisible on the thwart, though little else but bones and sinews, weighed as heavy as a sack of stones in the boat. At last the youngest of the Princes leaned on his oars to recover his breath. 'What', he sighed, 'can be amiss with this boat to-night? It never rowed so heavily.'

The youngest of the Princesses looked askance at him with fear in her eyes, for the boat was atilt with the weight of the old soldier and not trimmed true. Whereupon she turned her small head and looked towards that part of the boat where sat the old soldier, for there it dipped deepest in the water. In so doing, she gazed straight into his eyes, yet perceived nothing but the green water beyond. He smiled at her, and – though she knew not why – she was comforted. 'Maybe,' she said, turning to the Prince again and answering what he had said – 'maybe you are wearied because of the heat of the evening.' And he rowed on.[7]

Clearly the second passage sets the scene much more fully than the first. In Grimms' the concern is only with what happened next, and with cause and effect: the prince asks why the boat feels heavier, the princess offers a brief answer, and they row on. And this is true of the traditional tale generally: each item is only of interest as it furthers the one before. De La Mare stops to contemplate, to describe the wan light, the crystal windows of the palace, the princess's small head, the boat lagging and listing in the water. He portrays physical scenes and psychological states for themselves, almost in isolation. Very vivid is the picture of the boat leaning over where the invisible soldier sits; and vivid too the picture of the princess gazing straight into the soldier's eyes before this potential contact between them is removed once more by the 'perceived nothing but the green water beyond' – yet not wholly dispelled, for in a subtle way she has been reassured by the soldier's smile. In De La Mare's story people act upon one another, where in Grimms' events and characters tend to fit in with one another in a broad design.[8]

There is no mention in Grimms' version of how the other

boats pulled ahead, and the prince appears to feel the weight of the boat before starting out. But because De La Mare describes the boats rowing towards the island, and then says that the last boat lagged behind, the forward movement of the narrative is literally reversed as the reader is returned across the lake to the laden boat. There is a similar shift in time at the end of the passage when, after her long gaze at the dipping side of the boat, the princess speaks, 'turning to the Prince again and answering what he had said', which sends the reader back a paragraph to what the prince did say. Rarely does this kind of retrospection occur in traditional tales, where each event simply looks forward to the next. When the spindle in 'The Sleeping Beauty' has done its work, it is of no further interest; when Cinderella has become queen, her past life is forgotten.

There is even room for a form of literary effect in De La Mare's version: the reader is made aware of the boat suspended heavily on the water, and the slowness and backtracking of the passage could themselves be seen as enacting the slowness of the boat – even the repetition in 'for the boat was atilt with the weight of the old soldier and not trimmed true' could be taken to further this. Yet it is also true that De La Mare's passage gives a much more gradualist picture of psychological movement than that in Grimms'. Not till well under way does the prince notice the increased weight in the boat consciously, and the princess is shown coming gradually to her answer to his question: first there is her sight of the dipping of the boat, and then her eventual reassurance from mysterious causes.

Overall what is present in the modern retelling is the sense of a mind creating, reflecting on and delighting in the scene.[9] This element of consciousness is fundamental to the element of wonder in modern fairy tale. Wonder there is in traditional tale, but it is not lingered over – the trees of silver, gold and diamonds that the soldier encounters as he follows the princesses are in no way described.

This difference between traditional and modern fairy tale or fantasy can be further explored by comparison between Grimms' tales and an early Victorian fantasy which owes much to the traditional tale – Thackeray's *The Rose and the Ring* (1855). In traditional fairy tales supernatural gifts can be conferred in return for apparent trifles. In 'Donkey Cabbages'[10] an ugly old woman stops a huntsman and asks him for money for food and drink: when the huntsman takes pity on her and gives her what he can afford, she tells him how he may gain a cloak which will take him wherever he wishes, and a bird's heart which will provide him with a gold piece every morning. Clearly her request of the huntsman is purely an initiatory test, since she could with the magic objects have got all she wanted without his help.[11] Again, in 'The Golden Goose',[12] the hero Dummling, who unlike his brothers shares his food and drink with a dwarf he meets in the forest, is rewarded with a golden goose which eventually leads him to possession of a kingdom. Sometimes this introductory test is waived altogether. In 'The Devil with the Three Golden Hairs',[13] the Devil's grandmother discovers for the hero the three secrets of her monstrous relative and also plucks and gives to him the three hairs, whereby he gains wealth, a kingdom, a queenly bride and revenge on a royal enemy, all for nothing. The soldier in 'The Shoes that were Danced to Pieces' is helped by the old woman for no reward; De La Mare's version has him ingeniously catch her straying pig for her. The partiality of traditional fairy tales for youngest (and often seemingly weakest) sons and daughters is striking:[14] in 'The Three Feathers',[15] for example, it is purely the fact that the hero is the youngest and seemingly the most stupid of three sons that earns him success in the three tasks set, and the consequent reward of his father's kingdom.

In traditional tales there is often no explanation for the details of a story either. For example, the reader is not told why, in order to disenchant her husband the lion-prince, the heroine of 'The Singing, Soaring Lark'[16] must go to the Red Sea, where he is fighting with a dragon-princess, take the eleventh of a group of rods growing on the right shore of that sea, and strike the dragon with it. Nor is it clear why it should be a spindle in particular that in 'Little Briar-Rose'[17] causes the hundred-year sleep of the princess and all the court. The peculiar terms of trials or punishments seem often irrelevant to their objects. There is no explanation of what use it can be to a king, or of what congruity to gaining a kingdom, for the three sons in 'The Three Feathers' to have to compete to find the most beautiful carpet, ring and woman in existence, and for the ladies so discovered to compete at jumping through a ring hanging from the ceiling in the old king's hall. Magic objects are often incongruous with the actions they perform: the bird's heart in 'Donkey Cabbages', when eaten, produces a gold piece under the hero's pillow every morning; the apples in 'The Nose' fantastically enlarge the noses of all who eat them.[18]

The modern fairy tale or fantasy tends on the other hand to justify and explain. In *The Rose and the Ring* the role of the supernatural as fairy godmother and moral tutor provides a reason for its every action. At their christenings, Fairy Blackstick wishes upon both Princess Rosalba and Prince Giglio, her god-children, '"*a little misfortune*"'* because all her past christening gifts have been of no use to the spiritual welfare of their owners, and this in particular is what she wants to develop. Remarking the failure of her gifts of Rose and Ring, each of which beautifies the owners, to the infant wives-to-be of King Savio and Duke Padella, she comments:

'I gave them each a present, which was to render them charming in the eyes of their husbands, and secure the affection of those gentlemen as long as they lived. What good did my Rose and my Ring do these two women? None on earth. From having all their whims indulged by their husbands, they became capricious, lazy, ill-humoured, absurdly vain, and leered, and languished, and fancied themselves irresistibly beautiful, when they were really quite old and hideous, the ridiculous creatures! They used actually to patronize me when I went to pay them a visit.' (p. 12)

In the story the Rose and the Ring serve a more educative purpose. They do not (till the end) remain in the possession of one person. Thus Prince Giglio falls in love with Angelica, Rosalba and the repulsive lady-in-waiting Gruffanuff when they in turn have the Ring. All this – as with the doting lovers in Shakespeare's *A Midsummer Night's Dream* and the magic flower of Love-in-Idleness in that play – symbolises his spiritual ignorance, his lack of education in matters of the heart as much as of the head. When at the end he loves Rosalba for herself without magic aid, the reader knows he has reached wisdom. The supernatural objects are thus part of a moral pattern.

In *The Rose and the Ring* supernatural objects and actions are

---

* Mr M. A. Titmarsh [pseud. of W. M. Thackeray], *The Rose and the Ring; or, The History of Prince Giglio and Prince Bulbo, A Fireside Pantomime for Great and Small Children* (Smith, Elder and Co., 1855) pp. 12, 13. Page references hereafter are to this edition.

also clearly related to their functions. There is no more fitting punishment for the porter Jenkins Gruffanuff's impertinent door-keeping when Fairy Blackstick visits the Paflagonian palace, than that he should himself become a knocker, a door-knocker: and Thackeray enjoys a further pun on the situation, 'He *was* turned into metal! He was from being *brazen, brass!*' (p. 18).[19] Faced by the problem of how, in the traditional version of 'Hop o' my Thumb', the giant's seven-league boots fitted the tiny hero, Perrault rationalised:[20] and Thackeray acts similarly by making Giglio's magic bag extend when it has to hold objects as large as a sword, and by making the prince's trunk the container for other and still larger objects provided magically – the books for study first, and later the helmet and suit of armour (pp. 89, 93). The magic Rose and Ring suggest beauty and love respectively, and that is what in fact the first produces in its owner, and the second inspires in the beholder.

Supernatural action is made proportionate to desert and need. There is an episode in *The Rose and the Ring* which at first sight is directly reminiscent of those disproportionate supernatural gifts conferred in traditional tales. When Giglio is about to escape in a public coach from Paflagonia and his uncle's revenge, an ordinary-looking woman with a cough approaches, and is told by the coachman that she must spend the journey on the exposed top of the vehicle. Giglio at once gives up his seat to her. For this, the woman reveals herself as the Fairy Blackstick, and gives him a magic bag which will supply his every wish (pp. 85–6). Yet here the resemblance between Thackeray's treatment and that to be found in the traditional tale ends. In the latter, the episode alone would explain the magic gifts, but in *The Rose and the Ring* greater and more compelling reasons than a single act of kindness are behind Blackstick's generosity. In this story it is not merely Giglio's chivalry, but the fact that he *is* Giglio, rightful heir to the usurped throne of Paflagonia and persecuted lover of Rosalba, which makes the fairy intervene. She is concerned not only to better the fortunes of the prince himself, but – so far as the seriousness of the story goes – to re-establish the spiritual health of two kingdoms: she thus fulfils the role of guardian and educative angel in Thackeray's story. For this reason she not only gives Giglio a magic bag in the coach (the contents of which, incidentally, from bootbrushes to the sword, are always exactly proportioned to his day-to-day needs): she also gives him some good advice, and directs him to a year's course of study which will remove his considerable ignorance and fit him to be a king. This concern is in contrast to traditional fairy tales, where the interest is usually only in the means by which the hero becomes a king and not in his fitness to govern.

At the end of the story, when with the help of the magic bag Giglio has won the battle against King Padella of Crim Tartary and saved Rosalba, he becomes proud and tires of Fairy Blackstick, beginning to think that he has won by his own efforts. Her advice to him on how 'in all respects, to be a good King' (p. 119) irritates him, and he feels that he can do without her counsel. The fairy, therefore, will not help him when he is forced, on production of a past written promise, to agree to marry the hideous Gruffanuff instead of Rosalba. But when the pride of Giglio is humbled, and he has accepted his fate, Blackstick saves the situation. Thus a web of moral concern and justice can be traced throughout *The Rose and the Ring*.

Beside the emphasis on proportion, sense and moral value, there is nevertheless a strong element of the absurd in Thackeray's story. For instance, the reader learns of Fairy Blackstick that she

> had scores of royal godchildren; turned numberless wicked people into beasts, birds, millstones, clocks, pumps, bootjacks, umbrellas, or other absurd shapes; and in a word was one of the most active and officious of the whole College of fairies. (p. 11)

But this absurdity is only formally to be linked with the incongruities in the traditional fairy tale. What is present here is creative delight or play, the author enjoying extending the possibilities of his medium. This expresses itself in comic form, parody (of the traditional tale and the contemporary writer of melodramatic historical romance G. P. R. James) and conceit.

The entire story is shot through with exaggeration and caricature. Emotions expressed for characters in possession of the magic Rose or Ring are shown to be suspect by being preposterously overpitched. When Rosalba (known only at this stage as Betsinda the chambermaid) is wearing the magic Ring, Giglio declares:

> 'Oh, divine Betsinda! ... how have I lived fifteen years in thy company without seeing thy perfections? What woman in all Europe, Asia, Africa, and America, nay, in Australia, only it is

not yet discovered, can presume to be thy equal? Angelica? Pish! Gruffanuff? Phoo! The Queen? Ha, ha! Thou art my Queen. Thou art the real Angelica, because thou art really angelic.' (p. 53)

Bulbo is no less ridiculous in his amorous protestations (p. 51). Giglio's later dissertation on his past history to his student friends Jones and Smith similarly deflates itself (pp. 92–3) – though at this point Thackeray's comic zest has overflowed the moral bounds of the story, since Giglio's actual sentiments are here meant to be more accurate.

This zest expresses itself also in the ludicrous actions of the story. The vision of the jealous Bulbo tearing 'quantities of hair out of his head, till it covered the room like so much tow' (p. 53) shows Thackeray carrying on from Fielding's Partridge or Smollett's Strap. When Angelica hears that her beloved Bulbo is to be executed, and falls in a faint at the breakfast table, her father has a simple remedy: '"Turn the cock of the urn upon her Royal Highness", said the King, and the boiling water gradually revived her' (p. 67). At his battle with King Padella of Crim Tartary, Giglio has a magic sword which can lengthen and run through whole regiments at once, not to mention armour which shines blindingly with jewels, and is 'water-proof, gun-proof, and sword-proof' (pp. 113–14). With the added help of a magic horse which can gallop at any pace, Giglio pursues Padella, 'And, with his fairy sword, which elongated itself at will, his Majesty kept poking and prodding Padella in the back, until that wicked monarch roared with anguish' (p. 115). This cartoon performance continues when Padella finds that as he strikes Giglio with his colossal battle-axe, the weapon shrivels like butter on the magic armour of the prince.

The superb illustrations which Thackeray himself drew for *The Rose and the Ring* provide extra caricature of many of the characters, and also serve to bring out the grotesque in particular situations. The picture which attends the bending of King Valoroso's nose by Giglio (who hits him with a warming pan) is brilliant (p. 55). Later, when Rosalba rejects him, Count Hogginarmo of Crim Tartary flies into a great rage and 'kicking the two negroes [his servants] before him, he rushed away, his whiskers streaming in the wind' (p. 80): an apt illustration shows two rather melancholy negroes flying through the air before the mailed boot of their enraged master.

Thackeray constantly makes the reader aware of his presence as a mocking 'omniscient narrator' standing between him and the story, in the manner of his admired Fielding:[21] the tale becomes the expression of a particular consciousness. He describes Rosalba's dungeon in Crim Tartary as

> a most awful black hole, full of bats, rats, mice, toads, frogs, mosquitoes, bugs, fleas, serpents, and every kind of horror. No light was let into it ... [But] the toads in the dungeon came and kissed her feet, and the vipers wound round her neck and arms, and never hurt her, so charming was this poor Princess in the midst of her misfortunes.
>
> At last, after she had been kept in this place *ever so long* ... (pp. 81–2)

The shrill hyperbole of the opening list and the absurd pathetic fallacies which follow underline the lack of seriousness: the colloquial *'ever so long'* further deflates the scene. Thackeray is fond of sharing sly remarks about his characters with the reader. Of the portrait of the hideous Gruffanuff he asks, 'Would you not fancy, from this picture, that Gruffanuff must have been a person of the highest birth?' (p. 9). He remarks of Rosalba's distribution of honours to the members of her Army of Fidelity, 'you can't think how they quarrelled!' (p. 77). At the end of the story, with Gruffanuff foiled and everyone rejoicing that Giglio can now marry Rosalba, Thackeray adds, 'and as for Giglio, I leave you to imagine what *he* was doing, and if he kissed Rosalba once, twice – twenty thousand times, I'm sure I don't think he was wrong' (p. 128).

The reader himself is, as it were, thrown into consciousness by being given an ironic perspective on the characters. The story is told from a variety of points of view: the world is seen in turn through the eyes of Giglio, Bulbo, Valoroso and Gruffanuff. Further, the reader knows facts which are concealed from the other characters. For a long time only he knows the effects of the Ring, which first Angelica and then Gruffanuff cast so lightly aside (pp. 39, 50), and only he and Bulbo know the power of the Rose the latter carries – which gives special piquancy to the scene where Bulbo drops it, and when Angelica picks it up, he cannot, out of politeness, ask her to give it back again (pp. 69–

70). Similarly, only the reader knows that Fairy Blackstick has transformed Jenkins Gruffanuff into a door-knocker, and only he can fully appreciate the ironic reversal at the end when Jenkins is restored to his human form in time for his presence to save Giglio from enforced marriage to the supposedly widowed Gruffanuff. This sort of perspective is rarely provided in traditional fairy tale (though 'Little Snow-White' is a notable exception): usually there is only one point of view, that of the protagonist: the reader stays with him on his adventures and is not possessed of knowledge which he is without. In Thackeray's story the ironic mode can also be related to the theme of the story, which concerns the education of Giglio: when all is revealed and known at the end, so too he is 'knowing', his learning is complete and he can become king. Such artistic sophistication and overt concern with significance have no place in the traditional fairy tale.

As with De La Mare's story, what essentially distinguishes Thackeray's *The Rose and the Ring* from the traditional fairy tale is the presence of consciousness. It is here a consciousness which makes actions reasonable, moral, proportionate and comprehensible; which directly delights in its own creation; which engages in parody or imitation of other literary forms; which makes the reader aware of the personality of the author; which bestows significance on the story; which gives the narrative a sophisticated form imitating the content; which uses irony; and which throws the reader on his own consciousness. In a word, mind is separate from material: and the separation produces all the delight and organisation that have been seen. Naturally, such separation of mind does not occur in the same degree in all modern fantasies. In the fairy tales of the German Romantics and of George MacDonald particularly, can be found an attempt on the part of the writer to remove all his consciousness and become wholly one with his material in a kind of mystical self-surrender. But that aim in itself expresses the gulf felt, and indeed often fails of its object inasmuch as the conscious mind obtrudes.[22] In all modern fantasies the sense of a distance, and thus of a *relationship*, between the writer and his material, towards which he continually strives is permanent: and this is the basic condition from which the overt concern with wonder in all its forms is generated.

2 Fantasy as Praise: Charles Williams

Charles Williams's novels offer a striking individual instance of that simple praise of the identities of things which is the spring from which all the other aspects of fantasy considered in this book flow. In the case of Williams the praise and wonder are directed not so much at the creations of fantasy in themselves, as at this world as irradiated by them. His vision of reality is of an ordered dance in which all things, from the most evil to the most good, and from the most magnificent to the most sordid, offer in their own modes delight to the beholder and praise to the Creator. The ground of such delight and praise is for him the incarnational fact of Christ.

Williams's view of the universe was similar to that held by medieval and Renaissance theologians – ordered, hierarchical, ceremonial, inter-correspondent, a 'web of diagrammatized glory, of honourable beauty, of changing and interchanging adoration'.[1] Williams loved ceremony and order: he saw the essence of being as organic form. He agreed with Plato that '"God always geometrizes"';[2] in his *Thomas Cranmer of Canterbury* Cranmer is told of Heaven that there are 'none there to escape/ into the unformed shadow of mystery mere,/but find a strong order, a diagram clear'.[3] The more complex and highly wrought the form, the more fully it expresses God: it is evil that loses form and coherence. This is in large part why Williams deals with very elaborate patterns of supernatural being and action in his novels. Yet extreme complexity is simultaneously ultimate simplicity: the simple Unity that is the Stone made of the First Matter of Creation in *Many Dimensions* contains an infinite number of universes within it.

For Williams the universe existed by a kind of continuous charity which he called 'the Co-inherence', whereby each thing was most truly itself when giving itself for another. All things are inter-dependent; the universe is essentially civil, a 'City' or 'Republic'. All men owe their being to a woman who made herself a place for them before they were born; they depend on others for their food, and those others depend on them for the money that enables them to go on producing it; buildings rely on the law of gravity to remain standing. Thus seen, the condition of being is essentially one of exchange, whereby no-one can exist without giving and receiving from others. Of course man can refuse to exchange, as Adam refused to give himself back to God at the Fall; on the other hand he may choose to participate in the great supernatural act of exchange which restored to men the co-inherent nature of being that was lost with Adam – Christ's Incarnation, Passion, Death and Resurrection. As Williams sees it, living in the former mode man chooses to cut himself off increasingly from the universe; living by exchange he immerses himself more fully in it. Exchange is of the essence of God, and in God all places and times are eternally co-present, so that there Adam's sin and Christ's suffering are contemporary with the deeds of men today: hence, within the co-inherent web of divine charity, and through divine working in the soul, a man can give spiritual help to people far removed from him in space or time.[4] The vision of exchange explains why Williams's novels have not one isolated protagonist, but two or more friends or 'Companions of the Co-inherence'[5] acting together; and why, too (in contrast to such a figure as Bunyan's Christian, who develops his faith in isolation and lives for his personal salvation), the actions of the good are always for and towards others.

With the possible exception of *Descent into Hell* (1937) all the novels* subsume a basic pattern in which the supernatural makes its presence felt, for good or ill, in the domain of the natural before being removed. In *Shadows of Ecstasy* (written 1929; published 1933), a Lawrentian prophet of the passionate self of man, Nigel Considine, offers spiritual power to mankind, particularly the ability to direct human energy to the point of triumphing over death; on the verge of imposing his vision on the world through the victory of the African armies he controls, he is killed by a corrupt follower. In *War in Heaven* (1930) the Holy

---

* Page references are to the Faber editions of the novels – *All Hallows' Eve* (1945), *Descent into Hell* (1949), *War in Heaven* (1962), *Many Dimensions* (1963), *The Greater Trumps* (1964) and *The Place of the Lion* (1965).

Graal [*sic*] is found in modern England and is finally removed by its supernatural guardian, Prester John, when evil magicians seek to bend its powers to their own use. This pattern recurs in *Many Dimensions* (1931) and *The Place of the Lion* (1931) in which, respectively, a magic stone capable of healing and of moving people through time and space, and animal forms of the principles sustaining creation appear; here the removal of these intruders is carried out by mortals who make themselves willing agents of supernatural action. In *The Greater Trumps* (1932) the original pack of Tarot cards, made supernaturally by and in the image of the Cosmic Dance, and containing the power of the elements, the humours and such truths as Death, Love and Wisdom, appears and has to be controlled when misguided people let loose its energies. *All Hallows' Eve* (1945) describes the attempt of an evil modern magician, Simon Leclerc, to gain power in the realm of the afterlife: he is eventually destroyed when a mistake causes his magic to reverse itself until he is devoured by it, and thus the dead are once more separated from the living. A similar theme of propitiation of the vexed spirit occurs in *Descent into Hell*, where Pauline Anstruther is able to take upon herself the sufferings of a martyred ancestor, and her grandmother helps a contemporary suicide.

Williams's interest in the theme of a supernatural invasion of the world stems in part from his sense of how much, within the divine 'Co-inherence', the 'natural' is already shot through with the supernatural. But the fact that the supernatural 'invaders' are in a peculiarly extreme and disorderly condition is also used to highlight the delicate balance and pattern of the world in its 'normal' state. Further, the theme of invasion can be used to create another and larger pattern: its appearance often makes necessary Christ-like acts of vicariousness on the part of the protagonist of the novels to ensure the continued health of the world or simply of others. In *War in Heaven* the Archdeacon offers to sacrifice himself for his friends; in *Many Dimensions* Chloe Burnett accepts death by making herself a way for the magic Stone to be at one with its Maker; in *The Greater Trumps* Nancy and Sybil Coningsby act to protect their friends from the consequences of their having released the power of the magic Tarots; in *The Place of the Lion* Damaris Tighe, together with the Lamb, saves Quentin Sabot from his embodied supernatural terror; and in *Descent into Hell* and *All Hallows' Eve* characters take on themselves the physical and spiritual pains of others. In this way Williams's stories re-enact what was for him the central narrative of Christianity: the pattern they follow is a ritual one; and from a sacramental, or 'co-inherent' point of view, they *partake in* the story told in the Gospels.

The emphasis in Williams's novels is on the glory as revealed in this world. Williams never introduces other planets or worlds: he writes almost within a Ptolemaic conception of the universe, with the earth at the centre. (It is worth contrasting him here with the multi-centred universe in the work of his friend C. S. Lewis.) Things come in from 'outside' to the little, everyday English worlds of a Charles Williams novel: no-one goes on a journey in quest of them. Nor is the 'supernatural' (the term is of limited value to Williams) wholly 'other' or alien in the novels: it is often a (dangerous) crystallisation or concretion of 'natural' forces at work immanently within the known world – forces such as strength, subtlety, beauty, death, law, exchange, balance, wisdom. As such it may have to be removed, but it also reveals while present the true character of the reality in which this world participates. In short, it serves the purpose of transfiguration: it highlights the co-presence of the supernatural in the natural and of the absolute in the contingent. Hence, for example, the archetypal beasts of *The Place of the Lion*, which are found to be the principles sustaining life (see for example pp. 182–91); hence too the kind of perception evinced by Nancy Coningsby in *The Greater Trumps*, when she realises that the magic Tarots themselves 'were not more marvellous than the ordinary people she had so long unintelligently known' (p. 191).

This motif of transfiguration is also present in the novels in the way that a character may suddenly be seen in terms of the office he fills, and his office in the light of the eternal principle it embodies. This is the case throughout *Many Dimensions*, in the form of the Lord Chief Justice Arglay. In *The Place of the Lion* Anthony Durrant sees in the features of the local doctor, Rockbotham, the lineaments of Aesculapius (pp. 196–7); a patient railway porter in *All Hallows' Eve* expresses 'Golden-thighed Endurance, sun-shrouded Justice' (p. 76); a traffic policeman in *The Greater Trumps* appears to Nancy Coningsby as the Emperor of Trumps from the Tarot Pack,

helmed, in a white cloak, stretching out one sceptred arm, as if

Charlemagne, or one like him, stretched out his controlling sword over the tribes of Europe pouring from the forests and bade them pause or march as he would. The great roads ran below him, to Rome, to Paris, to Aix, to Byzantium, and the nations established themselves in cities upon them. The noise of all the pausing street came to her as the roar of many peoples; the white cloak held them by a gesture; order and law were there. It moved, it fell aside, the torrent of obedient movement flowed on, and they with it. (pp. 55–6; see also pp. 56–7)

Acts, too, are transfigured, as Lester Furnivall in *All Hallows' Eve* comes to see the simple action of her husband's bringing her water when she was thirsty at night:

and in her drowsiness a kind of vista of innumerable someones doing such things for innumerable someones stretched before her, but it was not as if they were being kind, for it was not water that they were bringing but their own joy, or perhaps it was water and joy at once ... [It] was a deed of such excelling merit on his part that all the choirs of heaven and birds of earth could never properly sing its praise. (p. 147)

Within the co-inherent web of the universe as Williams portrays it any being or act partakes in and dances with others of its kind in a ceremonial transcending time and place.

Similarly the characters of the novels can, through the exchanges made possible in the web of Co-inherence of which this world is a part, share in the nature of Christ or Adam or even Satan. Perhaps the most striking example of this is Anthony's transformation into Adam for the naming of the beasts that occurs at the end of *The Place of the Lion*. Again, as Lester takes Betty's sufferings on herself in *All Hallows' Eve* she feels herself sustained on a frame of wood (pp. 143–4). Gregory Persimmons in *War in Heaven* becomes for a time one with the nature of the devil; 'He was hungry – but not for food; he was thirsty – but not for drink; he was filled with passion – but not for flesh. He expanded in the rush of an ancient desire; he longed to be married to the whole universe for a bride'; he gains for a moment 'ecstasy of perfect mastery, marriage in hell, he who was Satan married to that beside which was Satan' (pp. 75, 76). The characteristic mode of Williams's novels might be described as one in which the human characters increasingly appear as actors in some great and eternal drama. From the standpoint of God, in whom all time is eternally present, 'It is finished; we ... do but play out the necessary ceremony.'[6]

The seemingly random is always part of a larger pattern, since everything exists within the Cosmic Dance. In *The Place of the Lion* the house in which the magician Berringer establishes a way for the Principles to enter our world is called The Joinings, and in a medium where good and evil are as it were precipitated out of solution we learn that Anthony Durrant is editor of a journal called *The Two Camps*; further, the names Foster, Wilmot, Durrant, Rockbotham and 17 Bypath Villas (the house of Richardson, the man of the mystical 'negative way') are not allegorical description, but divine truth. Sybil Coningsby in *The Greater Trumps* turns out to be 'a sibyl indeed' (pp. 53–4, 111), and the office of her brother Lothair as a Warden in Lunacy is neither accident nor artifice in a world where the central supernatural figure is that of the Fool of the Tarots. Similarly, apparently casual conversations can take on profound significance.[7]

The character of the universe is also expressed in the formal or diagrammatic mode by which the supernatural appears, exists and acts, and in the correspondingly ordered way in which the human characters have to come to an understanding of it. The Principles in *The Place of the Lion* appear in regular sequence: first the Lion, then the Serpent, the Butterfly, the Eagle, the Horse, the Unicorn, the Phoenix and the Lamb. Each Principle has its place in an elaborate dance, some apparently moving in spirals, others hovering, others rushing and falling, or simply staying still. In sequence they gradually extend their influence over the world they have invaded, each by gradual stages taking to itself the quality it is: creation goes into reverse, and particulars, instead of streaming out from universals, are pulled back. Yet even the mode of pulling happens formally as a dance. When the world's butterflies converge on the garden of Berringer's house to be united with their Archetype, Anthony Durrant sees them coming in in sweeping, multicoloured flights that eventually one after the other hover above the Principle, 'which rushed up towards them, and then, carrying a whirl of lesser iridescent fragilities with it, precipitated itself down its deep descent; and as it swept, and hovered, and again mounted, silent and unresting, it was alone' (p. 41).

The absorption of the world by the Principles follows certain laws. Those things most like themselves, or most purely beautiful or strong or subtle, are engulfed first, as the Principle that is Beauty draws the butterflies to itself and the Principle of Strength a lioness. The Principles also soon consume those people who have made themselves most like them in some aspect, as the power-seeking Foster is taken over by the Lion, and the scheming Miss Wilmot is turned physically into a serpent (pp. 114–16, 151–2). As the hold of these Archetypes over this world increases, it becomes clear to Anthony that all men who are not the harmony and balance of *all* the Principles that they ought to be – by which he means almost all men – will in time be drawn into that Universal to which they are most disposed. Meanwhile the archetypal Lion of the first circle of influence reaches the point of absorbing the strength of human artefacts. Here too there are precise gradations, a formality of action. Sections of railway crumble to dust, steel bends, wood snaps, hammers go awry, houses fall down. The disturbance affects a complete arc of the town of Smetham in which the novel is set: but initially it touches only those constructs which are not closely bound to human life by ties of constant use or love. Later, however, even inhabited buildings begin to be destroyed, and Anthony foresees the eventual result of the actions of the first and second, or Leonine and Serpentine, circles as a 'town full of a crowd of expressionless gaping mindless creatures, physical and mental energy passing out of them' (p. 155).

In *The Place of the Lion* and *The Greater Trumps* the fact that there is a *group* of supernatural objects supposes some kind of pattern amongst the various elements; and in the latter novel this is specifically portrayed as a continual movement which expresses the Cosmic Dance. In *Many Dimensions*, where there is only one magic object (if one capable of being infinitely multiplied), a different kind of order is portrayed. Here the concern is with the operation of precise, 'mathematical' logic through the Stone. This is particularly seen in the relation of its workings to time: if, by its means, someone wishes to be transported twelve hours into the past, he will remain in a constant temporal loop, for every time he returns to 'the present' it will be to find himself wishing himself twelve hours back again.

Faced by such logical behaviour, the characters themselves have to employ logic to overcome it – though humility is also needed. Indeed, if not logic, a peculiarly analytic approach is required of Williams's characters in understanding the nature and operation of the magic with which they are faced; the novels have often been compared to detective fiction, and one of them, *War in Heaven*, is in part concerned with a police inquiry into a murder. There is a passion for accuracy. In *The Place of the Lion* Anthony Durrant's friend Quentin wishes that Anthony would calm his fears by telling him that the strange lion they saw was really only a lioness that had escaped from a nearby zoo, but Anthony cannot do this:

> Quentin shrank back in his chair and Anthony cursed himself for being such a pig-headed precisian. But still, was it any conceivable good pretending – if the intellect had any authority at all? if there were any place for accuracy? In personal relationships it might, for dear love's sake, sometimes be necessary to lie, so complicated as they often were. But this, so far as Anthony could see, was a mere matter of a line to left or to right upon the wall, and his whole mind revolted at falsehood upon abstract things. It was like an insult to a geometrical pattern. (p. 48)

Later he reflects, 'Why did he always ask himself these silly questions? Always intellectualizing, he thought, always trying to find a pattern. Well, and why not? If Foster was right, every man – he himself – was precisely a pattern of these powers' (p. 71). It is the discovery of such patterns on which the protagonists, and even the antagonists, of *Many Dimensions*, *The Greater Trumps* and *The Place of the Lion* are engaged: they make the universe in each book progressively more intelligible. At the same time the style of the novels always aims at intellectual accuracy and definition.

In Williams's later novels *Descent into Hell* and *All Hallows' Eve*, there are no magic Graals, Stones, Principles or Cards. Where the earlier books are concerned more to portray the *being* of the living co-inherent web of the universe, the later ones show rather the *doings* of the web. Being and doing were for Williams interchangeable, 'categories of one Identity',[8] but that identity could be portrayed under its different aspects; further, 'The pattern of the glory is a pattern of acts.'[9] This pattern is portrayed in *Descent into Hell* and *All Hallows' Eve* in the acts of exchange. In *Descent into Hell*, where the central theme could be said to be acceptance or refusal of exchange, there are, on the one hand, those such as the historian Wentworth who progressively renounce relations with other people to the point where they are in hell; and, on the other, those such as Pauline Anstruther who learn to give themselves to and for others. What these acts variously portray is the nature and working of the Co-inherence through Christ. In *All Hallows' Eve* the Co-inherence is imaged in the City (here London), which in its webs of inter-relationship and dependence is the context of the acts done by the dead Lester Furnival on behalf of the living Betty Wallingford. Simon the magician sets himself in antagonism to exchange by trying to bend the wills of others to his own and seeking to invade the province of the dead: he is seen as attempting to break down that identity and separateness without which exchange is impossible. But he cannot finally escape relationship: by going against divine fact he invites that fact to go against him; at the end the Acts of the City destroy him through 'the operation of inflexible law' (p. 221).

Whether in the mode of being or of doing, the object of Williams's novels is to *show* something. To this extent plots are subservient to revelation; the novels are essentially masques (they can be seen as extensions of the masques Williams wrote between 1927 and 1929). The object for the hero in a Charles Williams novel is precisely to stop things changing, to keep them as they are. The supernatural is present to highlight the glory of what they are, and then is removed. The movement of the magic Tarots in *The Greater Trumps* encapsulates the dance of all created things; which Henry Lee describes as everlasting movement, rather than evolution to a new condition of being:

'Imagine that everything which exists takes part in the movement of a great dance – everything, the electrons, all growing and decaying things, all that seems alive and all that doesn't seem alive, men and beasts, trees and stones, everything that changes, and there is nothing anywhere that does not change. That change – that's what we know of the immortal dance; the law in the nature of things – that's the measure of the dance, why one thing changes swiftly and another slowly, why there is seeming accident and incalcul-

able alteration, why men hate and love and grow hungry, and
cities that have stood for centuries fall in a week, why the
smallest wheel and the mightiest world revolve, why blood
flows and the heart beats and the brain moves, why your body
is poised on your ankles and the Himalaya are rooted in the
earth – quick or slow, measurable or immeasurable, there is
nothing at all anywhere but the dance. Imagine it – imagine
it, see it all at once and in one!' (pp. 94–5)

The universe that Williams portrays, while formal and diagrammatic, is no static grid: it is a pattern in a constant state of
becoming and motion – like the style itself of the novels.
  One of the central themes in the novels is acceptance of things
as they are. In *All Hallows' Eve* Lester reflects on the debris she
sees floating in the Thames,

> The evacuations of the City had their place in the City; how
> else could the City be the City? Corruption (so to call it) was
> tolerable, even adequate and proper, even glorious. These
> things also were facts ... A sodden mass of cardboard and
> paper drifted by, but the soddenness was itself a joy, for this
> was what happened, and all that happened, in this great
> material world, was good. (p. 197)

Painful facts, too, are seen as glorious. Sybil Coningsby in *The
Greater Trumps*, going out into a violent snowstorm to rescue her
brother, goes, she says, to '"adore the mystery of love"' (p. 117).
Margaret Anstruther in *Descent into Hell* accepts the approaching
'joy of death' (p. 66), as does Lester that of eternal separation
from her husband in *All Hallows' Eve* (p. 226). Even hell, it is
maintained, is to the angels 'a fact, and, therefore, a fact of joy'
(*Descent into Hell*, p. 115).
  The evil in the novels are those who will not accept, who set
themselves against the universe, seeking to change it for their
own ends, existing and dying in antagonism, like Sir Giles
Tumulty in *Many Dimensions*, burned supernaturally to death by
his opposition to the true nature of the mystic Stone. But even
their actions are portrayed as serving only to testify to the Co-
inherence of all that is. Without Sir Giles the full range of the
laws by which the Stone operated in allowing time-travel would
not have been known; had it not been for the activities of the

magician Berringer in *The Place of the Lion* the wonder of the
Principles and thereby of life itself would have been hidden. Not
to accept reality is to remain shut on the ledge of the self, as
Anthony Durrant draws himself 'back both from safety and from
abandonment' on his tiny perch on the wall of the abyss that
seemed to open all round him in Berringer's house (*The Place of
the Lion*, p. 115); when he finally gives himself to the Eagle that
hovers before him, the images of the Celestials appear to him.
Such acts of acceptance thread all the novels, as Nancy
Coningsby in *The Greater Trumps* returns to Henry Lee despite his
attempt on her father's life, or Pauline Anstruther in *Descent into
Hell* overcomes her fears and takes to herself the pains and
terrors of others, or Lester in *All Hallows' Eve* accepts, despite all
her repugnance and fear of loss, that she must go into the house
where Betty Wallingford is and help her.

The theme of acceptance or refusal of fact is particularly
highly wrought in *Descent into Hell*. For Margaret Anstruther
there can be no beauty in experience unless 'you accepted what
joys the universe offered and did not seek to compel the universe
to offer you joys of your own definition' (p. 66). It is the latter
sort of joy that Lily Sammile (Lilith) seeks: she offers a refuge
from fact in illusion; she asks, '"Why not tell yourself a
comforting tale?"' and promises '"Everything lovely in you for a
perpetual companion, so that you'd never be frightened or
disappointed or ashamed any more"' (pp. 60–1). The historian
Wentworth, who vainly desires the young Adela Hunt, takes to
himself a succuba, in the form and with the personality of Adela,
but without her awkward and painful reality; he no longer
wishes 'to go back among the shapes that ran about, harsh and
menacing, outside the glade or the garden or the forest, outside
the mist. They betrayed and attacked him' (p. 86). As he refuses
one fact, so he refuses all facts: he twists historical evidence to
undermine his rival Aston Moffat's arguments, he rejects joy in
refusing to accept the knighthood given to Moffat, he says that
the uniforms for a play being rehearsed by several of the
characters are correct when they are not, he becomes increasingly unable to perceive or to hold a conversation with anyone else.
Wentworth's refusals give him the slumber of his soul and finally
the loss of meaning and therefore of joy which he has chosen;
Pauline's acceptances confer upon her joy or adoration in true
identity. The one is summed up in the succuba's eventually

becoming formless and finally a nonentity, the other in Pauline's vision of her previously haunting *Doppelgänger* as herself trans-figured by delight.

But if Williams thus asks acceptance or even adoration of things as they are, he asks it because for him these things are manifestations of God, His expression of Himself within Crea-tion. There is to be no worship of things without that larger sense of their contingency: the formula of the mystical way of 'affirmation of images' as it runs throughout Williams's writing is 'This also is Thou; neither is this Thou.'[10] But then, as Williams would see it, if something is truly adored, that wider perspective is present simultaneously, because adoration is not consumed in the object.

What then of the novels themselves, and their fictions: how is the reader himself to be led to 'accept' them? What is the status of fiction in the context of an insistence on not evading facts? Williams would say that no-one can know that 'real life' is any less of a fiction, a contingent reality, than the novels themselves; perhaps it is partly for this reason that he brings the supernatur-al into the everyday world in his fantasies. For him myth and fact are interchangeable, 'In a sense, of course, history is itself a myth; to the imaginative, engaged in considering these things, all is equally myth.'[11] By virtue of the Co-inherence all forms of exchange are possible. Williams would also say that much of man's experience of reality is a dialectical mixture of scepticism and belief, analogous to the literary suspension of disbelief. Certainly he embodies such a mixture of faith and reserve in several of his protagonists – Sir Bernard in *Shadows of Ecstasy*, Lord Arglay in *Many Dimensions* (e.g. pp. 101, 194) and, at one point, Richard Furnival in *All Hallows' Eve* (p. 134).

But these are declarations of how the reader should respond; and indeed much of what we have dealt with so far has been a matter of telling him how to look at things. How do Williams's novels work in trying to make his readers *feel* the adorations that they describe? One of the most striking features about them is the continuously intellectual, explicatory mode in which they are written. This, for instance, is a description of how from a distance, one character, Peter Stanhope, takes on the spiritual terrors of another, Pauline Anstruther, in *Descent into Hell*:

[He] settled himself more comfortably in his chair. A certain superficial attention, alert and effective in its degree, lay at the disposal of anyone who might need it, exactly as his body was prepared to draw in its long outstretched legs if anyone wanted to pass. Meanwhile he disposed the rest of his attention according to his promise. He recollected Pauline; he visualized her going along a road, any road; he visualized another Pauline coming to meet her. And as he did so his mind contemplated not the first but the second Pauline; he took trouble to apprehend the vision, he summoned through all his sensations an approaching fear. Deliberately he opened himself to that fear, laying aside for awhile every thought of why he was doing it, forgetting every principle and law, absorbing only the strangeness and the terror of that separate spiritual identity. His more active mind reflected it in an imagination of himself going into his house and seeing himself, but he dismissed that, for he desired to subdue himself not to his own natural sensations, but to hers first, and then to let hers, if so it should happen, be drawn back into his own. But it was necessary first intensely to receive all her spirit's conflict. He sat on, imagining to himself the long walk with its sinister possibility, the ogreish world lying around, the air with its treachery to all sane appearance. His own eyes began to seek and strain and shrink, his own feet, quiet though actually they were, began to weaken with the necessity of advance upon the road down which the girl was passing. The body of his flesh received her alien terror, his mind carried the burden of her world. The burden was inevitably lighter for him than for her, for the rage of a personal resentment was lacking. He endured her sensitiveness, but not her sin; the substitution there, if indeed there is a substitution, is hidden in the central mystery of Christendom which Christendom itself has never understood, nor can. (pp. 100–1)

The account is highly schematic: first the proper disposition of the self; then visualisation, first of Pauline, then of her *Doppelgänger*, then of her fear; then Stanhope's dismissal of his feeling for her, so that not sympathy but identification can occur; then the nature of the experience itself, defined in terms of its different registers on mind and body, and of precisely how much of it Stanhope takes to himself. The whole is shot through with abstractions. At no point is Pauline's fear realised for the reader:

he is made aware only of a pattern of actions being carried out on it. The paradox here is that it is precisely 'realisation' to the fullest extent on which Stanhope is engaged: he must feel it thoroughly in order to be able to deal with it; the reader, however, is told about it. The character enacts and experiences the pattern: the reader is shown him doing so; is shown, too, in the comments on sin, perhaps more of the pattern than the character grasps. The concern is always with definition, with the precise nature of the spiritual truths involved; the reader is at least like Stanhope in that he has to pay attention. Stanhope did not simply feel Pauline's fear: he summoned it. Every word is aimed at making an exact statement; the attention Stanhope leaves behind is 'alert and effective in its degree', his experience of the *Doppelgänger* is 'the strangeness and the terror of that separate spiritual identity'. It is his 'more active mind' that digresses to his own feelings; the 'body of his flesh' that receives her alien terror.

What is to be made of this? The reader may well feel that writing of this sort is not such as to move him greatly. But there is a whole series of possible answers from Williams's side to this, some of them theoretic or dogmatic, some of them perhaps not so. He might claim that, so far as he is concerned, his business is precisely not to let his readers' emotions in so that they feel or sympathise: 'when sensation slips from intellect, expect the tyrant'.[12] For Williams, 'Heaven is always exact'; while 'Hell is always inaccurate'.[13] The universe is diagrammatic, clear, exact: hence therefore a style of the same character, precise, denotational, conscious, is necessary to express it. This might seem the most convincing defence, for it extends an aspect central to the novels. Again, Williams might say that whatever his readers may feel about mind or intellect as divorced from 'reality', they are in truth not separate from objects or sensations. It is the intellectual reduction by Damaris Tighe in *The Place of the Lion* of the Principles to mere mental counters or abstractions that is overthrown by the living reality of the Principles themselves. In *The Greater Trumps*, by holding the suit of pentacles of the Tarot Pack and thinking hard of earth, Nancy Coningsby finds the cards moving in her hands and making actual piles of earth. For Williams at least, thinking and doing, mind and body, are not really divorced. But whether the reader can accept this on trust is another matter.

And actually Williams's style is not always so simply or starkly intellectual in any case. Another feature of his writing is the peculiar, rather alienating fervour with which it is often imbued. Thus Anthony Durrant, thinking about his friend Quentin in *The Place of the Lion*:

> His friend. The many moments of joy and deep content which their room had held had in them something of the nature of holy innocence. There had been something in them which was imparted, by Love to love, and which had willed to save them now. Much was possible to a man in solitude; perhaps the final transmutations and achievements in the zones on the yonder side of the central Knowledge were possible only to the spirit in solitude. But some things were possible only to a man in companionship, and of these the most important was balance. (p. 187)

Even while this is analytic, it seems to be half in love with the pattern the analysis reveals; the pitch seems monotonous, the lyrical rhythm cloying. There is a sense of the author doing the enthusing, prescribing how to react or behave, getting between the reader and free response. He speaks like an initiate, from the midst of an experience from which most readers are remote: he may know something of 'the final transmutations and achievements in the zones on the yonder side of the central Knowledge' but his reader does not, and the distance makes the phraseology seem absurd. Just before this passage Anthony's difficulty in reaccepting the Principles is attributed to the fact that 'reality is so evasive; self-consciousness, egotism, heaviness, solemnity, carelessness, even an over-personal fondness, continually miss it' (p. 182): Williams might here have been describing himself. Further, his taking over the separate identity of his fiction is precisely the kind of action that he condemns in the evil characters of his novels, even if it is done here for good purpose. What he said of poetry – 'It is not by the morals we draw from it or the maxims it inculcates or the melodies it releases that we shall be encouraged or consoled. We must enter into its own world'[14] – must therefore be seen implicitly as a criticism of his own work.

There are therefore limitations on how far the adorations of being asked by Williams's novels can be followed: how far, that is, the ideal of acceptance becomes fully realised in the reader himself. Nevertheless, style is not everything: the sheer originality, clarity, subtlety and beauty of Williams's vision are certainly at times sufficient to make his reader admire, if not love. And Williams might say that, given such a co-inherent universe as the one he describes, the reader cannot tell what further transmutations and achievements may be being accomplished unknown.

3 Conservatism in Fantasy: Ursula Le Guin

Most fantasies seek to conserve those things in which they take delight: indeed it is one of their weaknesses that they are tempted not to admit loss. Their frequent looking to the past is conservative in itself: and the order to which they look and seek to re-create is usually a medieval and hierarchic one, founded on the continuance of the *status quo*. Many of them portray the preservation of an existing state of things as their central subject. C. S. Lewis's *Perelandra* describes the maintenance of the innocence of a Venusian Adam and Eve, and his *The Lion, the Witch and the Wardrobe* portrays the recovery of the original condition of a land called Narnia through the Christ-like sacrifice of the lion Aslan. Tolkien's *The Lord of the Rings*, while admitting historical change, is concerned with the survival of being and individualism in Middle-earth, imaged in the destruction of the annihilating power of Sauron and the restoration of the rightful king to the throne of Gondor. E. Nesbit's fairy tales are conservative in that they often end with the return of parents or the recovery of an amulet or the restoration of a descendant to true inheritance. Charles Williams's novels portray the removal of a supernatural irruption which has itself illuminated the true character of reality. Many fantasies end in disenchantment and restoration of 'normality'. The *status quo* so preserved is no dead thing, but rather a living balance founded on continuous choice or on a delicately maintained frontier between the orders of nature and supernature. Conservatism and its concomitant balance are at the heart of the 'Earthsea' trilogy of Ursula Le Guin – *A Wizard of Earthsea* (1968), *The Tombs of Atuan* (1972) and *The Farthest Shore* (1973).*

---

* References are to the Gollancz editions, published respectively in 1971, 1972 and 1973 (and in one omnibus volume in 1977), and cited hereafter as *WE*, *TA* and *FS*.

Balance is the condition of being of Mrs Le Guin's fantastic world. When the apprentice mage[1] Ged, who is to be the hero of the trilogy, is at the school for wizards on the island of Roke, the Master Hand tells him,

> 'you must not change one thing, one pebble, one grain of sand, until you know what good and evil will follow on the act. The world is in balance, in Equilibrium. A wizard's power of Changing and of Summoning can shake the balance of the world. It is dangerous, that power. It is most perilous. It must follow knowledge, and serve need.' (*WE*, p. 54; see also *FS*, pp. 43, 74–5)

It is this balance which in *A Wizard of Earthsea* Ged upsets when, in arrogant contest with another apprentice mage Jasper, he summons up a spirit of the dead, and in doing so looses into the world a hideous black shadow which almost rends him to death (*WE*, p. 71); it takes all the power of the Archmage Nemmerle of Roke to save Ged, banish the shadow from Roke and close up the hole that has been made between the realms of life and death. The rest of the book describes Ged's attempt to restore the balance he has destroyed; and when finally he catches up with the shadow, he does so after voyaging 'towards the very centre of that balance, towards the place where light and darkness meet', and also to where land and sea merge in a unity out of time (*WE*, pp. 174–5, 184–6). In *The Farthest Shore* the mage Cob refuses to die, refuses that which is the balance of life (*FS*, pp. 188–9), and in doing so upsets the balance of the whole world and all but drains the life from it.

This balance is no static thing, but is part of the mobile fabric of life. In *The Farthest Shore* Ged (if rather explicitly) tells his companion, Prince Arren, '"Only what is mortal bears life, Arren. Only in death is there rebirth. The Balance is not a stillness. It is a movement – an eternal becoming"' (*FS*, p. 145). The balance has to do with a dialectically conceived world, where everything works by contraries. '"To light a candle is to cast a shadow"', says the Master Hand (*WE*, p. 54). Only by accepting death can one continue to live: in the land of the dead Ged tells Cob, of King Erreth-Akbe, '"Here is nothing, dust and shadows. There, he is the earth and sunlight, the leaves of trees, the eagle's flight. He is alive. And all who ever died, live; they are reborn, and have no end, nor will there ever be an end"' (*FS*, p. 189). As the epigraph from '*The Creation of Éa*' in *A Wizard of Earthsea* puts it, 'Only in silence the word,/only in dark the light,/only in dying life:/bright the hawk's flight/on the empty sky' (see also *WE*, pp. 28, 179, 189). The very nature of the fantastic world, Earthsea, paints a dialectical relation of earth and sea. The archipelago is not quite a 'land', since it is in fragments on an ocean. Yet it is united in legend and history, and as the huddle of the known world about such a centre as Roke, which sends out wizards to all parts of the world to preserve it from harm: it demonstrates the dialectic of unity in multiplicity in that the peoples are often insular and ignorant, and yet part of the larger, if often warring, group.

This 'dialectical balance' can be seen in the form of *A Wizard of Earthsea*, which is artistically the most satisfying book of the trilogy. Although Ged and the theme of the shadow are the central concern, there are many other topics not directly connected with it. These include the account of Ged's early life and education on Gont and Roke (*WE*, pp. 13–61); his career as mage of Low Torning and his vain attempt to bring back the sick child of the fisherman Pechvarry from the lands of the dead (pp. 88–93); his saving of Low Torning from the threat of the dragons of Pendor (pp. 94–102); the attempt of the Lord Benderesk and the Lady Serret on Osskil to persuade him to loose the evil power of the Terrenon stone (pp. 118–32); and Ged's encounter with the exiled king and queen on the mid-ocean shoal (pp. 145–52). But for his having loosed the shadow, Ged himself says, he would have explored much more of the diversity of Earthsea (p. 176). Unity is thus played against by multiplicity; and yet the multiplicity has in it the seeds of unity. For Ged's education as mage gives him both power and temptation (*WE*, pp. 31–5); the attempt to save the dying child is another, if more charitable, kind of the presumption that led him to try to call up a spirit of the dead; his battle with the dragons and his resistance of the old dragon Yevau's blandishments demonstrate his courage and purity of heart; his behaviour in rejecting the stone of the Terrenon further shows his learnt refusal to try to use evil for his own ends (an attempt which woud have led to his doom (*WE*, p. 128)); and his meeting with the old king and queen gives him one half of the Ring of Erreth-Akbe which is to be central to the plot of *The Tombs of*

Atuan. In short, what is portrayed in all save the last of these episodes is a moral development which helps to make comprehensible Ged's change, after the Terrenon adventure, from letting himself be hunted by the shadow to doing the hunting himself.

And that switch, from 'Hunted' to 'Hunting' (the titles of different chapters) is another instance of the formal balance of the book: chapters 5, 6 and 7 cover his attempts to flee the shadow and the next and last three cover his pursuit of it; and each section is of almost identical length. Again, in the 'Hunted' section Ged is in a sense directionless, going anywhere in the hope of escaping the shadow; but, 'Hunting', he has an increasing sense of where to trace the shadow: and in the end there is a trans-temporal fusion of these opposites when Ged travels across an empty sea with a fixed direction in mind, and meets the shadow on a featureless sandbank, where 'He strode forward, away from the boat, but in no direction. There were no directions here, no north or south or east or west, only towards and away' (*WE*, p. 186).

The Earthsea books have a formal structure expressing the theme of balance. Where in the first and third books Ged is journeying over Earthsea, in the second, *The Tombs of Atuan*, he remains in one place throughout, the labyrinth of the dark powers on the island of Atuan in the Kargad lands on the northeast of Earthsea. In *A Wizard of Earthsea* his journeying ends in a traverse of the East Reach, and in *The Farthest Shore* of the West Reach. Much is made of the number nine. There are nine lore masters on Roke,[2] nine months from the time that Ged leaves Roke after bringing his shadow into the world until he finally defeats it, nine chapters describing his development as a mage from the point of his apprenticeship to the wizard Ogion in *A Wizard of Earthsea* and nine great runes on the Ring of Erreth-Akbe. The course Ged follows in the first book, from Gont, via Roke, Low Torning, Pendor, Osskil, Gont, the shoal on which he finds the strange old couple, and Iffish, to the rendezvous with his shadow on the mid-ocean sand beyond the last land of the East Reach, traces out a figure 9 over the map of Earthsea; and the significant places stopped at also total nine. In *The Farthest Shore* the form of Ged's journey is that of a nine upside-down and reversed – a 6, starting at Roke, moving south-east to Hort Town, south-west to Lorbanery, Obehol, Wellogy and the floating town of the raft-people, then north up the West Reach to the Dragons' Run and Selidor: and here again there are nine places visited. The great constellation under the star Gobardon which dominates the sky of the West Reach and is in the shape of the Rune of Ending, Agnen, is in the shape of a figure 9 and has nine stars. In this way two journeys of the first and last books are balanced: one winds up, as it were, while the other winds down. The number nine is traditionally associated with the completion or 'winding up' of a spell (compare *Macbeth*, I, iii, 35–7: 'Thrice to thine, and thrice to mine,/And thrice again, to make up nine./ Peace! The charm's wound up'). In this case it is associated with the making of a maker of spells, a true mage, in terms both of education on Roke and of the spiritual journey of Ged thereafter. Under the influence of the reversed nine in *The Farthest Shore*, however, Ged's magical power is steadily unwound until at the end he leaves Roke as a mere man. Thus too Ged in the first book moves towards the East Reach, the direction of sunrise and beginnings, and in the last towards the West Reach and the sunset.

There is also a degree of formal balance at a thematic level. In the first book the concern is with a personal evil and a personal solution to it: Ged has loosed the dark shadow of his own arrogance (*WE*, p. 76), one which turns out in the end to have his own name; and the story describes how he learns the courage to face and hunt down this shadow, and thereby overcome his own evil nature. In *The Tombs of Atuan* the emphasis is both individual and social. The young priestess Arha (meaning 'The Eaten One') acquires throughout that growth of the self which will enable her to break free from her custodianship of the dark labyrinth which in one way figures the enclosed individual. But here that growth is stimulated and brought to fruition by outside agency in the form of Ged, who has symbolically penetrated the tunnels of the labyrinth in search of the other half of the Ring of Erreth-Akbe (and the uniting of the two halves of the Ring represents the marriage of Arha's will with Ged's). Similarly Ged himself could not have escaped from the labyrinth without the help of Arha. In *The Farthest Shore* the moral conflict of the first book has become wholly external, being between the heroic Ged (helped by Arren) and the depraved Cob; and the issue is now social and universal, for Cob is destroying the whole world.

At both an artistic and a thematic level the second book can be seen as a pivot or mid-point between the other two books. It seems fitting therefore that where the first and third books are centrifugal in character, involving long pursuits, with their object the banishing of beings out of the world, *The Tombs of Atuan* involves Ged's quest for a centre, the centre of the labyrinth, and the joining together of the long-divorced halves of the Ring of Erreth-Akbe; and at the end of the book Arha is 'reborn' into the world (*TA*, p. 144; see also p. 127).

The trilogy is also informed with the ethic of accepting[3] or of keeping things as they are, or allowing them to express their true being – that is, so long as they are goods. In *A Wizard of Earthsea* Ged eventually succeeds in taking to himself the shadow he has admitted into the world and in so doing makes himself whole (*WE*, pp. 187, 189); in *The Tombs of Atuan* he recovers the lost half of the Ring of Erreth-Akbe and gives Arha the life she should have; and in *The Farthest Shore* he gives Cob the death he is wrongly resisting, closes the breach made between life and death and restores being and vitality to Earthsea. The duty of all men as of mages is to preserve the Balance. Ged tells Arren:

'Do you see, Arren, how an act is not, as young men think, like a rock that one picks up and throws, and it hits or misses, and that's the end of it. When that rock is lifted the earth is lighter, the hand that bears it heavier. When it is thrown the circuits of the stars respond, and where it strikes or falls the universe is changed. On every act the balance of the whole depends. The winds and seas, the powers of water and earth and light, all that these do, and all that the beasts and green things do, is well done, and rightly done. All these act within the Equilibrium. From the hurricane and the great whale's sounding to the fall of a dry leaf and the gnat's flight, all they do is done within the balance of the whole. But we, insofar as we have power over the world and over one another, we must *learn* to do what the leaf and the whale and the wind do of their own nature. We must learn to keep the balance. Having intelligence, we must not act in ignorance. Having choice, we must not act without responsibility.' (*FS*, pp. 74–5)

In Mrs Le Guin's science fiction, by contrast, there is much more emphasis on alteration of the *status quo*. In *Planet of Exile* (1966) the last remnants of mankind are dying out on the distant planet they have made their home for six hundred years, and are able to survive only when they are forced into alliance and ultimate intermarriage with the humanoid hilfs of that planet under the assaults of an army of ravaging Gaal from the north. The ambassador Genly Ai in *The Left Hand of Darkness* (1969) eventually succeeds in bringing the backward planet Winter into the galactic federation of the Ekumen. *The Lathe of Heaven* (1971) describes a man who changes the world every time he dreams: normality is never fully restored. The scientist Shevek in *The Dispossessed* (1976) discovers an aspect of time which will revolutionise interstellar transport; and in his own way initiates by his very absence from it a revolution in the society of his own planet. The very fact that all three of Mrs Le Guin's fantasies are set in one place, Earthsea, where each of her science fiction novels creates a different world (and in *The Lathe of Heaven* our own is being fundamentally altered from chapter to chapter) is an index to the conservatism at the heart of the former.

Keeping things as they are means keeping them essentially as they always have been: the past is central. Yet only *essentially*, for each age alters the factors in the Balance, or sees different threats to it, or recovers more of the past than was previously known: it is, as it were, a case of tradition and the individual talent. The power of the mage is founded on his knowledge of the names of things in the Old Speech, the speech of Segoy when he created Earthsea, for those are the true names of things and have runic power over the creatures and objects they describe. Ged tells Arha:

'Knowing names is my job. My art. To weave the magic of a thing, you see, one must find its true name out. In my lands we keep our true names hidden all our lives long, from all but those whom we trust utterly; for there is great power, and great peril, in a name. Once, at the beginning of time, when Segoy raised the isles of Earthsea from the ocean deeps, all things bore their own true names. And all doing of magic, all wizardry, hangs still upon the knowledge – the relearning, the remembering – of that true and ancient language of the Making. There are spells to learn, of course, ways to use the words; and one must know the consequences too. But what a wizard spends his life at is finding out the names of things, and finding out how to find out the names of things.' (*TA*, pp. 119–20).

The task of the magician is therefore one of recovery.[4] But the past also exists in the present in the form of the dragons, who still speak in the Old Speech, in the lays and legends and sense of history that are part of the fabric of Earthsea society, and even at the level of the primordial memory – when Arren hears the Old Speech used by the dragon Orm Embar, 'he felt always that he was on the point of understanding, almost understanding: as if it were a language he had forgotten, not one he had never known' (*FS*, pp. 160–1). Yet while the past and the sense of it are at the heart of life in Earthsea, each generation may produce a new hero: the great figures of legend, Elfarran, the Grey Mage of Paln, Erreth-Akbe, are not greater than the mage Ged, who is a legend living in the present day of his world.

This reverence for the past may also be traced at the level of the indebtedness of Mrs Le Guin's fantasy to other works. The Earthsea trilogy, in common with most fantasy, owes much to literary tradition, and quite demonstratively. The concept of Earthsea, with the mapped journey, the nine wizard masters, the great Ring of Erreth-Akbe, the shadow, the sense of the past and precedent, the frequent reference to lay and legend, the emphasis on language and on magic as a craft, look back to Tolkien. The idea of the islands recalls C. S. Lewis's *Perelandra* (1943) or his *The Voyage of the 'Dawn Treader'* (1952), or perhaps Book 2 of Spenser's *Faerie Queene*, or *The Odyssey*. The theme of the evil shadow is also central in George MacDonald's *Phantastes* (1858) and *Lilith* (1895): in *Phantastes* the shadow is similarly released by an act of arrogant disobedience, and in *Lilith* there is also a theme concerning one's true name. The bestial, taloned form that the shadow first takes as it clings to Ged's face and tears his flesh is highly reminiscent of the appearance and behaviour of some of the horrible creatures in M. R. James's stories, particularly those in 'The Treasure of Abbot Thomas', 'The Tractate Middoth' and 'Mr. Humphreys and his Inheritance'.[5] The land of the dead, with its lightless towns and silence, recalls Dante and more directly James Thomson's poem *The City of Dreadful Night*. Ged's voyages in frail boats in *A Wizard of Earthsea* strongly suggest the legendary voyage of St Brendan, and the society and beliefs described in *The Tombs of Atuan* almost certainly look back to C. S. Lewis's *Till We Have Faces* (1956). Thus, just as Earthsea is profoundly traditional in character, so too are the books about it. Yet out of this indebtedness to the past Ursula Le Guin has made work which is uniquely hers.

The workings of magic in the Earthsea trilogy also express the conservative ethic of the fantasy. The accent is on magic not changing the nature of the world, except in cases of real need: as has been seen the job of the mage is to preserve the Balance. The arts of Changing and Summoning, whereby a wizard may transform himself or call other beings to him, are to be handled with peculiar care. It is his prideful summoning of Elfarran from the dead that causes Ged all his pain and fear in *A Wizard of Earthsea*. It is possible to change things for a short time and still be able to retract the deed, as Ged turns himself briefly into a dragon at Pendor to destroy the offspring of Yevau (*WE*, p. 97) or into a hawk to escape the servants of the dark powers of the Terrenon on Osskil (*WE*, pp. 131–3): but any longer would have risked permanent transformation. One may use magic to right an imbalance, as Ged slays the young dragons of Pendor or closes the breach Cob has made between the worlds; or to heal the imbalance caused by disease, as he heals the people of the village in the West Hand (*WE*, pp. 158–9); or to thank as he does the village-woman in *The Tombs of Atuan* for her hospitality by healing the infected udders of her goats (*TA*, pp. 147–8); but it is arrogant and dangerous to attempt to do more. The Master Summoner on Roke teaches his pupils to use spells over wind and sea 'only at need, since to summon up such earthly forces is to change the earth of which they are a part. '"Rain on Roke may be drouth in Osskil," he said, "and a calm in the East Reach may be storm and ruin in the West, unless you know what you are about"' (*WE*, pp. 63–4). When in *The Farthest Shore* Arren asks Ged why he does not work marvels with his magic he is told: '"The first lesson on Roke, and the last, is *Do what is needful*. And no more!"' (*FS*, p. 142). The reader may recall Ged's own impatience at the refusal of his early tutor Ogion to do miracles (*WE*, pp. 27–30).

Certain limits are inherent in the working of magic. Many of the true names of things in the Old Speech have been lost: Kurremkarmerruk, the Master Namer of Roke, tells Ged, '"some have been lost over the ages, and some have been hidden, and some are known only to dragons and to the Old Powers of Earth, and some are known to no living creature; and no man could learn them all. For there is no end to that language"' (*WE*, p. 57). And as he goes on to say, magic can work only locally, because the nature of Earthsea is such that generalisations are impossible:

> 'The sea's name is *inien*, well and good. But what we call the Inmost Sea has its own name also in the Old Speech. Since no thing can have two true names, *inien* can mean only "all the sea except the Inmost Sea". And of course it does not mean even that, for there are seas and bays and straits beyond counting that bear names of their own. So if some Mage-Seamaster were mad enough to try to lay a spell of storm or calm over all the ocean, his spell must say not only that word *inien*, but the names of every stretch and bit and part of the sea through all the Archipelago and all the Outer Reaches and beyond to where names cease. Thus, that which gives us power to work magic, sets the limits of that power. A mage can control only what is near him, what he can name exactly and wholly. And this is well. If it were not so, the wickedness of the powerful or the folly of the wise would long ago have sought to change what cannot be changed, and Equilibrium would fail. The unbalanced sea would overwhelm the islands where we perilously dwell, and in the old silence all voices and all names would be lost.'

(The last sentence is reminiscent of Ulysses' speech on degree in Shakespeare's *Troilus and Cressida*, I, iii, and indeed of the whole Renaissance emphasis on nature and universal order.) And, as Ged tells Arren, magic can be local in another sense: '"Do you know the old saying, *Rules change in the Reaches*? Seamen use it, but it is a wizard's saying, and it means that wizardry itself depends on place. A true spell on Roke may be mere words on Iffish"' (*FS*, p. 80). A further limit on magic is that it can be exhausted or confined. The Archmage Nemmerle loses all his power – and his life – through his actions after Ged has let the shadow into the world. By naming Ged with his true name the shadow removes for the time his power of wizardry (*WE*, pp. 115–16). Cob drains the powers of mages from the world and it takes the final exhaustion of Ged's powers to remove the damage he has done. Ged has to defy fatigue and resist sleep in order to keep together the magically synthesised boat of flotsam and jetsam in which he pursues the shadow (*WE*, pp. 153–6); his fellow-mage

Vetch wonders at Ged's powers in sustaining the magic wind that blows them both in their boat over the sea, where he 'felt his own power all weakened and astray' (*WE*, p. 184).

Magic is seen as part of, rather than opposed to, nature and 'normality'. A mage is born with his talent, just as another may be born a scholar or warrior. But, as with all talents, it has to be educated: the young mage is put to school to learn the lore of his craft. Thus Ged is found learning the skills of the Master Changer, the Master Namer, the Master Chanter, the Master Herbal, the Master Windkey, the Master Hand, the Master Summoner, the Master Patterner and the Master Doorkeeper, just as one might learn French or geometry or history, or do games (compare on the last *WE*, pp. 52–3). Primarily what the mage-scholar is bent on discovering is the inmost character of the things of nature (there is little technology in Earthsea) – the names of creatures, objects, forces, plants and places, their order, how to call them up, how to perform illusory and actual changes with them, the secrets of plants and animals, how to direct such forces as wind and tide, and above all how to respect and preserve the immanent metaphysical balance of nature. Indeed, knowledge of the essence of nature contained in the true names of things in the Old Speech is the most powerful key to magic. To do magic aright the mage must be in sympathy with nature. Ged comes to believe 'that the wise man is one who never sets himself apart from other living things, whether they have speech or not, and in later years he strove long to learn what can be learned, in silence, from the eyes of animals, the flight of birds, the great slow gestures of trees' (*WE*, p. 92). Thus magic becomes bound up with the created world, ' "the weaving of spells is itself interwoven with the earth and the water, the winds, the fall of light, of the place where it is cast" ' (*FS*, p. 80; see also pp. 41–2).

And, further to portray the magic as 'moderate', it is emphasised that some of the most difficult things in the world are done not only by magic but out of one's own nature. It is not only magic that enables Ged to defeat his shadow, but courage, integrity and insight; and his defeat of Cob also asks a deep love of the world and heroic self-sacrifice. The reader is told, too, of Ged's friend Vetch that, though he was a skilled mage, 'a greater, unlearned skill he possessed, which was the art of kindness' (*WE*, p. 52). Similarly, when Ged has to try to enter the school of Roke and cannot step over the threshold, he finds that no magic will help him, but only the simple act of asking the Doorkeeper for help (*WE*, pp. 44, 83–4). Frequently the wizard has to depend on the help of ordinary man, as Ged needs Arha to escape from the Tombs of Atuan (*TA*, pp. 127, 128, 131), and as he could not have found Cob without the assistance of Arren (*FS*, pp. 102, 131, 147–8).

The Earthsea trilogy is in large part panegyric, a celebration of things as they are. Centrally of course, this is done through the theme of the Balance: but there are other modes. *The Farthest Shore* is specifically about the loss of identity caused by Cob in the world, and its recovery when he is given, in his death, the true self he has so long refused. During Cob's refusal all meaning and distinctiveness had been largely drained out of Earthsea. The witch on Lorbanery who has lost her power tells Ged and Arren, '"I lost all the things I knew, all the words and names ... There is a hole in the world and the light is running out of it. And the words go with the light"' (*FS*, p. 92; see also p. 163). As mages all over the world forget their powers and lose their knowledge of the Old Speech, so eventually do some of the great wizards on Roke itself, the Summoner, the Changer and the Chanter (*FS*, pp. 148–54). The lustre goes from the famous blue dyes of Lorbanery (p. 88) and the dyers themselves have 'no lines and distinctions and colours clear in their heads' (p. 95). Arren himself loses faith in Ged and magery (pp. 107–8), coming to feel that

> reality was empty: without life, or warmth, or colour, or sound: without meaning. There were no heights or depths. All this lovely play of form and light and colour on the sea and in the eyes of men, was no more than that: a playing of illusions on the shallow void. (pp. 129–30)

But when at length free of the darkness caused by Cob, Arren can perceive the glory of the dragons' flight in the West Reach (pp. 155–6), and can see with Ged how the apparently unexciting island of Selidor is full of being in its streams and hills:

> 'In all the world, in all the worlds, in all the immensity of time, there is no other like each of those streams, rising cold out of the earth where no eye sees it, running through the

sunlight and the darkness to the sea. Deep are the springs of being, deeper than life, than death...' (p. 174; see also pp. 174–5)

In all three books of the Earthsea trilogy evil is a nonentity, a shadow, not substance. The evil powers in *The Tombs of Atuan* are the Nameless Ones; Cob's evil reduces people to shadows of themselves and eventually brings them into the land of shadows. Magic is centrally concerned with the identities of 'things as they are' in that it depends on knowing their true names, which are the names of their original making. Throughout the trilogy the reader is invited to feel a simple delight in the natures of things – a delight which is certainly 'thematic' but springs from the author herself[6] and her own pleasure in creation, or 'making', as Tolkien put it: in a sense she is analogous to her own Segoy and the creative joy he had in making Earthsea. So great is Mrs Le Guin's power of realisation of all the different places visited in *A Wizard of Earthsea* that she can make the sketchiest details conjure up a whole. When Ged leaves Low Torning after saving it from the threat of the dragons of Pendor,

> He went in a row-boat with a couple of young fishermen of Low Torning, who wanted the honour of being his boatmen. Always as they rowed on among the craft that crowd the eastern channels of the Ninety Isles, under the windows and balconies of houses that lean out over the water, past the wharves of Nesh, the rainy pastures of Dromgan, the malodorous oil-sheds of Geath, word of his deed had gone ahead of him. (*WE*, p. 104)

Each island has its character: even the bleak shoal where the old royal couple live receives an unforgettable thumbnail portrait (*WE*, p. 149). The result is that the reader feels that in the less than two hundred pages of this book he has covered an enormous canvas of highly individualised people and places, far more than (arguably) is present in all the eleven hundred of Tolkien's *The Lord of the Rings*. And all this comes from the thoroughness with which the author has seen things; the unsentimental realism with which she has presented them;[7] the metaphoric mode whereby she has so mingled the fantastic and the real that they give life to one another;[8] the originality of her descriptions and the re-creative force of her style (for example, *WE*, p. 29 and pp. 22–3, 37); and running through it all a lonely impulse of delight in all that is and is made.

4   The Union of Opposites in Fantasy: E. Nesbit

In the traditional fairy tale reality and magic are not radically separated. The hero catches a fish which grants him three wishes as the price of his freedom, receives a cloak of invisibility or a golden goose for his kindness, or is helped in the accomplishment of seemingly impossible tasks by helpful beasts or supernatural persons: but no time is lost in wonder save at good fortune, and the marvellous is presented in a matter-of-fact way, as though it was simply a part of the world. In modern fantasy, however, the two orders are often treated as though divided. For one thing, magic and miracle become rare, and sometimes manifest themselves only to certain types of people: E. Nesbit's Psammead and Phoenix are discovered after long concealments, and in George MacDonald's 'Curdie' books only faith and innocence of soul can reveal the princess Irene's mystic great-great-grandmother. For another, there is often much awe and amazement on the part of the protagonists at the supernatural – as with the response of Lewis's Ransom to the planetary angels he meets, or even the sheer stupefaction of F. Anstey's characters when they are turned into their fathers or pursued by amorous statues of Venus come to life. Again, several modern fantasies describe a journey from 'this' world to a supernatural one, as in David Lindsay's *A Voyage to Arcturus*, E. R. Eddison's *The Worm Ouroboros* or the fantasies of C. S. Lewis. Others set the reader in a wholly fantastic world without much reference to his reality: examples are William Morris's prose romances, Mervyn Peake's 'Titus' books, Tolkien's *The Hobbit* and *The Lord of the Rings* and Ursula Le Guin's 'Earthsea' trilogy. While a number of modern fantasies seek to show that the natural and supernatural orders are not so divided as might be thought – as, particularly, Christian fantasy – they do start from the assumption that the two are considered to be separate in the minds of their readers, as they are initially for their protagonists.

The separation of the two categories in modern fantasy allows for creative interplay between them. The process is metaphoric: the supernatural is 'naturalised' as it were, and vice versa. Just as God and the Archangel Michael appear as a travelling wine salesman and his assistant in T. F. Powys's *Mr. Weston's Good Wine*, so Prester John in Charles Williams's *War in Heaven* appears as 'a young man in a light grey suit and soft hat';[1] or, in the other direction, the patience of a railway porter in repeating information in Williams's *All Hallows' Eve* is seen as 'the thunder of the passage of a god dominant, miraculous and yet recurrent. Golden-thighed Endurance, sun-shrouded Justice, were in him, and his face was the deep confluence of the City.'[2] Thus too Kingsley's Mrs Bedonebyasyoudid in *The Water-Babies* behaves like a Victorian aunt, and the natural world of stream, river and ocean is shown as fantastic, 'the true fairy tale ... the true "Märchen allen Märchen"', as Kingsley himself put it referring to the workings of nature.[3] Lewis's Ransom in *Perelandra* becomes a type of Christ; the behaviour of the mortal characters in Thackeray's *The Rose and the Ring* is fantastically absurd while Fairy Blackstick is quite ordinary and sober; the magic in the fantasies of Tolkien and Ursula Le Guin is natural, in the sense both of being presented as a craft that can be learnt by those sufficiently gifted and of being concerned with knowing the secrets of nature. Sometimes the process is one of colloquialising, for instance in the work of F. Anstey, where magic creatures which might be expected to be grand and remote, such as a genie or the goddess Aphrodite, are made quite common, even vulgar; or in T. H. White's *The Once and Future King*, where the stylised mode of Malory is turned to the everyday, the vivid, the comic and the domestic.

The effect of this yoking together of apparent opposites in fantasy is to add new being and wonder to each side of the metaphor: nature becomes 'supernaturalised' or shot through with strangeness, and the supernatural becomes more vivid because infused with the everyday and the familiar. A very individual illustration of the successful application of the 'metaphoric' mode of fantasy can be seen in the work of E. Nesbit.

The fantasies or fairy stories of E. Nesbit (Mrs Hubert Bland) were all published, it might be said with chronological neatness, between 1900 and 1913,[4] starting with *The Book of Dragons* (first serialised in 1899) and ending with *Wet Magic*.* Naturally, given such dates, the commentator is drawn to see them as significant: to find E. Nesbit's work 'modern' rather than 'Victorian', and rather less modern than Edwardian.[5] In this aim he will not be frustrated, for it is true that E. Nesbit's stories are often much less didactic in final intent than those of her forbears, Mrs Ewing and Mrs Molesworth, in their reworkings of traditional fairy tale; and true too that class assumptions and clear values on which many of them depend vanished with the Great War. Yet such an account requires qualification. E. Nesbit wrote for children, and the relation between delighting and instructing a child is a perennial issue in children's literature, since the adult of any age stands at least partly in the role of instructor in relation to the child. A given author may equally write highly didactic and non-moral tales: the same George MacDonald who wrote *The Lost Princess* also wrote 'The Light Princess'; and E. Nesbit could with equal facility set about the purely witty 'Melisande' (*NUT*) as the more instructive 'Whereyouwantogoto' (*NUT*) or 'Justnowland' (*MW*). Then again, there must always be an element of 'class structure' in children's literature, not only because the adults who write them or appear as actors in the stories have to be leaders and repositories of value, but also because the child's mind is inveterately hierarchical, and his mental outlook is founded on rules, orders and stations. Nor was E. Nesbit the first to write her kind of fantasy. Her primary literary debt was to the work of F. Anstey, who, in such stories as *Vice Versa, or, A Lesson to Fathers* (1882), *The Tinted Venus, A Farcical Romance* (1885) and *The Brass Bottle* (1900), had developed the comic possibilities of fantasy beyond those exploited by Thackeray, Dickens or MacDonald:[6] though written within the 'Victorian' period, not one of his books attempts to be moral,

---

* Abbreviations used:

BD	Nesbit, *The Book of Dragons* (Harper and Bros, 1900)
FCI	——, *Five Children and It* (T. Fisher Unwin, 1902)
Moore	Doris Langley Moore, *E. Nesbit, A Biography*, rev. ed. (Ernest Benn, 1967)
MW	Nesbit, *The Magic World* (Macmillan, 1912)
NUT	——, *Nine Unlikely Tales for Children* (T. Fisher Unwin, 1901)
OBO	——, *Oswald Bastable and Others* (Wells Gardner, 1906)
PC	——, *The Phoenix and the Carpet* (George Newnes, 1904)
SA	——, *The Story of the Amulet* (T. Fisher Unwin, 1906)

and indeed in one of his stories, 'The Good Little Girl',[7] he gives us a young female prig who is cured of her penchant for making improving remarks by means of a spell which makes every 'sentence' she utters be accompanied by the dropping from her lips of jewels which are subsequently found to be fakes.

Nevertheless it is true that E. Nesbit is one of the first children's writers whose books, particularly her comic ones, are not largely concerned with moral issues and the instruction of a juvenile readership. E. Nesbit had an extraordinary gift for remembering her own childhood, and for putting herself inside the minds of her child-characters: she once said:

> You cannot hope to understand children by common-sense, by reason, by logic, nor by any science whatsoever. You cannot understand them by imagination – not even by love itself. There is only one way: to remember what you thought and felt and liked and hated when you yourself were a child. Not what you know now – or think you know – you ought to have thought and liked, but what you did then, in stark fact, like and think. There is no other way.[8]

If one is going to write from a 'child's eye' point of view in this way, the distance necessary for moral instruction is to a large degree removed. '"I make it a point of honour never to *write down* to a child"', E. Nesbit once declared (Moore, p. 178). A vast gulf separates her from earlier writers who began with a self-conscious preference for imaginative rather than moral stories for the young: E. Nesbit simply does not work from the outside like this, and it shows; she is not giving the child reader anything, for in a sense she is that reader. As her biographer has said: 'she understood children with a fellow-feeling rather than with the detachment of a psychologist' (Moore, p. 264).[9]

This special power of recall cannot readily be explained: certainly it has nothing to do with literary tradition or the time at which she wrote. To some extent it must be related to the vividness of her own childhood and character: yet the evidence here does not always point to a rosy youth. Her father died in 1862 when she was only four, and her mother took the family abroad for the sake of Edith's sister Mary's health (she was consumptive). It was not until she was fourteen, and after a variety of not often pleasant boarding schools in France,

Germany and Britain[10] that E. Nesbit had a lasting home again, at Halstead Hall in Kent. Longing for the return of a father, and a child's remote sense of the precariousness of the family fortunes are themes in many of her children's books – particularly *The Story of the Treasure Seekers* (1899), *The Would Be Goods* (1901), *The Railway Children* (1906) and *The Story of the Amulet* (1906). However, as a child E. Nesbit enjoyed endless games and 'scrapes' with her brothers Alfred and Harry, of which only a few mentions have survived[11] apart from those which doubtless found their way into her books. Without a father, and with her mother trying to carry on the agricultural school he had previously run, her early childhood must have been unusually free; and to this must be added the fact that her mother was far from strict.[12] What her early experience certainly did enforce on E. Nesbit was her sense of a family, and particularly of children: she hardly ever writes about the solitary child, but about the interactions of brothers and sisters, and always from a position of involvement, from the children's point of view (she was one of the first to do this).

E. Nesbit is not a writer with a definite philosophy or moral code which unifies or gives 'purpose' to her books. She herself flouted the conventions of her time, smoking cigarettes in public, wearing outrageous 'aesthetic' clothes (and making her children do so too),[13] and bringing up in her own family two of the children of her husband's extra-marital affairs.[14] Here again the lack of distance on her part in her children's books is explained. But the important point here is that she never committed herself to one thing in life (except her family), and had no fixed and narrow point of view.

One of the keys to an understanding of E. Nesbit is her passionate delight in life, and her wish to experience it to the full, to 'spread' herself in every direction. She threw herself with enthusiasm into everything she did. She was a prominent foundation member of the Fabian Society. She became a dedicated 'Aesthete' in the 1880s.[15] She made herself an accomplished hostess, and held many 'open house' weekends at Well Hall, her house in Sussex. She wrote articles as a poetry critic for the *Athenaeum*. For years she tried to identify Bacon with Shakespeare by means of logarithms.[16] She became fascinated with the construction of model cities out of household objects, writing a book, *The Magic City* (1910), on the subject, and exhibiting one of her cities at a stand at Olympia in 1912. And she was a writer of a vast number of books both for adults and children: of 'real-life' novels, melodramas, poems, magic books, horror tales and stories of childhood.

The range of her friendships and reading shows the same love of variety. She herself declared that she had read Hume, Locke and Berkeley, Percy's *Anecdotes* in 39 volumes, Burton's *Anatomy of Melancholy*, Buchner's *Man*, Mill's *Subjection of Women*, Louis Blanc's *Historical Revelations* and Sinnett's *Esoteric Buddhism*.[17] She was influenced by writers as diverse as Dickens, Mrs J. H. Ewing, Henry James, Kenneth Grahame, George Eliot, Mrs M. L. Molesworth, Thackeray, Wells, Anstey, Kipling, Charles Reade, George MacDonald and E. M. Forster; and she had a passion for drama, particularly Ibsen.[18] Laurence Housman actually assisted her with plots – and gave her the Phoenix.[19] Her 'sampler' of English poetry, *Poets' Whispers* (1895), speaks for itself of the breadth of her love for poetry; she and her husband Hubert Bland were members of the Browning and Shelley Societies. In 1908 she helped launch and edit the quarterly periodical *The Neolith*:[20] three of the contributors, with whose work she was at least partly familiar, were Lord Dunsany, Arthur Machen and Richard Middleton. E. Nesbit was influenced by the 'Decadent' mode too,[21] and herself contributed some work to the *Yellow Book*. Her circle of friends and acquaintances was vast: for example with Shaw, Wells, Kipling, Laurence Housman, Forster and Chesterton she was a particular friend, and she also knew William Morris, Yeats, Baron Corvo, Conrad, W. E. Henley, Oscar Wilde and Rider Haggard. It has been said in description of her character and reading that:

> Few writers have had a wider range of literary tastes than E. Nesbit or cultivated friendships with other writers so different in outlook and in accomplishments. A fervent Ibsen enthusiast ... she could shed tears over *Jessica's First Prayer*; a disciple of Kipling, she still perceived all the charm and delicacy of Henry James; she read the most advanced and challenging literature of the nineties and managed to appreciate it without any infidelity to her earlier loves – Dickens, Thackeray, George Eliot, and Charles Reade; fairy stories, adventure stories, contemplative poetry, political and religious works, anything in short that was good of its kind was

capable of providing entertainment for her. And when there was nothing better to be had, she was glad enough even of what was not good of its kind. As she once told a friend, she would sooner at any time in her life have read a railway time-table than nothing. As for her friendships, she seemed as she grew older to become rather more than less sensitive to the attractions of new intimacies, and the interesting possibilities of strangers. (Moore, p. 163)

Nesbit's character – her child-likeness, her refusal to be fixed on one activity or code in life, her sheer zest – is portrayed in the character of her books. It emerges in the form of episodic narratives organised not by 'themes' or deep meanings but by comic schemata which make witty conceits out of magic.

There is no recurrent theme or motif running through the variety of stories that she wrote (it has been said of the disparity between her adult and her children's books that 'it is almost impossible not to believe there were two Nesbits'[22]): and there is rarely a central idea in any single one of her works either. Her long stories often fall apart naturally into narrative vignettes. *Five Children and It* (1902) begins with the discovery by a family of children of a strange sand-fairy called a Psammead, which grants them a wish each morning with the proviso that the effects of the wish vanish at sunset. The book is thereafter a series of episodes, each centred on a wish granted, but all quite unrelated to one another. One day the children wish '"to be rich beyond the dreams of something or other"' (p. 44), and the Psammead fills the gravel pit near where they are standing with gold. But it is gold in the form of spade-guineas, which no shopkeeper will accept; and finally the children are taken to the police station to be charged with unlawful possession. Just as the worst is about to befall, however, the gold vanishes at sunset, and they are released, with reprimands. On another occasion they wish for wings, and are on the top of a locked church tower at sunset (chs 4, 5); on another Robert, who has just been unfairly beaten by the local baker's boy, wishes to be bigger than him, and the Psammead makes him a giant – by sunset he is being exhibited at a fairground (ch. 8). A similar technique is used in *The Phoenix and the Carpet* (1904). Several of E. Nesbit's magic books are simply collections of tales – *The Book of Dragons* (1900), *Nine Unlikely Tales* (1901), *Oswald Bastable and Others*

(1905), *The Magic World* (1912). In other stories there is a general narrative frame binding a series of episodes: thus in *The Story of the Amulet* the objective of the children is the search, by time-travelling, for the other half of a section of a magic amulet which they have found in a shop (the recovery of the whole will grant them their 'heart's desire'): but much of the story is a series of visits to different civilisations, and the entertaining effects to be derived from bringing a family of Edwardian children together with people from Stone Age, Babylonian, Roman or Phoenician cultures. E. Nesbit uses the same framing method in her 'domestic' children's novels: the general aim of the children in *The Treasure Seekers* is the restoration of the fortunes of the Bastable family by finding or making money, but the various attempts are complete and individual in themselves; and similarly with the general objective of *The Would Be Goods*.

E. Nesbit's books do not ask more than a literal level of reading. The search for the 'heart's desire' in *The Story of the Amulet* could conceivably have been made into a metaphor of spiritual pilgrimage, but, apart from one hint, the Amulet is treated simply as an object to be secured; and at the end, when it has been restored, the heart's desire thus gained is simply the return of the children's parents from abroad. The case is similar with E. Nesbit's more adult imaginative works. Where the subject of her 'modern melodrama', *Salome and the Head* (1909), would have been to a writer such as George MacDonald one rich in symbolic possibilities, it offered E. Nesbit simply the opportunity to exploit the full horror of the story by giving it a modern setting. In *Dormant* (1911), one of the characters, Antony Drelincourt, discovers through magical experiments the elixir of life, and with it wakens the beautiful Eugenia, who has been in a state of suspended animation for forty-five years. Alchemy is only the background for the romantic concern of the novel: Drelincourt, formerly pledged to one Rose Royal, abandons her for Eugenia; but later, while he is trying by means of the elixir to make himself more acceptable to Eugenia by becoming immortal, both of them are drowned. Charles Williams, whose fantasies are much concerned with the use and misuse of magic, would have made a theme out of Antony's blasphemy in his perversion of man's condition (as he does with Gregory Persimmons in *War in Heaven* (1930));[23] George MacDonald might have made the opposition of the two women a symbol of the waning subconscious; but E. Nesbit is more interested in using alchemy here simply as an exciting mechanism for the precipitation of amorous reversals.

Similarly, the supernatural characters in E. Nesbit's work have forms determined purely by the fancy of the creator.[24] This is the shape of the Psammead, the strangest of all:

> Its eyes were on long horns like a snail's eyes, and it could move them in and out like telescopes; it had ears like a bat's ears, and its tubby body was shaped like a spider's and covered with thick soft fur; its legs and arms were furry too, and it had hands and feet like a monkey's. (*FCI*, p. 14)

The Psammead's appearance is in no way symbolic, or expressive of a spiritual condition, as it would have been had George MacDonald been writing the story. In his *The Princess and Curdie* (1883), for example, MacDonald gives us a creature called Lina, which is similarly a 'mass of incongruities', but here the form is the projection of an inner state (the boy-hero Curdie is told that '"Shapes are only dresses, and dresses are only names"'):

> She had a very short body, and very long legs made like an elephant's, so that in lying down she kneeled with both pairs. Her tail, which dragged on the floor behind her, was twice as long and quite as thick as her body. Her head was something between that of a polar bear and a snake. Her eyes were dark green, with a yellow light in them. Her under teeth came up like a fringe of icicles, only very white, outside of her upper lip. Her throat looked as if the hair had been plucked off. It showed a skin white and smooth.[25]

E. Nesbit's description is simply additive: the Psammead is formed of a mingling of attractive and repulsive elements. The reader is moved from the snail's eyes to the more pleasing suggestion of a 'gadget' in the analogy with telescopes; thence from bats to tubbiness, from spiders to thick soft fur, and then, in different order, from furriness to monkeys. In MacDonald's account there is nothing very attractive in the portrait, unless the reader is determined over the tail: the 'skin white and smooth' might be pleasing but for the fact that it occurs where the hair has been removed, thus suggesting the lividness of scar tissue. What MacDonald juxtaposes here is the unfamiliar or displeasing with the unfamiliar. Elephants, polar bears, snakes and icicles are not common to most readers' experience. Nor of course do polar bears and snakes belong together, except in the one particular of shape of head, and the same goes for elephants and icicles. The picture is one of a body perverted: the reader is aware of a proportion which has been everywhere upset. The body is too short, the legs too long and thick; she cannot lie down properly; the tail is an unwieldy encumbrance; the bottom teeth are useless, except for rending; her throat hair is missing. The whole picture gives the sense of a mixture of laughable ungainliness, enormous power, ferocity (the mixture of dark green and yellow light in her eyes is peculiarly effective) and gentle, helpless innocence (the white skin) – precisely the spiritual state the form expresses. Where E. Nesbit's fusion of discordant qualities is a product of fancy, MacDonald's is one of the imagination. MacDonald himself described fancy as 'hunting after resemblances that carry with them no interpretation', and might have spoken of E. Nesbit as he did of Shelley:

> The evidences of pure imagination in his writings are unfrequent as compared with those of fancy; there are not half the instances of the direct embodiment of idea in form, that there are of the presentation of strange resemblances between external things.[26]

There are other differences between E. Nesbit's and more 'philosophical' fantasies. The children in her stories rarely have to be 'good' in order to meet the magic creatures, nor do they have to be gifted with imaginative vision, as in MacDonald's fairy tales. They simply happen on a Psammead in a gravel pit, or a magic amulet in a London curio shop, or a Phoenix egg rolled up in a new carpet.[27] To some extent E. Nesbit is playing on the adult sense of disproportion here. In some of her later magic books she tried to move towards a more mystical and 'poetic' treatment of the supernatural, and this involved spiritual considerations: but with the possible exception of *Harding's Luck* (1909) she was a little out of her element in so reaching for the 'significant' and the portentous, and these stories are not the expression of her peculiar genius.

E. Nesbit is not centrally interested in portraying spiritual development on the part of her child characters: she is not cut out for a writer of fantastic *Bildungsromanen*. In other fantasies, such as those of MacDonald, Charles Williams or C. S. Lewis, the supernatural may disappear at the end of the story, but it has left a permanent change in the souls of the protagonists: in E. Nesbit's work, 'Whereyouwantogoto' (the title of one of her stories) tends spiritually to end as Whereyoustartedfrom. Certainly her characters do gain and learn from their experiences, but the gaining and learning usually have little to do with transformation. A story may end with 'intellectual' benefit, as in the case of the fusion of the minds of the Learned Gentleman and Rekhmarā at the end of *The Story of the Amulet*, or Edwin's development as a mathematician thanks to the Arithmetic Fairy in 'The Sums that Came Right' (*NUT*). Parents return to children at the end of 'Justnowland' and *The Story of the Amulet*. Amabel's dislike for her aunt is removed by her experiences in 'The Aunt and Amabel' (*MW*). But however they are regarded, these are not *spiritual* benefits, particularly not that entry into and transformation of the soul by the supernatural implied in the notion here.

Even in those few of E. Nesbit's tales where moral education is at the centre of interest, the morality is often curiously linked with material values. In 'Whereyouwantogoto' (*NUT*, pp. 51–84) the children are taken by a magic ball to a sunny, sandy beach with rocks and caves, shells, seaweeds, a friendly dog, a seal, and a huge picnic lunch lying waiting for them. They have only to be good, and they will have these things for as long as they wish. But on the fourth day they quarrel over who is to make their fern-bed, and a housemaid appears to inform them that it is her place to make the beds, and that she will make sure the children are in them by seven every evening. A further quarrel turns the delicious food with which they are supplied into the kind of fare they have at home; and another brings a bathing machine, with a notice on it saying, '"You must not bathe any more except through me."' And so on, until they have turned the delightful beach into a hideous seaside resort. Their last act is to cut into the magic ball to see '"what makes him bounce"': upon which the scene is metamorphosed into the surroundings of their home, where they are punished by their aunt and uncle and sent to bed. The morality of this story is simply that being good is practical politics: there is no sense that it is a delightful experience in itself, only that it is a precondition. A story with a similarly 'materialistic' effect is 'The Cat-Hood of Maurice' (*MW*), where the ethics of putting oneself in another's position are worked out in the very physical terms of the boy Maurice's transformation into the cat he has so thoughtlessly bullied and teased, and the cat's temporary assumption of Maurice's body.[28]

There is some sense in which Evelyn Underhill's distinction, in her book *Mysticism* (1911), between attitudes to the unseen can be applied to E. Nesbit. Miss Underhill terms the two attitudes the 'way of magic' and the 'way of mysticism'. Magic is self-oriented, whether individually or socially: the magician wants to use the supernatural for his or humanity's ends. Mysticism, however, involves the struggle to remove the self through submission to an ultimate reality 'for no personal gain, to satisfy no transcendental curiosity, to obtain no other-worldly joys, but purely from an instinct of love'. In short 'magic wants to get, mysticism wants to give'.[29] This polarity at least provides an analogy for an understanding of E. Nesbit's fairy tales. The Amulet in *The Story of the Amulet* has the promise of goodness without effort:

> 'The complete Amulet can keep off all the things that make people unhappy – jealousy, bad-temper, pride, disagreeableness, greediness, selfishness, laziness. Evil spirits, people called them when the Amulet was made ... And it can give you strength and courage ... And virtue ... And it can give you your heart's desire.' (*SA*, pp. 51–2)

It is interesting to note, in relation to Miss Underhill's phrase 'transcendental curiosity' that in many of E. Nesbit's fairy tales magic is used to satisfy curiosity. Like her Mrs De Ward in 'Accidental Magic', E. Nesbit was fascinated by esoteric knowledge, by ' "all the things that people are not quite sure about – the things that are hidden and secret, wonderful and mysterious – the things people make discoveries about" ' (*MW*, pp. 58–9). Thus in *The Story of the Amulet*, *The House of Arden* (1908) and *Harding's Luck* part of the interest involves the 'discovery' of the unknown springs of action determining historical events, and the bringing-to-life of civilisations otherwise known only through fragmentary evidence. For instance, one of the episodes in *The Story of the Amulet* involves a visit to Atlantis, at the end of which the children watch the destruction of the civilisation by volcano and tidal wave; and in *The House of Arden* (ch. 8) the children are unwitting agents in the discovery of the Gunpowder Plot in 1605: here the 'unknown springs of action' are given to, rather than discovered in, the past.[30]

E. Nesbit exploits comic incongruities in several ways. For example, there is often a gap between the expectation and the reality of the supernatural. The appearance of the Psammead is hardly the standard conception of a fairy. E. Nesbit also plays against the notion of the remoteness of the supernatural: her magic creatures often have the hard definition and idiosyncrasy of realistic characters. The origin of the Psammead is within time, in the prehistoric past, and that past is made no more strange and remote than the everyday present:

'Why, almost everyone had Pterodactyl for breakfast in my time! ... I believe they were very good grilled ... People used to send their little boys down to the seashore early in the morning before breakfast to get the day's wishes, and very often the eldest boy in the family would be told to wish for a Megatherium, ready jointed for cooking ... when people had dinner-parties it was nearly always Megatheriums; and Ichthyosaurus, because his fins were a great delicacy and his tail made soup.' (*FCI*, pp. 18–19)

The 'day's wishes' is a marvellous piece of witty reduction: it shows how Nesbit's imagination works inwards to the brilliant *aperçu* rather than outward to large structures and themes. Both the Psammead and the Phoenix belong to a definite 'species', and though the Phoenix has semi-mythical origin, it is treated almost as a household pet. Such familiarity, with the Psammead in its paper bag, or sleeping in its bath of sand, and the Phoenix roosting 'on the cornice supporting the window-curtains of the boys' room' (*PC*, p. 23), is calculated deflation of mystery. As for their personalities, the Psammead hates water, and is bad-tempered, highly practical, cynical, contemptuous and jealous of being loved; the Phoenix loves anything to do with fire – including Fire Insurance Offices – and is aristocratic, conceited and pompous; and the Mouldiwarp is slow, rustic and tetchy.

The magic creatures are also given everyday speech. Shortly after the magic bird in *The Phoenix and the Carpet* has hatched from its fiery egg after a two-thousand-year sleep, it flies round the living room and, alighting on the tablecloth, scorches the material: at which, ' "It's only a very little scorched," said the Phoenix, apologetically; "it will come out in the wash" ' (*PC*, p. 17). The Phoenix can use London slang when called upon, and despite its long absence from the world, can converse in perfect French (*PC*, pp. 94–5, 121, 124). Similarly, when the Psammead sees its new travelling bag,

'Humph,' it said, sniffing a little contemptuously, yet at the same time affectionately, 'it's not so dusty.'
The Psammead seemed to pick up very easily the kind of things that people said nowadays. For a creature that had in its time associated with Megatheriums and Pterodactyls, its quickness was really wonderful. (*SA*, p. 176)

Few writers can have mentioned the actual *feel* of a supernatural creature as E. Nesbit does. When Anthea first discovers the Psammead burrowing away from her in the sand, what she feels is its fur (*FCI*, p. 13). The Psammead is 'to be felt' also in the bites it inflicts on the cruel shopkeeper and on the 'learned gentleman', and through its weight in Anthea's arms or in its waterproof bag.[31] Similarly the reader is made almost to feel the bulge of the Phoenix hidden beneath Robert's coat when he takes it to the theatre, where it emerges 'crushed and dishevelled' (*PC*, pp. 208–10).

The method here is the comic marriage of the strange and the familiar. In the shorter fairy tales there are genii which appear from magic rings in the forms of footmen and butlers, a princess who falls in love with a royal lift operator, a dragon which swims in a sea of treacle, another which, supposedly fierce, is won over with sugar-lumps, a dispossessed princess who is restored by an enchanted hedgehog, the transformation of an entire country's population into mussels, and a king who is metamorphosed by the laughter of a cockatoucan into 'a villa-residence, replete with every modern improvement'.[32]

At the same time the children in the magic books remain very real and intensely human.[33] It is one of E. Nesbit's strengths as a writer of fantasy that in the midst of magic nothing is lost of realism.

> 'Now I've been thinking' – [said Cyril].
> 'Not really?' whispered Robert.
> 'In the silent what's-its-names of the night. It's like suddenly being asked something out of history – the date of the Conquest or something; you know it all right all the time, but when you're asked it all goes out of your head. Ladies and gentlemen, you know jolly well that when we're all rotting about in the usual way heaps of things keep cropping up, and then real earnest wishes come into the heads of the beholder' –
> 'Hear, hear!' said Robert.
> '– of the beholder, however stupid he is,' Cyril went on. 'Why, even Robert might happen to think of a really useful wish if he didn't injure his poor little brains trying so hard to think.' (*FCI*, p. 198)

Cyril is a literary relative of Oswald Bastable: the sudden lapse from high-flown diction into child vernacular is superb, but even better is the complete mixture of metaphors which turns the children into decomposing vegetables and thoughts into fungi – not to mention, of course, the 'head*s* of the *beholder*'. E. Nesbit is fond of such linguistic interplay. When the children have succeeded in wishing themselves into being besieged in a castle by a troop of soldiers, Robert tries to address the leader in what language he can recall from his knowledge of historical romance: '"Sir Wulfric de Talbot," he said slowly, "should think foul scorn to – to keep a chap – I mean one who has done him no hurt – when he wants to cut off quietly – I mean to depart without violence"' (*FCI*, p. 166). In *The Story of the Amulet*, when the children are rescued from a Babylonian dungeon by the supernatural Nisroch, servant of the 'Great Ones', he asks them:

> 'Is there aught else that the Servant of the great Name can do for those that speak that name?'
> 'No – oh, *no*,' said Cyril. 'It's all right now. Thanks ever so.'
> 'You are a dear,' cried Anthea, not in the least knowing what she was saying. (*SA*, p. 167)

Of course one of the main types of comic interplay in the magic books is that between the children and the difficulties that magic makes for them. When they ask the Psammead to make them '"as beautiful as the day"' (*FCI*, p. 22), they become unrecognisable to one another, and their baby brother the Lamb, who has remained unchanged, does not know them and breaks into screams. When at last they reach home, Martha the nursemaid seizes the Lamb and bids the strangers be off, '"Go along with you, you nasty little Eyetalian monkey[s]"' (*FCI*, p. 30). The children are reduced to standing in a dry ditch, waiting for sunset and the end of their beauty. Perhaps the most amusing episode of this type is the one in which Cyril, irritated at the Lamb's having accidentally broken his watch, wishes without thinking that the Lamb were grown up. The subsequent struggles of the children to look after the now adult Lamb and prevent him from escorting a lady friend home on his bicycle are beautifully handled; the finest moment occurs when Martha, who, thanks to the Psammead, has now been made blind to any of the magic transformations of the children, picks up the slight but adult figure of the Lamb –

> 'Come to his own Martha, then – a precious poppet!'
> The grown-up Lamb ... struggled furiously. An expression of intense horror and annoyance was seen on his face. But Martha was stronger than he. She lifted him up and carried him into the house. None of the children will ever forget that picture. The neat grey-flannel-suited grown-up young man with the green tie and the little black moustache – fortunately, he was slightly built, and not tall – struggling in the sturdy arms of Martha, who bore him away helpless, imploring him, as she went, to be a good boy now, and come and have his nice brem-milk! (*FCI*, p. 250)

In E. Nesbit's finer magic books the strangeness of the creatures, places or peoples that the children see is always to some extent reduced. This is not done by evasion, or 'drawing a veil', because E. Nesbit will not insult the intelligence of her readers. Instead she often uses a technique which could loosely be called 'metaphoric' in its blending of the potentially frightening with the familiar. The strange city in which Philip and Lucy find themselves in *The Magic City* is an enlarged and animated version of the one they themselves previously built in their house out of books, finger-bowls, vases, cabinets, chessmen, pepper-pots and a host of other domestic objects, and the people in it are Philip's toys.[34] The same 'identification game' is the motif of the stories 'The Blue Mountain' (*NUT*), and 'The Town in the Library' (*NUT*).[35] When the children in *The Story of the Amulet* are watching the terrifying destruction of Atlantis, and the 'learned gentleman' puts everyone's lives at risk by refusing to return home through the Amulet till the last moment, the reader is suddenly brought back to the immediate scene when the enraged Psammead leaps out of its bag and bites his hand (*SA*, p. 229). Again, the music at the Babylonian banquet

> reminded Anthea of the band she and the others had once had on the fifth of November – with penny horns, a tin whistle, a tea tray, the tongs, a policeman's rattle, and a toy drum. They had enjoyed this band very much at the time. But it was quite different when someone else was making the same kind of music. Anthea understood now that Father had not been really heartless and unreasonable when he had told them to stop that infuriating din. (*SA*, p. 159)

The two contexts are married in Anthea's mind: Babylonian minstrelsy and policemen's rattles meet like the two halves of the Amulet.[36]

This interplay of natural and supernatural in E. Nesbit's magic books is in part the fusion of two personal and literary impulses in her life. On the one hand she was what may be called a 'realist'. Enough perhaps has been given of her biography to show how much she was a lady 'of her time', thoroughly involved with life both socially and intellectually. She wrote many poems on the folly of artistic or religious asceticism: one ends: 'Still there's the wisdom that wise men call folly,/Still one can go and pick daisies with Molly!'[37] Though professedly Catholics, neither she nor her husband Hubert Bland often attended church, and they seemed to take little account of whether they were 'in a state of Grace' (Moore, pp. 210–11). Occasionally in her poetry E. Nesbit sets out the possibilities of a life of contemplation, but only to return to 'this world' in the end.[38] She once wrote, on the Fabian Society, to a friend, 'There are two distinct elements in the F.S. ... The practical and the visionary – the first being much the strongest ... We belong – needless to say – to the practical party' (Moore, p. 107). Several of her poems concern the choice between town and country, and end by preferring to face the former: 'We fight for freedom and the souls of men –/Here, and not there, is fought and won our fight'.[39] The emphasis of her religious poetry is on the Incarnation,[40] and the theme of motherhood runs through all her verse.[41] Her poem *Jesus in London* (1908)[42] is a description not of Christ's divinity, but of how he would deal with the Mammon of the Edwardian age, and with the misery and repression of the lower classes.

E. Nesbit could be quite honestly materialistic: though her writing must have given her considerable pleasure, she was also very concerned to use it to provide money, not so often for the essentials of life, but to make comfort more comfortable. Thus, thinking of a boating holiday on the Medway, she points out how such joys have to be paid for in 'hard coin', by writing another chapter, 'And I will earn, working like mad,/The Medway, with the Psammead.'[43] Again, in her lines, 'To a Young Poet', she writes, 'Write for sale, and not for use./This is a commercial age!' and

> If your soul should droop and die,
> Bury it with undimmed eye.
> Never mind what memory says –
> Soul's a thing that never pays![44]

These various types of involvement with the 'real' world are to be contrasted with another side of her nature. The supernatural 'always had a strong fascination for her'.[45] For example, she believed in ghosts all her life, partly owing to an early experience in Brittany. She had gone for a ramble with her brothers, and they came across a dilapidated, locked chateau. The children found a boarded-up doorway at the back, and through the planks they could see a bare room with a heap of straw; but as they looked, the straw began to gather itself up and spin until it made a rope almost touching the ceiling. In their flight, the children passed a cottage, whence emerged an old woman who said, '"Je vois, mes enfants, que vous avez vu *la dame qui file*"' (Moore, pp. 66–7). They never found the castle again. There were many other traumatic experiences in E. Nesbit's childhood. Perhaps the most harrowing was her visit with her sisters to the 'mummies of Bordeaux' (she had wanted to go, because the name 'mummy' seemed so pleasant): the mummies turned out to be two hundred skeletons arranged in standing positions round three sides of a vault; skeletons with the flesh hardened to the bones and with long dry hair round their faces. As she put it later, 'The mummies of Bordeaux were the crowning horror of my childish life ... the shock of that sight branded it on my brain, and I never forgot it.'[46] For a girl who 'had no defence against the most cruel sensibility' (Moore, p. 54), the effects on her work of these early experiences were particularly far-reaching.[47] In addition she lived for most of her life in a series of reputedly haunted houses, which in itself must have been stimulus to her native morbidity of temperament, her fascination for 'searching into subjects which she herself found terrifying':

> Like a little girl fascinated with ghost stories whose after-effects she well knows to be disastrous, she would sit up at night writing tales of violence and death until she was afraid to go to bed. And she would read books and see sights which, as she was fully aware beforehand, were certain to upset her nerves. (Moore, p. 236)

Having been terrified at the thought of skeletons when she was a child, she tried the quaint and quite counter-productive expedient of familiarising her own children with such things by keeping a skull and a pile of bones to which she would introduce them (ibid.).

'[E. Nesbit's] sufferings ultimately resulted in an extraordinary dichotomy in her creative work' (Moore, p. 54). The fascinated terror of the supernatural and the horrifying found expression in many of the stories she wrote:[48] it is there in *Salome* and in *Dormant*, and in a number of smaller ghost and terror tales collected in *Grim Tales* (1893), *Man and Maid* (1906), *Fear* (1910) and *To the Adventurous* (1923).[49] While it is true that there was a *fin de siècle* vogue for such tales, and that E. Nesbit was one among such contemporary writers as Richard Middleton, Arthur Machen, Algernon Blackwood, M. R. James and W. H. Hodgson, her stories sometimes have a neurotic character all their own. For instance, 'The Power of Darkness' is set in a waxworks filled with grisly scenes of violence done in wax: one man lays a wager that another cannot spend a night there, and the one who accepts the challenge goes mad during his vigil.[50] In

'The House of Silence' a thief robs a wealthy but strangely silent house, and loses himself in tunnels leading off one of the rooms, until at the end of one tunnel he comes to a little sunlit courtyard where he sees a lady in green lying dead with a great black swarm of flies buzzing round her.[51] There is a peculiarly obsessional quality in these stories.[52]

The other, the 'realistic' side of E. Nesbit, went both into her 'Bastable' children's books and into a range of adult novels and stories such as *Thirteen Ways Home* (1901), *The Literary Sense* (1903), *The Red House* (1903), *The Incomplete Amorist* (1906), *Daphne in Fitzroy Street* (1909), *These Little Ones* (1909), *The Incredible Honeymoon* (1921) and *The Lark* (1922). Of the adult books only *The Literary Sense* and *The Red House* are memorable: the others are mostly on romantic themes well-worn by popular novelists of the time. *The Literary Sense* is a series of stories, most of them on the slightly Jamesian theme of self-dramatisation and its consequences, and *The Red House* describes family life in an idyllic manner, and, unusual for its day, married love. Its uninviting title E. Nesbit felt was probably the main cause of the poor sales of the former, but *The Red House* was a considerable success (Moore, pp. 198, 212–13).

These two sides of E. Nesbit – the 'realist' and the 'super-naturalist' – are brought together in her magic books, where magic is given a colloquial and comic face, and is brought into contact with very human children. This does not necessarily make the magic books the 'summit' of E. Nesbit's achievement – the Bastable stories are arguably as finely done[53] – but it does show that in those books she united opposed impulses in her own nature; or, to put it more theoretically, that there 'the most heterogeneous ideas are yoked by violence together'. This last phrase was applied by Dr Johnson to the method of the 'metaphysical' poets of the seventeenth century, and indeed the character of E. Nesbit's more successful work could be called 'conceited'. It is true that whereas a poet such as Donne compares constancy in love to a pair of compasses, that is, joins two opposed contexts to bring out his meaning more fully, Nesbit has no such meaning to clarify, and she wishes her readers to attend to incongruity rather than likeness between the terms. In this respect she is more akin to the more 'fanciful' Cleveland than to Donne. None the less, in all E. Nesbit's more characteristic magic books the central aim, and the one on which her strength depends, is the production of situations or images in which maximum comic energy is generated by a clash of contexts.

The opposites juxtaposed are not merely random: there is usually a law or principle, however tenuous, which gives the bringing together of the terms a certain inevitability; a reviewer has remarked, 'her magic was governed by inexorable rules of logic'.[54] For example, the purely superficial kinship between the Phoenix and the Phoenix Fire Office is sufficient to justify the bird's considering the latter as a temple erected to its fame. Thus the stage is set for the ludicrous events which take place when it visits the office and asks for the High Priest. When, also in *The Phoenix and the Carpet*, the children ask the magic Persian carpet to revisit its native land, '"and bring back the most beautiful and delightful productions of it you can"', the carpet is only being true to the laws of its own nature in returning with 199 very hungry and vocal Persian cats (*PC*, pp. 137, 140–1). There is a simultaneous centripetal and centrifugal movement which gives a special pleasure: the reader sees what thinly justifies bringing the terms together at the same time as they drive one another apart. The story 'Uncle James, or, the Purple Stranger' has behind it a law of reversal. The reader is told that the island of Rotundia was created when a pointed piece of rock impaled a lump of soft clay and both, spinning in the opposite direction to that of the earth, fell into the sea and came to rest. Thus it is that on the island elephants are tiny while guinea-pigs and rabbits are enormous; and thus too, 'all the things we have to make – buns and cake and shortbread – grow on trees and bushes, but in Rotundia they have to make their cauliflowers and cabbages and carrots and apples and onions, just as our cooks make puddings and turnovers' (*BD*, p. 50).

E. Nesbit is as fond of the use of arithmetic and logic in magical contexts as the metaphysical poets were in writing of love.[55] One of her best-known stories is 'Melisande, or, Long and Short Division' in which a Princess, doomed at birth by her wicked fairy godmother Malevola to be bald, uses a wish she is given when she is grown up to have golden hair a yard long, which will grow an inch every day, and twice as fast every time it is cut. The result is that she is soon growing balesfull of hair every minute, and the family have to advertise for 'a competent Prince' to try to find a way round the problem. The bright idea of cutting the Princess off the hair instead of the hair off the Princess results only in the Princess herself growing enormous while the hair stays still. After this error has been righted by cutting her hair off her again, Prince Florizel finds the solution to the whole problem by setting up a huge pair of scales, and putting the Princess into one scale-pan and the growing hair into another. When the weights are exactly equal he cuts the hair exactly at the fulcrum, so that, as he tells her, '"neither you nor your hair can possibly decide which ought to go on growing"', and the magic cancels out. At every stage, however absurd what happens, it all fits into a pattern of quasi-logic which makes it at once preposterous and appropriate.

Arithmetic is integrated with magic in 'The Island of the Nine Whirlpools' (*BD*). In this story, a Princess is imprisoned on an island guarded by a dragon and surrounded by nine whirlpools. As with every enchantment there is a loophole: the whirls are calm for five minutes in every twenty-four hours, and this period of calm begins five minutes earlier every day; and the dragon turns to stone and sleeps for five minutes each day and begins its sleep three minutes later every day. Prince Nigel, who comes to rescue the Princess, has to calculate when the quiescence of the whirls and of the dragon will interlock in such a way that if he lures the dragon into the water when the whirls are quiet it will begin its slumber just as they start again, and will be unable to save itself. Here the whole of the enchantment is actually organised on the lines of a mathematical problem: and thus magic can be conjoined with what amounts to a boy's homework exercise. This is overtly the case in another story, 'The Sums That Came Right' (*NUT*).

Sometimes a species of punning provides the 'yoking-together' element of E. Nesbit's tales. In 'Belinda and Bellamant', a Princess is doomed by a family of wicked bell-people to '"grow uglier every day, except Sundays, and every Sunday she shall be seven times prettier than the Sunday before"' (*MW*, p. 164), until she can find a bell '"that doesn't ring, and can't ring, and never will ring, and wasn't made to ring"'. Meanwhile, the wicked fairy godmothers of the corresponding Prince have rendered him quite physically incompatible by making him handsome all week and unbearably ugly on Sundays, until he can manage to stay underwater for more than two minutes. The requirements for the removal of the two curses seem to have no connection with one another, and the reader also expects something that *looks* like a ringing bell to be the salvation of the Princess: but in the end it is a diving bell which removes both curses. This story is a particularly fine example of E. Nesbit's method, for it can be seen that though the curses are opposed, they fit in with or are complementary to one another, in the same way that the Prince and Princess belong to one another. The situation is as neat as that in Marvell's 'The Definition of Love' – their love 'so truly parallel,/Though infinite, can never meet'. They do join forces to try to remove their curses ('the conjunction of the mind') but they cannot *marry* until that removal ('And opposition of the stars'). Best of all perhaps is the way that one object answers both curses: the witty fusion in the form of the diving bell joins the Prince and Princess in a shared release which itself effectively marries them. Another, if slightly less brilliant, story in this manner is 'The Princess and the Hedge-Pig', in which the Princess is doomed to be turned out of her kingdom, to have to face her enemies without a friend to help her and to be unable to return to her own again until she finds '"A thousand spears to follow her to battle"' (*MW*, p. 104). In the end a Prince who has been transformed into a hedgehog answers the requirement with his thousand spines.

There are of course degrees of appositeness in E. Nesbit's method. In 'The Cockatoucan' (*NUT*), the magic bird has the power to change people into *anything* when it laughs. Sometimes the transformation is fitting, as in the case of Pridmore, Matilda's grim nursemaid, who is turned into an automatic machine 'such as those which you see in a railway station' (*NUT*, p. 19); but this is not so much the case when the bird laughs on a public holiday meant to celebrate the return of the King's victorious army –

> The Cockatoucan laughed just as the reception was beautifully arranged. It laughed, and the general holiday was turned into an income tax; the magnificent reception changed itself into a royal reprimand, and the Army itself suddenly became a discontented Sunday-school treat, and had to be fed with buns and brought home in brakes, crying. (*NUT*, p. 33)

This is superb, but now because of the sheer disparity of the terms, particularly the last (the sentence gathers itself for it, and the transformations in the first two cases are less ambitious, making full weight fall on the third): it is partly the interplay of abstract and concrete – 'holiday' to 'income tax', 'reception' to 'reprimand', 'Army' to 'treat' and then back to a crowd of children. But it is only locally successful, and by the time the Cockatoucan has laughed again the reader has been taken to the realms of unmitigated fancy:

> 'There's your dear father – he's a desirable villa – the Prime Minister was a little boy, and he got back again, and now he's turned into a Comic Opera. Half the Palace housemaids are breakers, dashing themselves against the Palace crockery: the Navy, to a man, are changed to French poodles, and the Army to German sausages. Your favourite nurse is now a flourishing steam laundry, and I, alas! am too clever by half.' (*NUT*, p. 41)

Although this is great fun, it has no element of rule or logic behind it. Here, too, could be explored the twisting of the rules or the faulty causality in such tales as 'The Blue Mountain' (*NUT*), 'The Prince, Two Mice, and Some Kitchen-Maids' (*NUT*), 'Fortunatus Rex & Co.' (*NUT*) or 'The Princess and the Cat' (*OBO*). But the point should be sufficiently clear: the skill that goes into the better stories is a real one, requiring considerable subtlety and artistic discipline, and this can be seen by comparison with those tales in which it is not so fully brought to bear.

E. Nesbit's fantasy is not what would be called great literature: it is at its best without any deeply felt spiritual meaning, and it could be argued that the sensibility behind it is not particularly sophisticated – even that it is at times materialistic. To repeat the classification made here, her work is fanciful rather than imaginative. But fancy has its place: and it could be claimed that in E. Nesbit's work it reaches a high point of wit and ingenuity. She had her literary forbears – Thackeray, MacDonald, Carroll, Mrs Molesworth and particularly F. Anstey, all of whom played magic against humdrum real life for comic effect; but she gave the 'realistic' side more vitality by her special understanding of a child's mind, and the magic more scope by her use of rules and logic. The result is that the bringing-together of opposites in her magic books is of a variety, skill and comic potential unequalled before her or since.[56] But these books are also a picture of E. Nesbit's zest for life in almost any form: the 'conceited' method of juxtaposing opposites recalls the lady who was as happy with logarithms as with Ibsen, with Shaw as with Chesterton, with Fabianism as with the *Yellow Book*. Inventive powers and wit of the kind that she shows are not often recognised by literary criticism: perhaps there might be a healthy diminution of gravity if they were.

5   Circularity in Fantasy: George MacDonald

Unlike the traditional fairy tale, in which the hero often betters himself in the world and may move place, most modern fantasy involves the notion of a return to a starting point so that one ends where one began. This motif of circularity is an image of the preservation of things as they are, and thus one expression of fantasy's delight in 'being'. It may take the form simply of coming home at the end of one's adventures. Thus Gluck in Ruskin's *The King of the Golden River* returns to the wasted valley from which he and his cruel brothers were forced to leave, to find it blooming once more as at the beginning of the story; George MacDonald's Anodos in *Phantastes* and Vane in *Lilith* find themselves back in their castles after their journeys; William Morris's Ralph in *The Well at the World's End* returns to Upmeads, and Birdalone in *The Water of the Wondrous Isles* to Utterhay; E. Nesbit's children come back to London after their visits to the remote past in *The Story of the Amulet*; C. S. Lewis's Ransom returns to Earth from Mars and Venus; Tolkien's Bilbo and Frodo come back to the Shire from their distant adventures at the end of *The Hobbit; or, There and Back Again* and *The Lord of the Rings* respectively: Peake's Titus returns to Gormenghast (though Peake would have it believed that thereafter he left it finally); and Ursula Le Guin's *The Farthest Shore* begins and ends on the island of Roke in Earthsea. Sometimes there is the sense of circling about a fixed point, as when in David Lindsay's *A Voyage to Arcturus* the hero Maskull finds himself, at the culmination of his journey on the star Arcturus, in that same Scottish tower from which he set out originally from Earth (Lindsay owes something to MacDonald for this method).

Even when a character does not return to his actual place of origin, the impression is given that he has gone 'home'; that is, that he has returned to his rightful place, rather than that things have been changed. Kingsley's Tom, though he does not return to the Yorkshire town with which *The Water-Babies* began, is by the end linked with Ellie, with whom he goes 'home' – presumably to heaven. E. Nesbit's Dickie in *Harding's Luck* finds his true home in Elizabethan times. C. S. Lewis's 'Narnia' children, who find at the end of *The Last Battle* that they are no longer able to return to this world because in it they were killed in a train smash, travel home to heaven; and his Ransom, who felt on Perelandra that he was bound to that planet by primordial ties of longing, perhaps returns there at the end of *That Hideous Strength*. In some fantasies the plot itself can be circular. In E. R. Eddison's *The Worm Ouroboros*, the adventures of the characters are by divine gift at the end made recurrent; T.H. White's *The Once and Future King*, closing with the departure of Arthur, states beneath the text, 'THE BEGINNING'.

A further mode in which fantasy often returns to its starting point is in the departure of the supernatural. The magic realms, creatures, objects, actions or persons appear, disrupt 'normal' life and then depart once more at the end of the story. Thus Thackeray's Fairy Blackstick in *The Rose and the Ring* helps Giglio become a good king and then disappears; or in the works of F. Anstey, E. Nesbit and Charles Williams, a genie, a phoenix or a magic stone throw life into chaos until they are removed. Such removal need not always be final: the Psammead in Nesbit's *Five Children and It* is found again by the children at the start of their adventures in *The Story of the Amulet*. Nor does it suppose a return to happy ignorance or indifference. Thanks to the supernatural the world is by the end seen differently, and characters may have been altered spiritually through their experience of it, as in the work of Kingsley, MacDonald, Lindsay, Williams, Lewis, Tolkien, Peake, White or Le Guin. Here there is not only a circular mode of 'There and Back Again', but a spiral one, whereby the return is at a higher level of insight.

One of the most remarkable examples of the circular in fantasy may be observed by a comparison of George Mac-Donald's *Phantastes* (1858) with his *Lilith* (1895).[1]

Phantastes and *Lilith* stand out both among MacDonald's writings and Victorian literature generally as attempts to express and imitate the wholly unconscious mind.[2] MacDonald's deepest links are with extreme Romantic writers such as Novalis, Blake or the E. T. A. Hoffmann of *The Golden Pot* (1814).[3] Like them, if not always for the same reasons, he was absolute and uncompromising in his rejection of rationalist or empiricist approaches to the world and in his advocacy of the unconscious imagination as the source of truth. Unlike them, however, he valued the imagination because he believed it to be the dwelling-place of God in men, and hence the fount of absolute rather than possibly subjective truth. God, and not man, was for him the author of all thoughts in the mind, which 'from the vast unknown, where time and space are not ... suddenly appear in luminous writing upon the wall of ... consciousness'. For

> God sits in that chamber of our being in which the candle of our consciousness goes out in darkness, and sends forth from thence wonderful gifts into the light of that understanding which is His candle. Our hope lies in no most perfect mechanism even of the spirit, but in the wisdom wherein we live and move and have our being. Thence we hope for endless forms of beauty informed of truth. If the dark portion of our own being were the origin of our imaginations, we might well fear the apparition of such monsters as would be generated in the sickness of a decay which could never feel – only declare – a slow return towards primeval chaos. But the Maker is our Light.[4]

The human artist must therefore try to avoid imposing patterns or meanings on the gifts of his imagination, for he is expressing God's patterns, which can be understood only in the imagination and by the childlike mind, and not in the intellect: 'The greatest forces', MacDonald declared, 'lie in the region of the uncomprehended.'[5] *Phantastes* is prefixed by a quotation from Novalis on fairy tales (*Märchen*) as dream-like successions of images. *Lilith*, MacDonald told his son Greville, seemed to him to have been 'a mandate direct from God, for which he himself was to find form and clothing'.[6] At the close of *Lilith*, the central character Mr Vane is given a revelation of the true source of his dreams: 'When a man dreams his own dream, he is the sport of his dream; when Another gives it him, that Other is able to fulfil it.'* MacDonald especially valued *Phantastes* and *Lilith*, almost the first and last of his works, and his dearest literary aims[7] find expression in them.

MacDonald lived a life of almost total isolation from his intellectual and social milieu. He was a Highland Scot living in England, a minister deprived of a pulpit for heterodoxy, a man of uncompromising refusal to bend to the world's standards to make money, a soul longing for death as the door to meeting God; one who lived from the resources of his family and his own spirit rather than from any wider community.[8] This partly explains how he could write works so obscure and severed in character from those of his contemporaries. It may also explain why his work does not do the Victorian 'thing' and evolve, change in character or treat new ideas. Indeed the very fact that he ends his career with a work not dissimilar in basic form from one of his earliest[9] underlies this; it also closes the circle of his literary life just as he himself lived in a sense in a circle of his own.

The similarities of *Phantastes* and *Lilith* are clear enough. With the exception of the very different tale of Celtic second sight, *The Portent* (1864), they are the only romances for adults that MacDonald wrote. Both are dream-structured: that is to say, they each consist of a sequence of often inexplicable but suggestive images, described with a curious mixture of precision and vagueness;[10] and the landscape is that of both the unconscious mind and the world imaginatively seen. In both there are recurrent primordial images (most of them to be paralleled in the works of C. G. Jung, where they are given psychoanalytic explanation[11]) – mothers, the 'anima' figure, shadows, water, trees, caves, mirrors, and sun and moon. Both works describe death, whether out of the conscious self or life. In each there is one central and isolated human figure who has just come of age and into the management of his estate, and who goes from his house into a fairyland. In these fairylands each hero brings to life a woman enchanted or near death, is repulsed by her, and subsequently pursues her. At the end of each work the hero is returned to 'this' world to await a great good which he believes is coming to him (in both books evil is felt to be finally unreal (pp. 182, 262)). There are several smaller likenesses. Mirrors are

---

* George MacDonald, *Phantastes and Lilith* (Gollancz, 1962; Grand Rapids, Michigan, Wm. Eerdmans Publishing Co., 1964, repr. 1976) p. 420. Page references are to this edition.

used as magic apparatus in both works: Cosmo's mirror in the inset story in *Phantastes* has enslaved a princess to appear in the reflection of any room in which it is set; and the mirror-apparatus in Mr Vane's garret in *Lilith* is the means of his entry into the region of the seven dimensions. Anodos in *Phantastes* finds his evil shadow; Vane is opposed by a Great Shadow. There are feminine doubles in *Phantastes* such as the evil Maid of the Alder-tree and the pure white lady, and in *Lilith* there are a spotted leopardess that is Lilith and a white one that is Mara, child of Eve. The evil Ash and Alder of *Phantastes* have, like Lilith, a spiritual 'hole in the heart' which makes them devourers (pp. 39, 56–7, 325).[12] In both books songs have magical power, whether in binding Lilith (p. 319) or in loosing the white lady from imprisonment as a statue (pp. 45–8, 114–19). Both have halls of dancers (pp. 110–14, 262–6, 309–10), palaces, and cottages. In each the same poem on the home of life occurs in roughly the same position from the end:

> Many a wrong, and its curing song;
> Many a road, and many an inn;
> Room to roam, but only one home
> For all the world to win. (pp. 164, 398)

After that in *Lilith* Vane reflects, 'I thought I had heard the song before.'

Yet while there is not 'evolution' or difference in basic form between the two works, they are radically to be distinguished in subject-matter. Just as they circle MacDonald's literary life, so the one completes the circle begun by the other. That circle has nothing to do with development, but rather with completing a pattern. For *Phantastes* deals with some of the First Things; and *Lilith* with the Last. *Phantastes* has as its subject a man embarking on life, and describes a fall (Anodos's enslavement to his evil shadow after an act of disobedience) and a Christ-like act of sacrifice for others by Anodos in the evil forest-church at the end; after which, back in his own world, he finds that his wicked shadow has gone. Anodos concludes: 'Thus I, who set out to find my Ideal, came back rejoicing that I had lost my Shadow' (p. 182). The narrative in *Lilith*, however, moves towards the Last Days, and describes the morning of eternity when resur-rected souls make their way into heaven; the story focuses on the gradual acceptance by the recalcitrant hero Mr Vane of his need to lie down and sleep with the dead in Adam's house so that he may waken to eternity. In a sense *Phantastes* and *Lilith* together make up a single fantasy.

Throughout *Phantastes* Anodos is occupied in waking people up. In a cave he finds a block of alabaster in which he can see the indistinct outline of a woman: on an impulse he sits by this '"antenatal tomb"' (p. 45) and sets about waking the woman by singing a song against sleep, darkness and death, until the lady actually breaks free from the stone and glides away into the surrounding woods (p. 47). Again by song Anodos later renders visible the figure of the lady in a hall of statues in a fairy palace; and when he seizes her from the black pedestal on which she is set she comes to life and escapes from him (pp. 115–20). Anodos's last act in Fairy Land is designed to waken his master the knight to the evil of the religious ceremony in the forest church (p. 175). The story of Cosmo and his mirror is also one of an awakening: first the princess, who has hitherto been a passive victim of the mirror, not knowing that she is seen in it, becomes aware of Cosmo; and then, when by an act of sacrifice which prefigures that of Anodos Cosmo dies to smash the mirror, she is released from its power and from the deadly trances it produces. In *Lilith*, however, the object of Mr Raven, or Adam, is to persuade people to lie down and sleep in his house of death. Where Anodos invokes movement and consciousness – '"Rest is now filled full of beauty,/and can give thee up, I ween;/Come thou forth, for other duty/Motion pineth for her queen"' (p. 46) – all motion in *Lilith* save the one act of climbing on to one of the slabs in the dormitory of the cold sleepers and losing consciousness is seen as evanescent.

Phantastes could be said to portray the gradual wakening of the hero, who is at first unconscious. Though the first words of the book are 'I awoke one morning' the mode of Anodos's entry into Fairy Land is like a gradual lapse out of consciousness, into a dream:

[I] became aware of the sound of running water near me; and looking out of bed, I saw that a large green marble basin, in which I was wont to wash, and which stood on a low pedestal of the same material in a corner of my room, was overflowing like a spring; and that a stream of clear water was running over the carpet, all the length of the room, finding its outlet I knew not where. And, stranger still, where this carpet, which I had myself designed to imitate a field of grass and daisies, bordered the course of the little stream, the grass-blades and daisies seemed to wave in a tiny breeze that followed the water's flow; while under the rivulet they bent and swayed with every motion of the changeful current, as if they were about to dissolve with it, and, forsaking their fixed form, become fluent as the waters.

My dressing-table was an old-fashioned piece of furniture of black oak, with drawers all down the front. These were elaborately carved in foliage, of which ivy formed the chief part. The nearer end of this table remained just as it had been, but on the further end a singular change had commenced. I happened to fix my eye on a little cluster of ivy-leaves. The first of these was evidently the work of the carver; the next looked curious; the third was unmistakably ivy; and just beyond it a tendril of clematis had twined itself about the gilt handle of one of the drawers. Hearing next a slight motion above me, I looked up, and saw that the branches and leaves designed upon the curtains of my bed were slightly in motion. Not knowing what change might follow next, I thought it time to get up; and, springing from the bed, my bare feet alighted upon a cool green sward; and although I dressed in all haste, I found myself completing my toilet under the boughs of a great tree, whose top waved in the golden stream of the sunrise with many interchanging lights, and with shadows of leaf and branch gliding over leaf and branch, as the cool morning wind swung it to and fro, like a sinking sea-wave. (pp. 19–20)

Throughout the passage (which is very reminiscent of Hoffmann's *The Golden Pot*[13]) there is a steady increase of change from one mode of being to another, mirroring the collapse of the empirical mode of presentation and entry into the unconscious mind and the world it perceives. (It is of a piece with the character of *Phantastes* as a whole that what is described is not only a change of being, but a shift from stillness into motion.) First it could appear that the basin was overflowing for quite ordinary reasons, and that the stream of water was equally natural – though rather more of a spreading flood might be expected; and despite Anodos's 'stranger still' it would still be possible to believe that his impression of the movement of the grass and daisies of the carpet both beside and beneath the stream was an optical illusion. But the possibility of illusion is removed in the same way that the solidity of the carvings of leaves on the oak dressing-table turns through increasing uncertainty into twisting vegetation. With the movement of the branches and leaves on the bed-curtains being heard as well as seen, the reader is still further in; and when Anodos leaps out of bed on to a lawn instead of a carpet, the reader feels sure that little remains of the bedroom itself. The ironic fact is that when Anodos finally rises from his bed he is most fully asleep.[14]

During the first half of the story Anodos (whose name is the Greek for 'pathless', or 'having no way') experiences events in a chance manner, without any specific object in view: he wanders into the cave containing the lady in alabaster, he meets the Ash and Alder by apparent accident, a stream leads him to the fairy palace, he sojourns in the palace for some time. Though he wanders in a generally eastwards direction,[15] he does not know why, and can speak of 'my custom since I entered Fairy Land, of taking for a guide whatever I first found moving in any direction' (p. 75). Random impulse governs many of his actions, such as his clearing the moss from the alabaster in which the white lady is imprisoned, and then singing to release her (pp. 44, 45); entering the cottage of an ogress and, despite her warning, opening the door of her cupboard and thus being found by his evil shadow (pp. 62, 63); or singing in the fairy palace (p. 109). He declares, 'it is no use trying to account for things in Fairy Land; and one who travels there soon learns to forget the very idea of doing so, and takes everything as it comes; like a child, who, being in a chronic condition of wonder, is surprised at nothing' (p. 33). This is partly true, but Anodos has to learn how to unite child-likeness with true consciousness. He finds false consciousness in the form of his shadow-self, which is a symbol of intellectual and materialist modes of perception, and removes enchantment from all about him: it turns a beautiful fairy child with magic toys into 'a commonplace boy, with a ... multiplying glass and a kaleidoscope' (p. 66), and leads Anodos to covet, seize and so break the wonderful music-emitting globe of a little girl (pp. 68–9).

In the fairy palace he begins to be more purposive, and to plan ahead. Around the central hall of the palace are twelve radiating halls, each filled with human statues and curtained off. Anodos becomes convinced that the statues are often dancing and tries to surprise them at it, but in vain, for they are always motionless on their pedestals when he enters. He discovers that 'a premeditated attempt at surprise, though executed with the utmost care and rapidity, was of no avail' (p. 113): if he has any preformed intention of catching the statues before he lifts one of the curtains he is bound to fail, for what is needed is 'a sudden thought suddenly executed' (ibid.). By trial and error, giving his mind to other thoughts and images than the dancers, he arrives at a moment when the impulse to catch them comes just as he is next to one of the curtains, and can dart through on the instant. Clearly there has to be a fusion of conscious and unconscious intention: the wish to surprise the statues must be 'put to sleep' until the right moment arrives. Elsewhere in the second half of *Phantastes* there is emphasis on the notion of being at once prepared and unprepared. Faced by the evil Ash-tree, the knight of the rusty armour knows that '"earthly arms availed not against such as he; and that my soul must meet him in its naked strength"' (p. 139); and later he tells Anodos that a man will do none the worse in Faërie for not being '"burdened with provision and precaution"' (p. 169). In the battle with the giants the brothers and Anodos have no time to don their carefully prepared armour (p. 155), though their resolution, training and some of their weapons remain to them. In the church in the forest, when Anodos wishes to expose the evil he feels there, he hands his battle-axe to one of the congregation, 'for I wished to test the matter unarmed, and, if it was a man that sat upon the throne, to attack him with hands bare' (p. 176).[16]

Thus the reader finds that, in the second part of *Phantastes*, Anodos's actions emerge from rather more sustained desires and sequences of motive and act than hitherto, though these are combined with the previous unconscious mode.[17] When, early on, he brought to life the white lady in the alabaster, his search for her lasted little further than his unhappy confusion of her with the Maid of the Alder. But when he makes her both visible and mobile in the fairy palace he sets off in a pursuit of her which becomes an intermittent motif during the remainder of his experience in Fairy Land. Gradually, however, he learns to yield her to the knight of the (formerly) rusty armour, whom she loves; and eventually he serves the knight as his squire; in his death the two lay him in his grave. Interpolated with this is another causal sequence, beginning with the old lady of the strange island cottage in the ocean, who sends Anodos forth to help two princes slay a group of giants that are despoiling their country; Anodos, the sole survivor of the contest, is fêted by the people, and then, becoming vain of his prowess, meets a double of himself in the forest, and is shut up in a tower until he learns humility. This motif, and that of the white lady, are, however, relatively disconnected from one another, and there are still numbers of episodes with no clear relation to either of them – the island-cottage itself with its four mystic doors, the dead dragon with which Anodos finds the knight of the rusty armour encumbered (pp. 166–9), and the little girl who is searching for butterflies to make wings for herself but who is continually being knocked over by invisible wooden creatures (pp. 169–72).

In the end, Anodos finally loses his evil shadow in what is an act at once conscious and unconscious: he senses in his soul that there is evil in the forest church, and he perceives with his keen eyesight that something suspicious is being done to the people led to the central throne (p. 174). Together these sensations bring him to a decision and an act which is more his own than anything previously in the book (if there is still an evil tincture of revenge in his motivation (p.176)). It is the culmination of a development of true consciousness, and with it the false consciousness of the shadow goes for ever. The product of that consciousness is also death, but it is a death in which Anodos's perceptions are more fully awake than ever before.

> The hot fever of life had gone by, and I breathed the clear mountain-air of the land of Death. I had never dreamed of such blessedness. It was not that I had in any way ceased to be what I had been ... If my passions were dead, the souls of the passions, those essential mysteries of the spirit which had imbodied themselves in the passions, and had given to them all their glory and wonderment, yet lived, yet glowed, with a pure, undying fire. They rose above their vanishing earthly garments, and disclosed themselves angels of light. But oh, how beautiful beyond the old form! (p. 178)

This was anticipated by the framing stanza of the song Anodos sang to the princes before the battle with the giants: '"Oh, well for him who breaks his dream/With the blow that ends the strife;/And, waking, knows the peace that flows/Around the noise of life!''' (p. 154). In that peace, waking and dreaming, conscious and unconscious, are one.[18] Anodos has one further stage to go, however, for he has to 'die' back out of Fairy Land into this world and mortality once more; so that in a sense, just as he is divided from Faërie, so he is divided from the true unconscious life once more.

The idea that to be truly dead or asleep is to be truly alive and awake is also central in *Lilith*, but is demonstrated from the opposite direction (illustrating the words of the song in both works – 'Many a road .../... but only one home/For all the world to win' (pp. 164, 398)). In *Lilith*, the hero moves from a condition of stubborn consciousness into unconsciousness. The means by which Mr Vane finds himself in the region of the seven dimensions[19] is an apparatus whose magical workings are described in quasi-scientific terms concerning the polarisation of light: it is a mirror, which in this context is a symbol of the intellect, the conscious self,[20] and is thus quite opposite in character to the gateway to Fairy Land in *Phantastes*. Unlike Anodos, Vane enters the strange realm of his story in a wakeful, questioning state, and in pursuit of something specific, the strange librarian, Mr Raven. He is constantly surprised at what he sees, and unlike Anodos spends much time inquiring into the nature of the new world he has entered: 'Could it be that I was dead, I thought, and did not know it? Was I in what we used to call the world beyond the grave? and must I wander about seeking my place in it? How was I to find myself at home?' (pp. 196–7). Mr Raven, whom he meets in this other world, baffles his questions with riddles and paradoxes which themselves continue the intellectual, conscious element – for example, '"you have not yet left your house, neither has your house left you. At the same time it cannot contain you, or you inhabit it!"' (p. 202). Later he tells Vane by intellectual means that he must do without intellect (pp. 326–7). The 'wakeful' condition of Vane throughout *Lilith* is part of the reason for that work's being more consistently connected in structure and motivation than *Phantastes*.

The topography of the region of the seven dimensions is clear, with the Bad Burrow, the Evil Wood, the dried watercourse, the two cottages, the home of the Little Ones and the giants, and the town of Bulika all fairly clearly placed in relation to one another. Vane follows a steady sequence of motive and act in a way that Anodos does not till near the end of his history. He refuses Mr Raven's invitation to lie down in the house of the dead; he meets the Little Ones and eventually leaves them in the hope of eventually helping them in their development and in their difficulties with the giants; he finds the almost-dead Lilith and revives her; he pursues her to Bulika where she feigns love for him in order to gain access to 'this' world, whence she is beaten off by Mr Raven. Once more offered death by Mr Raven, Vane refuses and sets off on the horse of his futile passions (pp. 329–33) to help the Little Ones, but finds them already prepared, under the guidance of Lilith's daughter Lona, to do battle against the giants and set off to assault Bulika and Lilith. The latter aim results in the capture of Lilith, who eventually agrees to lie down with the dead, whereupon Vane does also. Vane remains at a consistent level of truant wakefulness for much of *Lilith*, unlike Anodos, who as we have seen, gradually loses his state of simple, passive unconsciousness.

In keeping with the injunction to more consciousness in *Phantastes* and less in *Lilith* – and also with the fact that Anodos in the former is portrayed as a spiritual child at first – the reader finds that where Anodos is often asked to resist something, Vane and Lilith are required to give way. Anodos is forbidden to touch his fairy-grandmother (p. 17), told to guard against the evil Ash and Alder trees, and warned by the ogress of the peril of opening the cupboard door in her cottage. Despite the inscription ' "TOUCH NOT!" ' (p. 111), he lays hands on the female statue he renders visible by his singing in the fairy palace, and then pursues her through a door over which is the command, ' "*No one enters here without the leave of the Queen*" ' (pp. 119–20). Later he is told in vain by the old lady of the cottage in the sea not to go through the fourth door of the cottage, the door of the Timeless: as a result he has to leave and the sea rises to cover the cottage for a year (pp. 143–5). Lilith and Vane, on the other hand, are told to do rather than not to do something. They wrongfully resist for long the injunction to lie down and sleep. Where Anodos is asked to refuse, they are asked to accept. Lilith is told that to do so is to do what her deepest and truest will wants, and that ' "There is no slave but the creature that wills against its creator" ' (pp. 371–2).[21] The imperative here is to go with the

grain of the universe, in which one finds oneself borne forward
by a will deeper than one's own; while for Anodos the need is
often to stand back, to remove himself from absorption in himself
and phenomena. In a sense Anodos finds his true self by a
process of separation, Vane by one of immersion: the one has to
do with what is needed for living, the other with dying.

Much of this difference stems from the theme of maternity in
Phantastes, and the fact that the history of Anodos is one of
gradual removal from over-dependence on mother-figures and a
condition of unthinking passivity.[22] These mother-figures include the fairy he meets before his adventures (p. 18), the Beech-
tree in the fairy forest who protects him from the ravening Ash
(pp. 37–40), the 'old nursing earth' itself (p. 50), the matron of
the second forest cottage (p. 56), 'mother Nature' as he floats
down a river (p. 72) and the old lady of the mid-ocean cottage
who soothes his distress (pp. 131, 144). It is when the last finally
sends him forth saying, '"Go, my son, and do something worth
doing"', that he feels 'as if I were leaving my mother for the first
time' (p. 145). Thereafter Anodos meets no more mother-figures
during his time in Fairy Land: when at one point he feels
'unmanned' by a weak desire for maternal comfort, he 'dashe[s]
away the tears, ashamed of a weakness which I thought I had
abandoned' (p. 162). In his death, however, which is the product
of a fully 'adult' decision and sacrifice, he enters that higher
childhood of union with earth, of solid self with solid self, which
the earlier mothers have in part prefigured, 'I seemed to feel the
great heart of the mother beating into mine, and feeding me with
her own life, her own essential being and nature' (p. 178).[23]

After Anodos leaves the island cottage, his journey is no longer
connected with water or baths, symbols both of the womb and of
the melting of one's identity in an infant state of dependency on
the mother: there are no more streams, deep rivers, or seas, but
only dry land, the upland of the conflict with the giants, the royal
city and the forest. In *Lilith*, however, Vane is to be seen as an
adult who, with an adult's consciousness, is active rather than
passive, until he learns a self-surrender which has nothing to do
with flight to a refuge, but is rather the opening of the self to the
living stream of the universe. For much of *Lilith* the landscape is
waterless and arid, reflecting this insistence on the conscious and
personal self: when Lilith gives herself up, the river wells up from
the subterranean depths in which it was lost (p. 394).[24]

One of the central themes of *Phantastes* is possession. To seek to get' is to be possessed or helpless.[25] Even the voracious Ash-tree, with its need to devour all that it meets, is in a sense a passive victim: the Beech-tree tells Anodos that '"he has a hole in his heart that nobody knows of but one or two; and he is always trying to fill it up, but he cannot"' (p. 39). It is because Anodos lacks a truly 'born' self that he himself feels the need to possess things, to lay hands on the lady of the fairy palace, or, through the effect on him of his evil shadow, to seize the little girl's beautiful crystalline ball of harmony (pp. 68–9). Because most of his acts of seizing are impulsive and childlike rather than actively malignant, he is frequently being mothered. But when he learns to be a separate individual, he learns also to let things be separate from him. He sees the course of his story as a gradual doing without greed and pride, for these are functions of infancy: 'I learned that he that will be a hero, will barely be a man; that he that will be nothing but a doer of his work, is sure of his manhood' (p. 165). Thus at the end of the story he finds his true self by giving rather than getting, in his sacrifice in the forest church.

In the first part of *Phantastes* there is a sense of enclosure: Anodos is wandering through forests, or entering cottages or palaces. After he leaves the sea-cottage there is more sense of openness in the upland site of the battle with the giants. Later he returns to woodland: but the tower of his pride in which Anodos is shut is one out of which he can walk simply by opening the door (p. 163).[26] The forest church in which he later finds himself is full of the sense of being confined, 'enclosed by four walls of yew ... These trees grew to a very great height, and did not divide from each other till close to the top' (p. 173). (The yew tree is a death-symbol.[27]) The eyes of the circular congregation are directed inwards, the avenue of white-robed men narrows in the distance, and it is growing dark in 'the enclosure' (p. 174). The sacrificial victims are constantly 'surrounded' and 'crowded' towards the central throne (pp. 174–5). It is out of this constriction that Anodos breaks, by smashing the idol and suffering death. In the account of his brief 'life after death' in Fairy Land (pp. 177–80), confinement and freedom, like all other opposites, are reconciled. Anodos lies down in his grave 'like a tired child ... in his white bed ... with a more luxurious satisfaction of repose than I knew'; but he also then rises above

the ground, first in the form of a primrose, and then floating on
cloud in the free air. But then he is returned into this mortal
world, becoming 'once again conscious of a more limited, even
bodily and earthly life', sinking from his 'state of ideal bliss, into
the world of shadows which again closed around and infolded
me' (p. 180). He now has to await the final deliverance of death
out of this world. But at least he has broken free of the womb
and can truly begin his life (at the opening of the story it was
emphasised that he was just twenty-one); thus the description of
his return to this world is somewhat like that of a birth, 'a pang
and a terrible shudder went through me; a writhing as of death
convulsed me; and I became once again conscious of a more
limited, even a bodily and earthly life'.

In *Lilith* the procedure is the reverse: a man who wanders for
much of the narrative in the open country ends by entering the
house of Adam. But the houses in each story are on the whole
different: in *Phantastes* it is the house of life, from which one must
break free to realise one's own being; in *Lilith* it is the house of
death, in which one is once more joined with the earth (but
difference ceases in the death-states of the protagonists, when life
and death, womb and grave are reconciled). Life is circular, but
for MacDonald as for Blake, in spiral form: one must move from
innocence to experience as in *Phantastes*, but thence to a higher
innocence which is a return at a different level to the childlike
state.

Anodos in *Phantastes* follows a roughly linear path, if the
direction is not always constant. He is told by the woman of the
second cottage he comes to, ' "I have heard, that, for those who
enter Fairy Land, there is no way of going back. They must go
on, and go through it. How, I do not in the least know" ' (p. 61).
Thus Anodos never covers the same ground twice, but is always
happening on new experiences. First he journeys through the
fairy forest, encountering the Ash, the Alder and the Beech, the
lady in the alabaster and his own shadow; then he moves down
river to his sojourn in the fairy palace with its statue-halls; and
thereafter through the sequence of subterranean journey, wintry
sea, island cottage, battle with giants, tower in forest, forest
church, death, resurrection and return to this world. Narrative is
matched by spiritual progression, as we have seen: *Phantastes* is
Bildungsroman, Anodos's experience gradually bringing him
nearer true selfhood and humility.

The book is also in a sense centrifugal. Anodos leaves his castle to enter Fairy Land; he starts two female statues into motion and flight; his story is interspersed with other narratives, such as those of the strange 'loveless' planet and of Cosmo that he reads in the library of the fairy palace (pp. 82–108), or the ballad sung to him by the woman of the island cottage about Sir Aglovaile and his ghost-wife (pp. 131–5); in the fairy library he often lapses out of his own consciousness into those of the authors or characters of the books he reads:

> if the book was one of travels, I found myself the traveller. New lands, fresh experiences, novel customs, rose around me. I walked, I discovered, I fought, I suffered, I rejoiced in my success. Was it a history? I was the chief actor therein. I suffered my own blame; I was glad in my own praise. With a fiction it was the same. Mine was the whole story. For I took the place of the character who was most like myself, and his story was mine. (pp. 81–2; see also pp. 53, 87, 89)

In *Lilith*, however, Vane in a sense never moves from his house: Mr Raven tells him: '"you have not yet left your house, neither has your house left you"' (p. 202). In *Lilith* MacDonald portrays a condition in which objects from different dimensions can co-exist in the same place; this is the burden of the epigraph to the book from Thoreau's 'Walking'. In the realm beyond the mirror Mr Raven shows Vane a tree which '"stands on the hearth of your kitchen, and grows nearly straight up its chimney"', and says that some heads of Faërian wild hyacinth are among the strings of the piano that Vane's housekeeper's niece is playing in the breakfast-room of the house, '"and give that peculiar sweetness to her playing"' (pp. 203–4). Another tree grows '"in the ruins of the church on your home-farm"' (p. 205). Later Vane is smitten with terror, 'I was lost in a space larger than imagination; for if here two things, or any parts of them, could occupy the same space, why not twenty or ten thousand?' (p. 215). Distance is telescoped: Vane is told by Mr Raven that the closet in the library of his house, into which he emerged immediately on leaving the vaults of the dead (as he does on leaving heaven at the end of the story (p. 419)) '"is no nearer our cottage, and no farther from it, than any or every other place"' (p. 326). Thus it is that during the narrative Vane several times returns to his house as Anodos did not (pp. 197, 217, 315, 405).

Unlike Anodos's wanderings, those of Vane are centripetal, about the cottage of the dead he for much of the narrative resists, and he traverses the same landscape continually, visiting the Little Ones twice, Bulika twice and the Bad Burrow of hideous monsters four times. Where Anodos follows a linear path, that of Vane is a circular or spiral one. There is mention of an ancestor Sir Upward (pp. 190, 219–21), and at the end Vane is told of his awakening, '"here all is upwardness and love and gladness"' (p. 408). To reach the mirror-apparatus in his house Vane must ascend a spiral staircase (p. 197). MacDonald found deep and sacramental meaning in spirals, stairs, heights and church-spires. He found 'co-substance between the stairs of a cathedral-spire and man's own "secret stair" up to the wider vision';[28] and declared: 'the movements of man's life are in spirals: we go back whence we came, ever returning on our former traces, only upon a higher level, on the next upward coil of the spiral, so that it is a going back and a going forward ever and both at once'.[29]

This linear/spiral, centrifugal/centripetal contrast between *Phantastes* and *Lilith* partly reflects the fact that while Anodos develops spiritually throughout, Vane does not. For most of *Lilith* Vane is simply truant, trying to cling to the ledge of what he considers to be his identity, despite being twice invited to lie down with the dead (pp. 209–17, 327–32). He is constantly in the spiritual condition described by MacDonald in one of his *Unspoken Sermons*:

> The liberty of the God that would have his creature free, is in contest with the slavery of the creature who would cut his own stem from his root that he might call it his own and love it; who rejoices in his own consciousness, instead of the life of that consciousness; who poises himself on the tottering wall of his own being, instead of the rock on which that being is built. Such a one regards his own dominion over himself – the rule of the greater by the less, inasmuch as the conscious self is less than the self – as a freedom infinitely greater than the range of the universe of God's being.[30]

Hence, in part, the name 'Vane'. All he has to do is to give way, to stop, whereas Anodos has to move and change. With

Phantastes the question is: 'What is it properly to be?'; with *Lilith* it is, 'What is being?': the one is concerned with ethics, the other with ontology. Vane and Lilith do not *become*: they simply find out what they are. Thus Lilith is brought to Mara's house solely to relinquish her fancied picture of herself, and to see herself as she really is (pp. 371–8). Such a seeing will involve transformation into what God meant her to be. During the process, Mara tells Vane: '"The central fire of the universe is radiating into her the knowledge of good and evil, the knowledge of what she is. She sees at last the good she is not, the evil she is"' (p. 373).

Mr Raven's first question of Vane is, '"Who are you, pray?"'', at which:

> I became at once aware that I could give him no notion of who I was. Indeed, who was I? It would be no answer to say I was who! Then I understood that I did not know myself, did not know what I was, had no grounds on which to determine that I was one thing and not another. As for the name I went by in my own world, I had forgotten it, and did not care to recall it, for it meant nothing, and what it might be was plainly of no consequence here. I had indeed almost forgotten that there it was a custom for everybody to have a name! So I held my peace, and it was my wisdom; for what should I say to a creature such as this raven, who saw through accident into entity? (pp. 195–6; see also p. 198)

Mr Raven then declares, '"No one can say he is himself, until first he knows that he *is*, and then what *himself* is. In fact, nobody is himself, and himself is nobody"' (p. 196). Later again, the issue of Vane's true self is raised, when he finds that he cannot even remember his own name, and Mara tells him, '"Your real name, indeed, is written on your forehead, but at present it whirls about so irregularly that nobody can read it"' (p. 253).[31] (It may occur to the reader here that 'Vane' is a partial anagram of 'Raven'.) There is a motif of metamorphosis, or uncertainty of identity, in *Lilith*, which is not to be found so much in *Phantastes*. Lilith and Mara can change to leopardesses and back again. Mr Raven keeps shifting between appearing as a raven and as a librarian (pp. 196, 210, 271, 273, 315, 329). In the Evil Wood the trees and leaves keep turning, to Vane's sight, into the shapes of beasts or men or dancing cadavers and back again (pp. 232–4, 262–6).

Because of the emphasis on finding what one truly is, rather than what one may become, time and place are of less moment in *Lilith* than in *Phantastes*. Regarding place, it has been seen that the story circles about one centre, Adam's cottage, and that there is stress on the notion of 'bi-locality'. Mr Raven tells Vane:

> 'Home is ever so far away in the palm of your hand, and how to get there it is of no use to tell you. But you will get there; you must get there; you have to get there. Everybody who is not at home, has to go home. You thought you were at home where I found you: if that had been your home, you could not have left it. Nobody can leave home. And nobody ever was or ever will be at home without having gone there.' (pp. 225–6)

And Vane later reflects: 'But what mattered *where* while *everywhere* was the same as *nowhere*! I had not yet, by doing something in it, made *anywhere* into a place!' (p. 261). As for time, when Vane apologises for his lateness in lying down with the dead, he is told: '"There is no early or late here"' (p. 399); and while he is asleep he remarks: 'For centuries I dreamed – or was it chiliads? or only one long night? – But why ask? for time had nothing to do with me; I was in the land of thought – farther in, higher up than the seven dimensions, the ten senses: I think I was where I am – in the heart of God' (pp. 400–1). There is not even a clear finality to the duration of the universe: the sleepers in the house of the dead rise and go to heaven at different times; the last chapter is entitled 'The "Endless Ending"'.

What idea of development there is in *Lilith* refers primarily to the state of death, not what one does when one is 'alive'; and it is a circular rather than a linear concept of growth, whereby one goes forward by going backwards. Vane learns that his mother lying in the house of the dead '"will go on steadily growing younger until she reaches the perfection of her womanhood – a splendour beyond foresight"' (p. 399); and the Little One, Odu, after his wakening from the dead, is told of the still cold princess Lilith, '"Her wake is not ripe yet ... she is busy forgetting. When she has forgotten enough to remember enough, then she will soon be ripe, and wake"' (p. 411). It is Lilith in her corrupt state who thinks of ripening and development in purely linear terms of forward movement: '"the older we grow, the nearer we are to our perfection ... ours is a ceaseless ripening. I am not yet ripe, and have lived thousands of your years"' (p. 305). But true change in *Lilith* involves a return, through experience, to childhood. Lilith is told, '"A slave thou art that shall one day be a child!"' (p. 378). The rhetorical correlative of this process of going forward by going back is the use of paradox throughout the book. Thus Mr Raven informs Vane that '"the more doors you go out of, the farther you get in"' (p. 194), '"No one who will not sleep can ever wake"' (p. 225), '"Nothing but truth can appear; and whatever is must seem"' (p. 272), '"you will be dead, so long as you refuse to die"' (p. 331); and Vane himself says – when he has found his true being in death – '"no one can die who does not long to live"' (p. 395).

Lilith involves a losing of the self, a merging with others. The title of the book speaks of a figure who shares the central position in the novel with Vane, a figure who like Vane refuses to yield her will and go to sleep in Adam's house. In the end Vane lies down together with Lilith and the Little Ones in the company of the vast hosts of the dead, in a universal dormitory; the grave in *Lilith* is no fine and private place. Beings appear constantly in groups – Adam and Eve, the Little Ones, the giants, the dancing dead, the quarrelsome skeletons (pp. 266–71), the Bad Burrow full of monsters, the 'society' of Bulika. *Phantastes*, on the other hand, which is much more concerned with progressive growth and separation of the self, usually involves single figures – the women of each of the three cottages, the Ash, the Alder, the Beech, the knight of the rusty armour, the lady in the alabaster, the fairy child, the girl with the globe, the statue in the fairy palace. Even the story of Cosmo and his mirror involves his not meeting his beloved princess until he has his death-wound;[32] and the reader learns that on the strange planet of which Anodos reads in another story, when two people fall in love, 'instead of drawing nearer to each other, they wander away each alone, into solitary places, and die of their desire' (p. 87). Though towards the end of the story Anodos becomes somewhat more social, in helping the brothers against the giants, or acting as squire to the knight, his isolation from the white lady is constantly felt, and at the end of his life in Fairy Land his act of sacrifice in the forest church is uniquely his own, no others seeing the evil till he reveals it.

Anodos's dream clearly springs from his own unconscious, but Vane is often not sure whether he is dreaming or being dreamt by others. In the black hall of Lilith's palace, he realises that 'in the black ellipsoid I had been in the brain of the princess!' (p. 313; cf. p. 303); and when at the end he seems to have been returned once more to his house and severed from his fellow-dead, he says: 'I had fled from my dream! The dream was not of my making, any more than was my life: I ought to have seen it to the end!' (p. 406). In *Phantastes* the concern is with the individual, in *Lilith* with the corporate subconscious.[33] Even the individual in *Lilith* is multiple: Mr Raven, the bird-man, tells Vane:

> 'Every one, as you ought to know, has a beast-self – and a bird-self, and a stupid fish-self, ay, and a creeping serpent-self too – which it takes a deal of crushing to kill! In truth he has also a tree-self and a crystal-self, and I don't know how many selves more – all to get into harmony.' (p. 211)

The motif of metamorphosis, by which apparent identity is not sacrosanct but rather shared with other modes of being, is here again significant: all the figures in *Lilith* are, as it were, parts of one huge imagination. Even unconsciousness itself is not certain: increasingly towards the end Vane does not know whether he is waking or dreaming: 'Can it be that that last waking also was in the dream? that I am still in the chamber of death, asleep and dreaming, not yet ripe enough to wake?' (p. 419). The root of this multiple identity, this corporate mind, is God: thinking does not come from the one, but from the Many who is also the One. MacDonald said, writing of the human imagination, 'a man is rather *being thought* than *thinking*, when a new thought arises in his mind';[34] and young Harry Arnold in his *David Elginbrod* (1863) says: '"I never dream dreams; the dreams dream me"'.[35]

The landscape of *Lilith* is shared by all minds, and is ultimately God's dream; that of *Phantastes*, however, is usually felt to be an extension of the mind of the solitary hero Anodos.[36] In *Phantastes* Anodos finds his evil shadow; in *Lilith* Vane encounters the Great Shadow. In *Phantastes* Anodos tells the reader that he set out to find his Ideal (p. 182). The lady in the alabaster seems to him 'perfectly lovely; more near the face that had been born with me in my soul, than anything I had seen before in nature or art' (pp. 44–5). It is this personal image of the desirable that he seeks in this lady, in the Maid of the Alder and in the statue-lady in the fairy palace. In his search he at length learns to go beyond the merely personal and the possessive, but his journey remains one into the interior, to discover some hint of the root of his true being. Unlike Vane, however, he never directly encounters God, who is the ultimate source of his desire or *Sehnsucht*, immanent in, but not to be identified with, the white lady he for long tries to possess. *Lilith*, on the other hand, is directly concerned with matters of heaven and hell (for example, pp. 322–3, 408). Vane, standing 'in the burial ground of the universe' (p. 208), moves outward to an understanding of the nature of all being: the figures in his story constitute the whole human race, and in particular the great personages of Christian history – Adam, Eve, Lilith, the Great Shadow, Mara (probably Mary), Christ; and finally God Himself, met, if not quite face to face, in the journey to heaven of the risen sleepers at the end.[37]

Phantastes is geared to mortal, *Lilith* to immortal, existence. Perhaps expressing this difference, *Phantastes* is rather more dialectical in character. Anodos has to learn to live the dialectic of desiring without seeking to possess. In Fairy Land he finds good and evil forms of his white lady; his experiences with his evil shadow partly embody the ancient struggle of darkness with light which the ogress describes before he opens the forbidden cupboard door (pp. 62–3). The book is shot through with such opposites as art and nature (the ladies Anodos brings to life are both originally statues), active and passive, conscious and unconscious, dream and reality, opacity and translucency,[38] age and youth. Many of these are, as has been seen, married in Anodos's death. Yet at the very end Fairy Land and this world remain divided: Anodos accepts that he is no longer in the Faërian realm and wonders: 'Could I translate the experience of my travels there, into common life? This was the question. Or must I live it all over again, and learn it all over again, in the other forms that belong to the world of men, whose experience yet runs parallel to that of Fairy Land?' He goes on: 'These questions I cannot yet answer. But I fear' (p. 181).

Vane, however, does not know whether he is awake in this world or still sleeping and dreaming in Adam's house (p. 419). This uncertainty in part expresses the greater emphasis on the reconciliation of opposites that is found prefigured throughout *Lilith*. The book could be called apocalyptic in that it continually looks to a future, to death and resurrection. *Lilith* is eschatology, and eschatology is not finally dialectical. '"When you are quite dead, you will dream no false dream"' (p. 403). Evil will cease: Lilith lies down among the dead in peace, and the Great Shadow will do so also (p. 388). Where Anodos seeks to remove his evil shadow, the Shadow in *Lilith* is to be redeemed.[39] This bringing of things together is expressed in the motif of atonement. Eve tells Lilith of the latter's daughter Lona, '"Death shall be the atonemaker; you shall sleep together"' (p. 386). When Vane wakes on his resurrection-morning,

> Nothing cast a shadow; all things interchanged a little light. Every growing thing showed me, by its shape and colour, its indwelling idea – the informing thought, that is, which was its being, and sent it out. My bare feet seemed to love every plant they trod upon. The world and my being, its life and mine, were one. The microcosm and the macrocosm were at length atoned, at length in harmony! I lived in everything; everything entered and lived in me. (p. 412)

The language of paradox in *Lilith*, in which opposites are yoked together, is also functional here.

A sentence from MacDonald's *Unspoken Sermons* serves to describe the circle that is begun in *Phantastes* and completed in *Lilith*: 'The final end of the separation is not individuality; that is but a means to it: the final end is oneness – an impossibility without it.'[40] Seen in this light *Phantastes* and *Lilith* themselves together form a larger dialectic: the one concerning itself with the First Things, and with true birth, self-realisation and movement into the world; the other treating the Last Things, and true death and the merging of the self with the greater consciousness which is its root. Yet there is, as has been seen, something of an 'atonement' between the two works also, in the marriage of opposites in the death-state which the one briefly describes and the other continually praises and prefigures. Having lived in his imagination, and hence, for him, in God, through the total pattern of Christian history, MacDonald felt himself to have moved out of time towards eternity. Shortly after the publication of *Lilith* he entered a long silent vigil that preluded the death (in 1905) to which he had looked forward all his life.

6 Fantasy and Loss: T. H. White

T. H. White's *The Once and Future King* admits more loss and pain than most fantasies. In rewriting the Matter of Britain from Malory's account White had to portray the failure of Arthur's ideals, the downfall of the Round Table and the departure of the wounded king from the world. All that he loves and celebrates for much of the book has to go: being is in the end swept into nonentity. Other writers of fantasy preserve their worlds with happier endings, earned or unearned. The fact that White does not, and that he is no less devoted to his creations, produces tensions and divisions in his work.

White's book has much in common with many modern fantasies which draw part of their inspiration from the meaning of the medieval world order to their authors – for example, the works of William Morris, Lord Dunsany, E. R. Eddison, James Branch Cabell, Charles Williams, C. S. Lewis, J. R. R. Tolkien or Mervyn Peake. In these works the impulse is on the whole nostalgia for a world simpler, less populated, better ordered and more natural than the writer's own, although this nostalgia may be extended to a mystic longing (Lewis) or even the belief that such apparently lost worlds are eternally co-present with this one (Williams). The 'medieval revival', which began in the eighteenth century, grew from a variety of impulses: antiquarian research; relativism (the sense, illustrated by Richard Hurd's *Letters on Chivalry and Romance* (1762) that eighteenth-century standards could no longer be used to evaluate other ages); aesthetics (the growing 'pre-Romantic' belief that Gothic was more natural than Palladian); primitivism; and sensationalism, whereby medieval landscapes and buildings were used in literature to evoke melancholy, or, in the Gothic novel from Walpole's *The Castle of Otranto* (1764) onwards, terror. In the nineteenth century, beginning with Scott, the interest shifted and narrowed under the increasing impact of industrialism towards plain longing for a world felt to be more certain, more beautiful and more ordered than the doubting, grimy and vulgar condition which scientific progress had bestowed on man.[1] White's book is definitely a backward view in this sense. Industrialism was for him one great enemy of culture and of the imagination,[2] the other being the decay of both personal initiative and the hierarchic arrangement of society, with the corresponding growth of 'communistic' doctrines, particularly 'the demonstrably false proposition of Washington, that all men are born equal'.[3] On his own admission he was the opposite of what he called a 'farewell-stater' – 'a snob and a gentleman';[4] one 'dedicated to the cause of gentleness', who bitterly resented what he saw as Britain's decline.[5] The only and inevitable irony here is that White placed his terminal date for civilisation around 1914, so that in his fine elegy *Farewell Victoria* (1933) – which is in many ways a prolegomenon to his Arthuriad – he could find something beautiful 'something medieval ... something feudal'[6] in that very Victorian period from which writers of his stamp who lived then themselves sought to escape.

Before White is classed as an 'escapist', due weight should be given to his view that the twentieth century in which he lived was itself escapist – a time in which man had lost touch with reality by becoming over-intellectual:

> The curse of England is industry, as Cobbett realised. But who reads Cobbett now? Who knows nowadays which way the wind was blowing when he got up, and whether it has changed since? We are mechanically introverted, unable to see the world about us, unable to cope with it with our hands, even unable to cope with ourselves. It is astonishing to see the intellectuals, who know all about communism and the European situation, trying to live their own lives, even indoors. They lean against the mantelpiece at the wrong angle, and the fender slips, and bang goes one of the candle-sticks, broken. They can't cope even with their own centres of gravity. I saw a presumably 'modern' boy the other day, who was so little conscious of the position of his own body that he fell backwards off a chair while thinking of something else.

All truly good and great men are interested in laying and lighting fires ...[7]

The image of the incompetence of the intellectual is reminiscent of that in Swift's Laputa.[8] The aim that results from it is similar to J. R. R. Tolkien's concept of 'Recovery' – an attempt to get back to grips with the world in a society which has lost touch with (or 'escaped from') it; the regaining of a clear view of things which have become so familiar to men that they no longer notice them.[9] However, White adds to the need for a change in perception the Swiftian prescription for a change in *action*.

White tried to live his whole life on these principles. After 1936 (when he resigned from his job as head of the English department at Stowe School) he had no profession save that of writer, and spent much of his life in such miscellaneous 'outdoor' activities as learning to be a pilot, rearing goshawks, hunting, ploughing, painting, fishing, bugle-playing, shooting, diving and meteorology. Many of his books are written in celebration of rural values, sport, or 'the things that won't fail with the services'.[10] A fox-hunt begins the early detective story *Dead Mr. Nixon* (1931); *Earth Stopped; or, Mr. Marx's Sporting Tour* (1934) describes the initiation into field sports of a communist intellectual; most of the stories in *Gone to Ground* (1935) have a 'sporting' context; *England Have My Bones* (1936) is 'a book about things, for people who have lost them', 'an empirical book, an attempt to return to the various world';[11] *Burke's Steerage; or, The Amateur Gentleman's Introduction to Noble Sports and Pastimes* (1938) is a satire on those who take no delight in sport for itself, but use it either to flatter themselves or to work out their neuroses on the animal kingdom; *The Goshawk* (1951) is an account of White's ultimately unsuccessful attempt during 1937 to train a singularly recalcitrant bird of prey; and *The Elephant and the Kangaroo* (New York, 1947) and *The Godstone and the Blackymor* (1959) are portraits of Ireland, the country itself and the country people White knew when he lived there during the war.

In all of these books White is, not always implicitly, prescribing a return to country life and values. In one way, of course, this limits his 'relevance', since most of his readers will be unable to do more than wish for the kind of life he portrays: for instance, few would dare to follow White's suggestion in *England Have My Bones* that we rediscover the special character of each day by naming it by the then prevailing wind, rather than by the date (p. 227). White himself seems to have seen that his was a closed world in this sense, and that the only way in which more than a few might be brought to it would be through a holocaust which destroyed civilisation – the technique he uses in *Earth Stopped* and *Gone to Ground*. However, it may be said that insofar as the reader can bring to his own world the clearness of vision and the humanity that White offers him, this rural ideal need not remain wholly an ideal; such, at least, was Tolkien's hope with his own fantasy.

In the story of Arthur and the Round Table, White found a perfect context for the expression of his aims and ideals. In the first place, for him as for Ruskin or William Morris, the medieval world was one in which craftsmanship and not the production line was behind everything made: and thereby making gave particular pleasure, and the product was individual. The scale ran from cooking:

> In the kitchens the famous cooks were preparing menus which included, for one course alone: ballock broth, caudle ferry, lampreys en galentine, oysters in civey, eels in sorré, baked trout, brawn in mustard, numbles of a hart, pigs farsed, cockintryce, goose in hoggepotte, venison in frumenty, hens in brewet, roast squirrels, haggis, capon-neck pudding, garbage, tripe, blaundesorye, caboges, buttered worts, apple mousse, gingerbread, fruit tart, blancmange, quinces in comfit, stilton cheese and causs boby.*

to castles:

> It was plastered. They had put chrome in the plaster, so that it was faintly gold. Its slated turrets, conical in the French fashion, crowded from complicated battlements in a hundred unexpected aspirations. There were little fantastic bridges, covered like the Bridge of Sighs, from this chapel to that tower. There were outside staircases, going heaven knows where – perhaps to heaven. Chimneys suddenly soared out of machicolations. Real stained-glass windows, high up and out of danger, gleamed where once there had been blank walls . . .
> (p. 621)

---

* T. H. White, *The Once and Future King* (Collins, 1958) p. 446. (Page references hereafter are to this edition.)[12]

Unexpectedness is here part of the effect: the exotic and the common, caboges and buttered worts, lie side by side, heightening their identities by their juxtaposition; and while the theme of the castle is aspiration, the modes in which this is realised continually surprise. There is also an element of what in narrowly practical terms would be waste. The courses could never all be eaten, and the castle's decoration serves no function but to express the creative – or *sportive* – exuberance of the builder. Lastly there is the sense of variety and detail, the special clarity and minuteness of description which is White's *forte*.

The Arthuriad also offered White a world, predominantly rural, in which sport and the craft of sport were of the essence. Hunting and falconry there found their natural home: and the basis on which the Round Table was founded was the chivalrous and practised conduct of arms. White enters fully into the description of the training of a knight, whether of the Wart (the young Arthur) or of Lancelot – the various strokes that may be used in tilting, training by means of a quintain or a ring, types of armour and crest, jousting spears, horses (pp. 330–7).[13] He compares jousting to cricket, even down to the scoring pavilion:

> When the sword-play had begun, the combatants stood opposite each other in the green acre like batsman and bowler – except that they stood closer together – and perhaps Sir Gawaine would start with an in-swinger, which Sir Lancelot would put away to leg with a beautiful leg-glide, and then Lancelot would reply with a yorker under Gawaine's guard – it was called 'foining' – and all the people round the field would clap. (p. 330)

Sport was for White a form of art; full of snatched graces. He once wrote that the guilt the hunter may at first feel in killing a beautiful animal can be gradually dulled, '*provided that in destroying that beauty he can at the same time congratulate himself upon having created another beauty, the beautiful shot*'.[14] And if sport is an art, might not art be a sport? – simply done for 'the achieve of, the mastery of the thing', as Hopkins, White's most admired poet, once put it? This will have to be borne in mind when considering how far *The Once and Future King* was created out of delight and how far for a definite purpose.

If there is one more general motive which led White not only to the writing of his Arthuriad, but to his celebrations of other ages in *Farewell Victoria* (1933), *The Age of Scandal* (1950) and *The Scandalmonger* (1952), it is his delight in identity. In the eighteenth century, and even in Victorian and Edwardian England, he found a social order which allowed the individual to express himself to the full. At the end of *The Scandalmonger* White turns to remark:

> All the fantastic kings and noblemen of the age which we have been discussing have given way before the demonstrably false proposition of Washington, that all men are born equal. They are not. Dr. Johnson was born with scrofula, while Sixteen-string Jack the highwayman was born with a perfect body; Selwyn was born a fool, while Porson came into the world with the brain of a great scholar. I for one am sorry to see the old distinctions go.[15]

The change from the Victorian to the modern era he sees as 'a sway from man to men'[16]: communism, in its many forms, had banished the individual for the mass. In nearly every book he wrote White set his face against this. *The Scandalmonger* and *The Age of Scandal* are both a series of vignettes of eighteenth-century life, covering every activity of man, but with a special eye for the individual and the eccentric. *The Book of Beasts* (1954), White's translation of a medieval bestiary, was done out of what he shared with his source – 'a reverence for the wonders of life'.[17] We find this pleasure in the particularity of every living thing expressed with peculiar poignancy in *The Once and Future King*, as, to a lesser estent, in *Farewell Victoria*, for in these books White is portraying a theme painfully close to him – the end of an age; not the deaths of individuals so much as the death of individualism.

The Once and Future King can be seen as a pastoral,[18] with an epic orientation. Modern fantasy often belongs to the pastoral genre; indeed is now probably one of the main vessels of its continuance: thus, for example, Kingley's *The Water-Babies* is a submarine pastoral, Lewis's *Perelandra* is an idyll of another planet and Tolkien's 'rural' *The Lord of the Rings*, like White's book, is a myth of history – in Tolkien's case, of *pre*history as it ought to have been. Within the walls of the form, however, there need be no escapism, no evasion of the hard facts generated from the pastoral world itself; and in this sense the pastoral is no less 'realistic' than any other literary form. There are those who do refuse the challenges of the world they have made – Tolkien, for example, who never allows the suffering that the terms of his world demand for his heroes.[19] White, however, faces the pain his story implies, as he faces and tries to accept it in any of the pastoral worlds he creates. *The Once and Future King* moves from the idyllic side of pastoral in the first book, *The Sword in the Stone*, to an increasingly elegiac vision, in which is shown the slow decay of the Round Table and the erosion of all that Lancelot, Guenever and Arthur represent. Time is at the centre of White's work as it is only at the end in Malory: the reader watches the Dark become the Middle Ages, and the Middle turn into the later Middle Ages; and he sees the central characters ageing. The story may have been given to White, but his peculiar emphasis on the fading of the dream and on the movement of time heighten the poignancy of the loss – even more because White is denying himself. The first book celebrates a condition of being; the later ones show a process of becoming, a process which erodes all attempts to look backward, whether by White, in his love of the passing medieval world, or by Arthur, in his continual attempt to make life recover his boyhood idyll.

Nevertheless, at the risk of digression here, some qualifications have to be made. Although White 'accepts' the facts of loss or death, he refuses them their final plangency. Like William Cowper, he is fascinated by the process of 'becoming' in life, the sense that 'Nature's threads ... to the cause/Of their best tone their dissolution owe':[20] but he avoids any bleak sense of transience by seeing death as itself a continuation of living. In one of his poems, a king (like Arthur) says that when he is dead, 'No one will say of me then/He came, nor now he is; always he comes.'[21] The maggots White watches on a dead sheep in *The Goshawk* are like 'live oats, busy, dry-sounding, crackling with life'; and he reflects, 'The air of death; I smelt it vigorously. It was a challenge to life. It was a tonic ... They were living and busy maggots, clean, vital, symbolical of an essential life-force perfectly persisting.'[22] This view of an *élan vital* which precludes finality is seen again in a letter White wrote to his friend David Garnett on the imminent death of Garnett's wife Ray: '*I* don't believe people do die in the full sense of that word. I believe in the law of conservation of energy, or something of that sort, and

I don't think the electric current has gone just because you switch the bulb off.'[23] The 'or something like that' is a painful indication that White's 'belief' is as much need as belief. Sometimes an Olympian view can help to remove the sting of perishability: thus he says of himself and the goshawk that their very tininess beside all the other creatures of the world makes them huge: 'so insignificant as to be significant, so transitory as to be eternal, so finite as to be infinite and a part of the Becoming. How should we feel fear or impatience, being so large and small?'[24] Similar is the description of Mundy at the end of *Farewell Victoria*, watching the creatures in the rock pool struggling for survival:[25] a writer such as Kingsley (to whom, incidentally, White owes much[26]) would have tried to make divine sense of the scene by seeing the law at work as the survival of the *morally* fittest, but White does accept the fact, while trying to rejoice in it as part of becoming. This is the White who lived all his life in terror of death.

> I have always been afraid of things: of looking a fool, of being hurt, of death. Death particularly, and probably more than with most people ... The fear of death has always been something living, an idea of being shut conscious in a black box with worms and earth, or, as that passed, of what the dead people miss. It is the penalty paid for sensibility. If one likes the shape of clouds and people, or the sun on one's knees; if one is aware of pleasures, can see and feel; if one is avaricious, ravening for more life: death is a sense of loss. One has to avert one's mind from it.[27]

If one loves the created individualities of life (or of one's own literature), White is saying, one will desperately refuse death the right to obliterate them. This may explain White's various attempts to alleviate the collapse of the Round Table in *The Once and Future King*. It may have been the very fact that in Malory Arthur is 'Rex Quondam Rexque Futurus' – that is, his end is not conceived as final, but as a station from which continually to become – that partly drew White to this story; at the end of the book he announces a circularity characteristic of fantasy – 'THE BEGINNING'. To this traditional 'alleviation' White has added several features of his own. Minor perhaps, is Arthur's charge to his page-boy, one Thomas Malory, on the night before the final battle, that he return home to write down the whole story of the Round Table for posterity. More significant is White's attempt to give Arthur's lifelong search for an English utopia a final fillip in his last-minute discovery that what has been at the bottom of the enmities and passions he has sought to check in his kingdom has been a sense of frontiers, and that the answer for this is a world-state with no national boundaries. This last try at making sense of the apparently senseless was 'imported' into the fourth book from the unpublished fifth, 'The Book of Merlyn', in which White, through Merlyn, expatiated at length to Arthur on what is gained in loss. With only this perfunctory discovery of an answer, *The Once and Future King* ends more painfully than White *consciously* intended it to.

However, while one side of White may have wished for a more consolatory conclusion, a side less recognised by him does not. The fifth book was an afterthought; 'these fragments I have shored against my ruins', and he felt that the first four books were the limit and the circuit of his inspiration.[28] Whatever White may have wished, the inmost nature of his being made his epic properly finish where it does, in an uncertain atmosphere of final loss and posited continuance. In that sense his Arthuriad does not manage to mitigate death and loss: despite the efforts of its author, it cannot escape them.

The first book of *The Once and Future King*, *The Sword in the Stone*, deals with the boyhood of Arthur, and has, apart from the concluding episode where he draws the sword from the stone, an air of the timeless about it: there is in a sense nothing but to be 'boy eternal' within the charmed circle of Sir Ector's castle and Merlyn's magical tuition. True, Arthur is learning, whether in the empire of the mindless ants or in the mess-hall of the militaristic falcons, facts that will be useful to him in later life: but at this stage the learning seems largely a pleasure taken for its own sake, and it is in these terms that Merlyn describes it – "pure science, the only purity there is" ' (p. 186). Sir Ector's castle and the Forest Sauvage are images of the happy communal life of boyhood and of the boyish lust for adventure: whether in Vat and the Dog Boy rolling about in the kennels, or the riotous party when Twiti the king's huntsman arrives; or in the adventure with Robin Hood in which the Wart and Kay release Morgan le Fay's captives from the fairy castle of food and later slay the griffin guard.[29] It is a boy's vision, and one to which

White only for the time subscribes: and in this sense it would be mistaken to attribute the 'prep-school' fun of Sir Pellinore's chaotic pursuit of the Questing Beast, or Sir Pellinore's ludicrous joust with Sir Grummore in the forest simply to the author. It is true that White misses out the nastier side of boyhood, the side that is seen in the sordid slaying of the unicorn by the Orkney children in the next book, *The Queen of Air and Darkness*; but that is part of the point of idyll. Occasionally, however, he pokes light fun at the picture, as in his account of the weather, which, if not eternal spring, is at least the seasons as Cowper painted them:

> in the Old England ... The weather behaved itself.
> In the spring, the little flowers came out obediently in the meads, and the dew sparkled, and the birds sang. In the summer it was beautifully hot for no less than four months and, if it did rain just enough for agricultural purposes, they managed to arrange it so that it rained while you were in bed. In the autumn the leaves flamed and rattled before the west winds, tempering their sad adieu with glory. And in the winter, which was confined by statute to two months, the snow lay evenly, three feet thick, but never turned into slush.
> It was Christmas night in the Castle of the Forest Sauvage, and all around the castle the snow lay as it ought to lie. It hung heavily on the battlements, like thick icing on a very good cake, and in a few convenient places it modestly turned itself into the clearest icicles of the greatest possible length.
> (p. 137)

A little further on the reader is told how round this scene 'the old English wolves wandered about slavering in an appropriate manner' (p. 138). It is an arranged world: there are fewer and less pleasant destinal arrangements in the world Arthur finds when he becomes king; and most of the other arrangements have to be made by Arthur himself – as Merlyn shortly to leave him warns: '"Stand up for yourself, that's the ticket. Asking advice is the fatal thing"' (p. 227); '"the important thing is this thinking for-yourself business"' (p. 228).

The destinal arrangements of the adult world may be simply described. Arthur, left ignorant of his true parentage and hence of his relations, is to be seduced by his half-sister Morgause, and Mordred, the child that results, is to destroy his father. The various episodes in which Mordred just escapes with his life – such as Arthur's attempt to have him drowned, or the occasion when Gawaine nearly stabs him, or that when he is the only one to escape with his life during the attempt to arrest Lancelot while he is with Guenever – all serve to heighten the sense of inevitability. For White this made the story of Arthur 'a perfectly Aristotelian tragedy'.[30]

Yet at the same time the reader is made strongly aware of the concatenation of human wills which puts Arthur and the Round Table at risk. Throughout his kingship Arthur searches for an 'arrangement' which will bring civilisation and peace to Gramarye: seeks, that is, the establishment by humanity of a state which may approximate to the idyll that is always lost with childhood. Faced by the violence of human nature, or, more locally, continual internecine strife among the barons, he resolves to try to harness violence, or Might, to a good end, or Right.[31] He establishes the Round Table and a code of chivalry by which member knights will be expected to fight for the weak and oppressed. For some time the idea works – until most wrongs in the kingdom have been righted. Then violence turns inward and becomes more selfish: first developing into 'games-mania', or competition to see who can come out top of the ousting averages; and then degenerating further, through the Gawaine faction, into renewed enmities and murder. Arthur tries to find a new channel for frustrated Might in a *spiritual* goal – the quest for the Grail; but all that happens is that he loses half of his knights, and the rest, apart from Lancelot, who is 'mad on God in any case' (p. 499), return to Camelot enraged at the impurities within them which have been made manifest by the guardians of the Grail. Frustrated again, Arthur begins to think towards abolishing Might altogether by establishing an absolute code of Right: 'He was groping towards Right as a criterion of its own – towards Justice as an abstract thing which did not lean upon power. In a few years he would be inventing Civil Law' (p. 508).

The irony is that the arrival of Civil Law is to facilitate the final destruction of the Round Table. Lancelot and Guenever are lovers: hitherto anyone who wished to prove this had to defend his case in personal combat, and since Lancelot was unbeatable, the point could never be carried. But under the new law code, trial by combat may be waived for trial by jury, and the burden of proof shifts from prowess to hard evidence. Agravaine of the Mordred faction (he hates Lancelot, and Mordred Arthur) realises how justice may be used to further his enmity, and sets about supplying proof of Guenever's infidelity. Now what began as the harnessing of Might by Right is reversed. Agravaine anachronistically exults to himself as he finds out from Arthur how he may proceed, '"Hoist with his own petard!"' (p. 589) After this the context is one of more or less naked wills. Agravaine secures his proof, though at the cost of his own life and of all save Mordred's of the knights who try to arrest Lancelot. The queen is adjudged to the fire and Lancelot arrives as expected not only by the queen but by Arthur and Gawaine to rescue her. In the struggle he slays two unarmed knights whom in his haste he fails to recognise: Gareth and Gaherys, loved brothers of Gawaine, and close friends of Lancelot. Thereafter Gawaine is out for Lancelot's blood, and Arthur is dragged reluctantly to France to lay siege to Lancelot's castle of Benwick. In the interim Mordred (who, since Arthur is otherwise childless, is in the line of succession) is left as regent, seizes power, and Arthur returns to face him in the final battle.

Before that battle Arthur reviews his long struggle to establish Right, searching for an answer to the native hostility of the human heart. Eventually he traces the cause to 'Suspicion and fear: possessiveness and greed: resentment for ancestral wrong' (p. 671), and in the depths of despair suddenly hits on an answer which leaves him 'refreshed, clear-headed, almost ready to begin again' (p. 676): the removal of frontiers between man and man, nation and nation, along the lines of the tribes of the geese which know no boundaries – in short the establishment of something like a world state.[32] And this he sees as being done through culture: just as the survival of Sir Thomas Malory and of the story of Arthur are what are created rather than simply left by the whole fall of the Round Table, so out of strength and ignorance may come sweetness and knowledge:

> There would be a day – there must be a day – when he would come back to Gramarye with a new Round Table which had no corners, just as the world had none – a table without boundaries between the nations who would sit to feast there. The hope of making it would lie in culture. If people could be

persuaded to read and write, not just to eat and make love, there was still a chance that they might come to reason. (p. 676)

The reader will recall, however, what he has previously concluded on the idea of people's 'sharing everything – even thoughts, feelings, lives' (p. 670):

> Obviously you might cure a cancer of the womb by not having a womb in the first place. Sweeping and drastic remedies could cut out anything – and life with the cut. Ideal advice, which nobody was built to follow, was no advice at all. (p. 671)

Arthur – and White – continue to worry the bone of this debate in the unpublished fifth book.

The manner of Arthur's attempts to reconcile Might and Right is reminiscent of an experiment. It is as if to say 'Here are the difficulties of human nature: let us try and find a means of smoothing them away'; and then to proceed, as experimenters do, by patient trial and error, till all possibilities have been explored. This is typical of White. *The Once and Future King* is in this sense another version of *The Goshawk*, where the attempt is also (unsuccessfully) made to train and redirect the savagery of a raptor. Without the attempt nature is simply random, brutish and unintelligent. In fact, what White and Arthur are trying to do is to put intelligibility into the world. In one way it is a curious aim for a man who detested intellectuals – 'Fundamentally I don't like intelligence. I have never been in love with an intellectual person':[33] but White did claim that what he meant by this was intelligence considered in isolation from the body it inhabited – 'it is useless to rely on the intelligence only. The desirable specimen is the specimen, I take it, whose physical and emotional efficiency is at least on a par with that of his intelligence.'[34] This last is the point of the satire on the central figure in *The Master* (1957). When, however, White is found arguing for the removal of dualities ('The static noun and the active verb correspond to the other exploded dualities: space and time, matter and mind ... mind and matter coalesce into aspects of something else'[35]), it can only be felt that he is trying to reduce a doubleness in his own nature and vision. This doubleness is

seen portrayed in *The Once and Future King*, where on the one side
there is incorrigible, stupid fact, and on the other, intelligence
trying to marshal and organise it – to the final breakdown even
of a marriage of opposites.

It would appear that there is a radical disjunction between the
White who wants to tell the story for its own sake, and the White
– here as Arthur – who wants not only to put sense into it, but to
put sense into the actors themselves. And this is made manifest
by the delight he takes for much of the story in the sheer fact of
things, whether in describing a castle or a love-affair: one side of
the book is a celebration of the single and separate identities
of things, and particularly of an age when those identities were
most fully expressed:

> Lancelot and Guenever were gazing on the Age of Individuals.
>   What an amazing time the age of chivalry was! Everybody
> was essentially himself – was riotously busy fulfilling the
> vagaries of human nature. There was such a gusto about the
> landscape which stretched before their window, such a riot of
> unexpected people and things, that you hardly knew how to
> begin describing it. (pp. 561–2)

The society of the ants, in which each member merges its
identity in the collective, is meant as an Awful Warning to the
Wart. Thus it is that we can find White taking a certain pleasure
in describing that very chaotic violence of Might which he
elsewhere condemns:

> It had been no uncommon sight to see a man-at-arms
> whistling like a lobster, and looking like porridge, because
> they had emptied a bucket of boiling bran over his armour
> during a siege. Other spectacles even more dramatic have
> been mentioned by Chaucer ...
>
>   .   .   .   .
>
> All the tyrannous giants were dead, all the dangerous
> dragons – some of which used to come down with a burr like
> the peregrine's stoop – had been put out of action. Where the
> raiding parties had once streamed along the highways with
> fluttering pennoncels, now there were merry bands of pilgrims
> telling each other dirty stories on the way to Canterbury.
> (pp. 444, 445)

On the other hand, while Arthur is portrayed by White as a simple, well-meaning man, and his early mental struggles before his tutor Merlyn to find a way of containing Might with Right are gently satirised, it would be quite wrong to argue that White intended Arthur's debate with his kingdom to be seen throughout in an ironic light. The position is rather that White is certainly on the side of Arthur and the idealistic search for life as it may be, but is equally involved with life as it is. Like Malory he finds it hard to condemn the adulterous relation of Lancelot and Guenever: here Arthur, who turns a blind and possibly less than fully heterosexual eye, is White himself.[36] The love relation has little obvious place in the theme of Might versus Right either,[37] and escapes condemnation from that source also. What makes Lancelot fall in love with Guenever is something that no statute or code can legislate away: he is a self-suppressed sadist,[38] and one day despite himself he causes Guenever pain, and sees her suffer. 'He might never have noticed her as a person, if he had not seen the pain in her eyes' (p. 353; see also p. 348). In his Lancelot and Guenever White has created the most full-bodied characters and the most convincing portrait of a heterosexual love-relation in all his work.[39]

> One explanation of Guenever, for what it is worth, is that she was what they used to call a 'real' person. She was not the kind that can be fitted away safely under some label or other, as 'loyal' or 'disloyal' or 'self-sacrificing' or 'jealous'. Sometimes she was loyal and sometimes she was disloyal. She behaved like herself. And there must have been something in this self, some sincerity of heart, or she would not have held two people like Arthur and Lancelot. Like likes like, they say – and at least they are certain that her men were generous. She must have been generous too. It is difficult to write about a real person. (p. 497)

The psychological penetration of the account of the lovers is considerable. A good instance is the moment of Lancelot's meeting Guenever when he has arrived to rescue her from the clutches of the besotted Meliagrance. For some time since his experience on the Quest for the Grail, Lancelot has separated himself from Guenever to purify his devotion to his God: now

Guenever gives him the freedom she had not previously allowed.

> When Guenever saw him, and he saw her, the old electric
> message went between their eyes before they spoke a word. It
> was as if Elaine and the whole Quest for the Grail had never
> been. So far as we can make it out, she had accepted her
> defeat. He must have seen in her eyes that she had given in to
> him, that she was prepared to leave him to be himself – to love
> his God, and to do whatever he pleased – so long as he was
> only Lancelot. She was serene and sane again. She had
> renounced her possessive madness and was joyful to see him
> living, whatever he did ... And, in truly yielding, she had won
> the battle by mistake. (p. 531)

There are, it is true, moments when White lurches into
sentimental applause for the lovers: 'It is a story of love in the old
days, when adults loved faithfully – not a story of the present, in
which adolescents pursue the ignoble spasms of the cinemato-
graph' (p. 539).[40] But on the whole the portrait is founded on the
understanding of real characters.

Realism and idealism are in a sense the two impulses of *The
Once and Future King*, and White cannot finally reconcile them.
The drive of events seems to be towards the defeat of any ideal,
of any attempt to make sense of human affairs, yet Arthur
rescues further hope from the approaching collapse. The question becomes: should one accept things for what they are, or
should one judge, discriminate and try to better them? At one
point White introduces the reader to what he calls the 'seventh
sense'. The sixth he considers to be the physical balance implicit
in learning to walk; the seventh that spiritual balance by which
one puts up with things without trying to change them. The
latter comes, particularly to women, with middle age. With it
one 'can go on living – not by principle, not by deduction, not by
knowledge of good and evil, but simply by a peculiar and shifting
sense of balance which defies each of these things often' (p. 394).
This discovery of the seventh sense is no triumph: it is a final
deadening of feeling and of the knowledge 'that there could have
been a time when we were young bodies flaming with the
impetus of life'. Yet, bitter though White may be at the seventh
sense, his picture of idealistic youth that goes before it is not
without irony:

But there was a time when each of us stood naked before the world, confronting life as a serious problem with which we were intimately and passionately concerned. There was a time when it was of vital interest to us to find out whether there was a God or not. Obviously the existence or otherwise of a future life must be of the very first importance to somebody who is going to live her present one, because her manner of living it must hinge on the problem. There was a time when Free Love versus Catholic Morality was a question of as much importance to our hot bodies as if a pistol had been clapped to our heads. (p. 395)

The seventh sense is disgusting, but it is as inevitable as time, and in a way more real than these vital youthful questions. White loves the idealism of Arthur, could not do without it, but he is drawn as strongly by 'the hard fact of things'. Arthur has, in one way, tried to pull both sides together, the coarse realism of Might and the ideal of Right, but by using the very categories of Might and Right he has renounced any complete synthesis. So too for White: there can be no middle ground between the seventh sense and idealism, and no third factor which transcends them: the passage shifts its unproductive irony from one to the other. In a way, it might be added, the picture is one of a final incompatibility between man and woman. White doubts whether women ever 'live by seeking the truth' (p. 394).[41] Guenever does not see what is wrong with the Round Table that makes it necessary for Arthur to send his knights on the Grail Quest. As Arthur and Lancelot grow boyishly excited at the plan, the reader is made aware of Guenever watching them enthusing over their hobby (pp. 455–8). The plan itself is an almost total failure: it affords White an excellent opportunity for condemnation of what he sees as the facile judgments made on Arthur's knights by a set of spiritual standards to which they cannot hope to aspire; but the reader is left to wonder what place there is for any standards after it – particularly as White is found portraying Lancelot's continued devotion to God rather than Guenever as faintly absurd.

The whole theme of Might and Right is in one way periphrastic, only 'a way of putting it', so far as the growth and decay of the Round Table are concerned. The *matière*, as the Arthurian *matière* is prone to do, resists the *sens*. Fate is one of the primary causes of failure. Another is quite simply time. Malory, particularly in his final book, used time and the seasons in a similar manner, but there is not the pervasive insistence on mutability, on youth and decay that is to be found throughout White's treatment of the story. Arthur, as has been said, is trying to re-create in the adult world the idyll of his childhood as it is portrayed in *The Sword in the Stone*: trying, that is, to go back by going forward;[42] which may be one reason for the reader's sense of him as so perpetually youthful. He is seeking permanence in a world of flux. His methods of establishing a utopian relation between Might and Right have to be adjusted throughout, through failure after failure, until there is no place for them save in the blind and willed idealism of the close. Everything wears out to naught: 'If you achieve perfection, you die' (p. 504); and so too if you simply live: when Lancelot sees Guenever as no longer young,

> It was his old love for a girl of twenty, standing proudly by her throne with the present of captives about her – but now the same girl was standing in other surroundings, the surroundings of bad make-up and loud silks, by which she was trying to defy the invincible doom of human destiny. He saw her as the passionate spirit of innocent youth, now beleaguered by the trick which is played on youth – the trick of treachery in the body, which turns flesh into green bones. (p. 483; see also pp. 442, 559)

At the court, after the Quest, there is a new atmosphere 'which had begun to pull away from ... [Arthur] instead of with him' (p. 505). Here White telescopes the shift from the Early to the High Middle Ages, relating the principle that 'the younger rises when the old doth fall' not only to the effects of the Quest, but to a larger shift in culture and fashion in which Arthur, Lancelot and Guenever are more out of place.

> The best knights had gone to perfection, leaving the worst to hold their sieges. A leaven of love was left, it is true – Lancelot, Gareth, Aglovale and a few old dodderers like Sir Grummore and Sir Palomides: but the tone was set elsewhere. It came from the surly angers of Gawaine, the fripperies of Mordred, and the sarcasms of Agravaine. Tristram had done no good to

it in Cornwall ... Marital fidelity had become 'news'. Clothes became fantastic ... The court was modern.

So there were eyes on Guenever now – not the eyes of strong suspicion or of warm connivance, but the bored looks of calculation and the cold ones of society. (pp. 504–5)

'Strong suspicion' implies some standards of value, but cynicism does not: 'Mordred and Agravaine thought Arthur hypocritical – as all decent men must be, if you assume that decency can't exist' (p. 505). This, as White sees it, is the basis for the civil war which is to destroy both Arthur and Mordred, for the division is a final one: it is not so much passion against passion, but passion against that which denies the existence of passion.[43]

The causes of the fall of the Round Table in White's story are perhaps both as various and obscure as the explanations that Arthur tries to find at the end for human warfare and enmity. White refuses judgment on Arthur for having tried to kill Mordred in infancy by setting him adrift in a boat, but the bare fact partly explains Mordred's hatred of him; and similarly Lancelot is not fully *blamed* for slaying the unarmed Gareth and Gaherys when he rescues Guenever from the stake, but the consequence in terms of Gawaine's hatred is inevitable: it is a tragic vision of evil far outweighing the act which admitted it. White refuses to make the Arthuriad a moral tale in which the Round Table meets its just deserts, as Malory's French sources – particularly the *Mort Artu* – had done: for him the Quest for the Grail was not an exposure of the spiritual corruption and vainglory of the earthly chivalry of Arthur's court, but an experimental extension of the continued debate between Might and Right; and, in the event, an irrelevant and destructive one. Malory islanded the Quest story within his Arthuriad: the valuations made on Arthur's knights within that story do not reverberate beyond it. (White was so struck by this point that he made the joking claim that Malory did not write it[44] – which in a sense, given that Malory was trying to follow his sources, is true.) But Eugene Vinaver's claim that Malory 'made Corbenic a province of Camelot'[45] is truer of White. White goes the full distance towards refusing the reader a set of clear valuations which will blunt the painfully tragic element with any sense that the disaster was deserved. Much, no doubt, is due here to his love of the characters Arthur, Lancelot and Guenever, and the

Order of which they are a part; but as much, in effect, since he is true to the facts of the story, to the bleak awareness of evil begotten out of the finest intentions: 'There lives within the very flame of love/A kind of wick or snuff that will abate it.'[46] Ultimately, since causes are left largely obscure, it could be said that White is simply, lovingly, and painfully recording facts: facts which make even the glosses on them in terms of Might and Right finally meaningless. And, if that is so, the true determinant of the fall of chivalry is to be found in the empty flux of process, in the cyclic movement from growth to decay. Claudius, it will be recalled, went on, 'And nothing is at a like goodness still;/For goodness, growing to a pleurisy,/Dies in his own too much.'

There is here none of the triumphant stoicism of Mundy surveying the rock-pool in *Farewell Victoria*, but there is some victory in having faced it. One might say that there are two poles in *The Once and Future King* – being and nonentity. Neither one is more real than the other: life is conceived not as a swallow flying from darkness into a brightly lit hall and back into darkness, but as a continual cycle from death to life, an endless process of becoming. It seems almost a necessary part of White's lifelong concern for the sheer identity of created things that he should have as powerful a sense of the reverse: the reduction of being into nothingness. It is perhaps the peculiarly Romantic duality that is seen, for example, in Keats: the more one is fascinated by the existence of things, the more one can become subconsciously drawn to the opposite of that existence in night and death. (It is interesting, in relation to this tension between conscious and unconscious, to note that there are very few night scenes in *The Once and Future King*, and that of these the most memorable is an account of the destroying wind.) Lancelot, Guenever, Arthur, even Mordred, are the fully realised beings of White's Arthuriad; so also are the details – rendered with peculiar clarity – of the shifting medieval backcloth. That backcloth goes in the significantly named 'The Candle in the Wind', where the main figures are isolated;[47] and finally they themselves all go, leaving, apart from the *voulu* Sir Thomas Malory, only the wind – 'Anguish of Ireland had once dreamed of a wind which blew down all their castles and towns – and this one was conspiring to do it' (p. 659). This is the wind that the Wart found on the mud flats at night when Merlyn changed him to a goose:

The place in which he found himself was absolutely flat. In the human world we seldom see flatness, for the trees and houses and hedges give a serrated edge to the landscape. Even the grass sticks up with its myriad blades. But here, in the belly of the night, the illimitable, flat, wet mud was as featureless as a dark junket. If it had been wet sand, even, it would have had those little wave marks, like the palate of your mouth.

In this enormous flatness, there lived one element – the wind ... In the human world, the wind comes from some-where, and goes somewhere, and, as it goes, it passes through somewhere – through trees or streets or hedgerows. This wind came from nowhere. It was going through the flatness of nowhere, to no place. Horizontal, soundless except for a peculiar boom, tangible, infinite, the astounding dimensional weight of it streamed across the mud ...

The Wart, facing into this wind, felt that he was uncreated. Except for the wet solidity under his webbed feet, he was living in nothing – a solid nothing, like chaos. (p. 166)

This is a picture of identity totally lost: it is White's *le néant* to his *l'être*.

When White first wrote this passage, in different form, in 1938, for a projected story entitled 'Grief for the Grey Geese', he ended it: 'The wind in this place had no human characteristics: it did not punish or lament or exult or despair. It was mindless, in a country without mind.'[48] White himself was seen by one friend as 'chased by a mad black wind. Not always distraught, of course, sometimes gay, often wildly enthusiastic, tremendously moved, especially by natural beauty, then often quickly lapsing into melancholy because that beauty was so transient.'[49] The same friend said, of this man whose every book is in large part a vision of delight, 'I think he was 75 per cent of his time unhappy and often *very unhappy*; probably about nothing in particular. Terror and awe mysteriously affected him. He couldn't bear to think about death ...'[50] The price the spirit exacts for over-simplifications needs no labouring: flight from the nonentity of the modern age, flight from misery, or from death become in a sense the measure of fascination with them. In *The Once and Future King*, however, this polarity in White's nature is *understood* within the story of Arthur. White is perhaps recognising himself in the tale concerning the inevitability of fate which Merlyn tells

Arthur – the story of the man of Damascus who fled from a prevision of his imminent death, only to find that his prevision related to Aleppo, whither he had fled (p. 295).[51] In the picture of man on the mud-flats, White has given substance to a vision which haunted him all his life: man alone, exposed to the meaninglessness, the total loss of vacancy.

> The unseeking sea
> Cruelly purposes nothing,
> Has no thread,
> Engulfs purpose,
> In vacuum smooths over
> The assimilated insentient
> Insentiently,
> Us, dead![52]

The extent to which, as in White, love of being can tip over into equal fascination with nothingness demonstrates a process of emotional action and reaction which must perhaps always be a potential threat to the delights of creation expressed in fantasy. The process can work in the opposite direction too: David Lindsay's strange fantasy *A Voyage to Arcturus* (1920), which sets out to show all the pleasures of life as empty and corrupt, does so through a series of images so vivid, striking and abundant that the impression at least equally conveyed is a love of creation. But such a dialectic is not always demonstrably present, as here with T. H. White. Many fantasies, such as those of MacDonald, Lewis, Tolkien, Peake or Le Guin, make nothingness the evil that must be crushed, whether in the form of Anodos's shadow, the Un-man, Sauron, Steerpike or Cob. Here it is only by turning the moral oppositions into psychological inner conflicts, by saying that the writer makes nonentity the evil because he is repressing a fascination for it in himself, that the existence of such a duality can be claimed.[53] Nevertheless the duality is potentially there: and this seems demonstrated by the fact that White's fantasy admits more loss than most, and in doing so exacerbates and exposes tensions which would be otherwise assuaged in the triumph of the good and the preservation of joy.

7 Fantasy and Mind: Mervyn Peake

Many modern fantasies show a dissociation between 'mind' and 'matter': the images or objects of the story become divided from the more intellectual aspects of the work. Something of this has already been seen with T. H. White, where there is a gap between the raw material of the Arthuriad and the sense Arthur and White try to make of it. It can be seen also in Kingsley's *The Water-Babies*, where the wonderful variety of the underwater creatures presented has little to do with the theme of moral (d)evolution, or of the soul making the body, in the book; or in C. S. Lewis's *Perelandra*, where there is a split between the sections describing the fantastic appearance of the planet and its creatures and those dealing with lengthy debates over whether or not the unfallen Lady of Perelandra should disobey the prohibition of God. In the fantasy of George MacDonald the author is not wholly prepared to let the wonderful imaginative imagery of his story work on the unconscious minds of his readers, but feels the need to enter with discordant explanation or didacticism. In Mervyn Peake's *Gormenghast*, the second book of his 'Titus' trilogy, is found a breakdown of the unity of 'objects' and significance that prevailed in its predecessor *Titus Groan*, into either too much argumentation or excess of description for its own sake.[1] It seems true to say of fantasy that its concern with wonder at being is responsible for this isolation of the intellect.

Peake's work shows this separation in further modes. The first two of his three novels about Titus the seventy-seventh Earl of Groan – *Titus Groan* (1946), *Gormenghast* (1950) and *Titus Alone* (1959) – are set in an isolated castle called Gormenghast. Nobody comes to this castle from beyond the horizon, and no-one within it is described as ever having gone more than a few miles from it. The reader knows nothing of where Gormenghast is, or of any other place. This condition is in *Titus Groan* also reflected in the inhabitants of the castle, who, so far as they can, live in total isolation from one another – Sepulchrave the seventy-sixth Earl of Groan in his library, his wife the Countess Gertrude with her cats and birds in her rooms, their daughter Fuchsia in her attics, the Aunts Cora and Clarice, Sepulchrave's sisters, in their strange Room of Roots, the old curator Rottcodd in his Hall of Bright Carvings. If there is much in the portrayal of the castle (with its sprawling aspect, its subterranean labyrinth and its way of appearing to grow as the book proceeds) which suggests the character of a brain, then the limbs it is supposed to control have in large part a life of their own.

But the same can be seen in *Titus Groan* at the level of the individual character. Parts of bodies often appear to take on independent activity, without much reference to a controlling mind. The face of the poet of Gormenghast is thus described:

> It was a wedge, a sliver, a grotesque slice in which it seemed the features had been forced to stake their claims, and it appeared that they had done so in a great hurry and with no attempt to form any kind of symmetrical pattern for their mutual advantage. The nose had evidently been the first upon the scene and had spread itself down the entire length of the wedge, beginning among the grey stubble of the hair and ending among the grey stubble of the beard, and spreading on both sides with a ruthless disregard for the eyes and mouth which found precarious purchase. The mouth was forced by the lie of the terrain left to it, to slant at an angle which gave to its right-hand side an expression of grim amusement and to its left, which dipped downwards across the chin, a remorseless twist. It was forced by not only the unfriendly monopoly of the nose, but also by the tapering character of the head to be a short mouth; but it was obvious by its very nature, that under normal conditions it would have covered twice the area. The eyes in whose expression might be read the unending grudge they bore against the nose were as small as marbles and peered out between the grey grass of the hair. (*TG*, p. 139)*

---

* References are to the Eyre and Spottiswoode (second) editions of the novels (identical to the subsequent Penguin editions): *Titus Groan* (1968), *Gormenghast* (1968) and *Titus Alone* (1970), cited as *TG*, *G* and *TA*.

The features have not grown together by any inner and unifying directive, but have as it were settled from outside and fought for living space in a facial 'scramble for Africa': the result is that each tries not only to claim as much space but effectively as much attention for itself as possible, and together they appear as a cluster of diverse fragments. At the same time these separate parts of the face appear to have taken on independent life and intelligence: the features 'stake their claims', the nose has 'ruthless disregard' and 'unfriendly monopoly' and the eyes bear an 'unending grudge'.

In other portraits it is often the eyes which take on a life of their own. As Rottcodd walks in his Hall of Bright Carvings, his head and optics are 'constantly on the move ... the head wobbling in a mechanical way from side to side ... and the eyes, as though taking their cue from the parent sphere to which they were attached, peering here, there, and everywhere at nothing in particular' (*TG*, p. 17; compare pp. 19–20). The eyes are not following the dictates of any brain in the parent sphere, but simply copying the physical movements of the head; and all the movements are purposeless – 'peering ... at nothing in particular'. Later one of Swelter the cook's eyes comes into play as he hears two apprentices arguing on his return to the kitchen:

> His eye, moving around the panel of the door, is like something detached, self-sufficient, and having no need of the voluminous head that follows it nor for that matter of the mountainous masses undulating to the crutch, and the soft, trunk-like legs. So alive is it, this eye, quick as an adder, veined like a blood-alley ... As the eye rounds the corner of the door it devours the long double line of skinny apprentices as a squid might engulf and devour some long-shaped creature of the deeps. As it sucks in the line of boys through the pupil, the knowledge of his power over them spreads sensuously across his trunk like a delicious gooseflesh. (*TG*, pp. 361–2)

The eye operates almost independently of body and mind alike: it has become Swelter in microcosm. Only in the last sentence does the account return to the possessive 'his', and then it is Swelter's body which registers knowledge, not any brain he may have. Again, when Swelter encounters Flay, servant to Sepulchrave, the antipathy between them is described in terms of that between each pair of eyes (*TG*, pp. 364–5).

Voices too are sometimes portrayed as though they are independent agents. When Countess Gertrude, requiring the presence of Dr Prunesquallor, bellows '"SQUALLOR!"', 'The word echoed along the corridors and down the stairs, and creeping under the door and along the black rug in the Cold-room, just managed, after climbing the doctor's body, to find its way into both his ears simultaneously, in a peremptory i modified condition' (*TG*, p. 59). When at the Christening ceremony Sepulchrave has to call for his son Titus to be brought in, 'His voice moved down the corridor and turned about the stone corner' (*TG*, p. 115).

The bodily dissociations in *Titus Groan* relate mainly to parts of the head, thus perhaps accentuating independence from mind by proximity. There are exceptions – the withered leg of Barquentine, Master of the castle's Ritual, is described as on one occasion blushing at the violence of his oaths with 'an awakened sense of shame at what the upper part of the body could *descend* to' (*TG*, pp. 491–2). And while not acting quite this independently, other parts of the body can form obstacles to mental intentions – Sourdust's beard caught in the door of an iron cupboard during an act of Ritual (*TG*, pp. 295–6), or Flay's cracking knee-joints and Swelter's vast bulk when they are stalking one another.

These portrayals of bodies fragmenting into independent life can in part be related to the way that many of the characters pour all their humanity and love into that which is not human, rather than relating to each other: the aloof Outer Dwellers into their beautiful carvings, the Countess into her cats and birds, Fuchsia into her attic and the imaginary figures with which she has peopled it, Pentecost the gardener into his apple trees, Sepulchrave into his books, Sourdust into the Ritual, Cora and Clarice into their tree and its roots. Frequently the castle i described as being so much a part of the characters' lives as to b felt by them as part of their bodies (*TG*, pp. 62, 273; *G*, p. 341) and the result is that it takes on a life of its own (*G*, pp. 340–1 359).

It can also be argued that this fragmentation expresses a wide lack of control in Gormenghast in *Titus Groan*. The titular centr of the book is a helpless and inarticulate baby. Authority has fo the time gone from 'the kingly crowned head',[2] for Sepulchrave has made himself wholly the slave of the Ritual and has not tried to rule. The Ritual itself is a mass of observances of which the meaning has been forgotten. The book is full of people without minds, whether the automata Rottcodd, Cora, Clarice and Sourdust, the baby Titus or the finally mad Sepulchrave: symbolising this, perhaps, is Steerpike's theft of the skull from Sourdust's skeleton. Without control, rebellion becomes possible, and the villainous youth Steerpike, Cora and Clarice, Fuchsia and even Titus variously challenge the *status quo.* Certainly in *Gormenghast*, where the Countess Gertrude asserts her authority and there is much more will and awareness at the centre of the castle, there are fewer references to fragmented bodies: for example the whole account of the courtship of Bellgrove, headmaster of Gormenghast's school, and Irma, sister of Dr Prunesquallor, is specifically about the success of the mind in controlling recalcitrant body (*G*, pp. 207, 218, 221–6, 242–7).

However it is clear too that Peake simply delights in this idiom, and in people having worlds which are supremely their own, 'the world of their centre where their lives burn genuinely and with a free flame' (*TG*, p. 77). For instance, after Flay has cut off Swelter's ear during their mortal fight in the strange Hall of Spiders, Peake as narrator comments: 'it swung to and fro in a spider-made hammock a foot above the floor-boards at the far end of the room. And what voluptuary ever lolled with half the languor of that boneless thing!' (*TG*, p. 434). The vision in *Titus Groan* of mind having only frail control over body can be seen morally and thematically, but it is also very much Peake's own. In the subsequent Titus books it manifests itself in different and less artistic modes.

In *Gormenghast* the motives given for characters' behaviour are often unconvincing or inconsistent. In his *Modern Fantasy* the present writer has tried to show how Peake has considerable difficulty in providing Titus with reasons for rebelling against and eventually leaving Gormenghast;[3] and this will not be repeated here. But the motivation of Steerpike, the other central figure, is also obscure. It is hard for the reader to understand why, for example, if Steerpike has a cold and tameless 'greed for personal power' (*G*, p. 164), he does not gather some followers and seize it for himself quickly. He could have destroyed almost the entirety of the leading figures of Gormenghast in the library burning in *Titus Groan*. It is true that there is some evidence that he may prefer the gradual getting to the actual having: on two occasions it is stated that he wishes to become Master of Ritual in order to learn 'the innermost secrets of Gormenghast', and gradually over years to bend the Ritual to his own purposes (*TG*, p. 333; *G*, pp. 163–4): but such gradualist aims are in conflict with others. If the reader accepts that he is resigned, after his murder of Barquentine, to a ten-year period of consolidating a position as saintly Master of Ritual, and if, more particularly, Steerpike is aware of how carefully he must now tread to allay the powerful suspicions in the castle (*G*, p. 304), it must be wondered too why he continues to woo Fuchsia, thus risking exposure. Quite what his object is, is unclear. For the reader next learns that he is seeking to seduce Fuchsia in order to gain power over her (*G*, p. 345), and then that he wishes to slay Titus by cunning, so that 'the Countess alone would stand between him and a virtual dictatorship' (p. 349). In *Titus Groan* it is once said that he has 'along with his faculty for making swift and bold decisions, an unending patience' (*TG*, p. 224), but here there is not the sense that these two faculties are united, and the reader loses touch with Steerpike and what drives him.

Others of his actions are left without explanation. Why he kept the Aunts alive for so many years, especially when they had found out that he had tricked them, is not clear. Their accidental deaths by starvation were, he admits, 'an untidy business' (*G*, p. 305). By not having despatched them and destroyed their remains as one would expect him to do, he runs the risk of discovery, and in the end *is* discovered, in being followed when he goes to check that the Aunts are indeed dead in their distant chamber – for the years have brought the vigilant Flay (banished from Gormenghast in *Titus Groan*) back to watch over the castle by night. At the end of *Gormenghast*, during the flood, it is hard to understand why Steerpike does not seek to make a boat or to steal one before he does, for he could have escaped to the safer purlieus of the nearby Gormenghast Mountain; and this becomes even more of a question when he has stolen Titus's canoe.

There is often similar lack of explanation for the behaviour of lesser characters. When it is revealed that Barquentine has a son (*G*, p. 268) the reader wonders why he has not sought to replace Steerpike with him before, since he has increasingly distrusted him. Barquentine himself was the son of the previous Master of Ritual, Sourdust, and when unearthed was found to be thoroughly versed in the Ritual; his own son is at least forty years old (*G*, p. 268); and it is the norm for the Mastership to pass from father to son (*G*, p. 302): it is therefore all the more surprising that he has not taken any steps to ensure that his knowledge is transmitted to one of his own blood, or even tried to see his son during all these years. It is worth noting, however, that all these mentions of Barquentine's son stand in contradiction of his own assertion in *Titus Groan* that he does not have one (*TG*, p. 454).   Scott Donner

It is also difficult for the reader to understand how the Aunts, who have been consistently characterised as stupid to the point of being incapable of thought (for example, *TG*, pp. 244 ff.), and who had to be rehearsed continually by Steerpike in the simple task of setting fire to the library when everything else had been done for them (*TG*, p. 268), could yet have constructed so elaborate a trap for Steerpike as the delicately-hung axe-head above the door on the inside of their chamber (*G*, pp. 259–60, 379) – and then have given its existence away (*G*, p. 260). Similarly puzzling is the fact that Titus and Prunesquallor could break down the locked door of the Aunts' chamber, while the desperate Cora and Clarice, who had at least one axe-head and were credited with considerable mechanical aptitude, were supposedly unable to escape.

What is present in this loss of motive for actions is a different version of the fragmentation and loss of control of mind over body evident in *Titus Groan*, and one stemming from a different cause. It expresses itself also in the dissociation between the comic and serious sides of the book, the isolation of the lengthy account of the academy of Gormenghast from the main plot of Steerpike, Titus and his foster-sister the Thing. There is a breakdown of the union that prevailed in *Titus Groan* of significance and insignificance: now there are situations which are either only absurd or else labour under their gravity.[4] Now the reasons for behaviour are either explicit and imposed, or else lacking; now there are either too many of them or too few.

In *Titus Alone* there is a further kind of fragmentation. In his *Modern Fantasy* the present writer has argued that no scene or character in the book is given anything like the reality of the people of Gormenghast: what we have is a great number of figures and places, none of them kept with or really felt, and the book is full of short-term episodes.[5] Part of this may be traced to the weakness of the reasons given for Titus's escape from Gormenghast: not having adequate reason for being in this new world, neither he nor it can have much reality. Hence Titus returns to Gormenghast; and although he then leaves it once more the feeling is that he will continue to return.[6]

Almost the central motif of *Titus Alone* is that of the fragment.[7] Titus carries a fragment of stone from the Tower of Flints of Gormenghast, and is himself 'a chip of stone' from Gormenghast (*TA*, p. 102; see also pp. 9–10). He is 'Alone', cut off from final intimacy with the people he meets: Juno, his love, finds in the end that 'He was an island surrounded by deep water. There was no isthmus leading to her bounty; no causeway to her continent of love' (*TA*, pp. 98–9). The city in which he eventually finds himself is itself cut off from its surrounding country: 'how isolated in the wide world was the arena with its bright circumference of crystal buildings ... how unrelated it was to the bone-white, cave-pocked, barren mountains, the fever-swamps and jungles to the south, the thirsty lands, the hungry cities, and the tracts beyond of the wolf and the outlaw' (*TA*, p. 35). Gormenghast was different in its isolation: it had country immediately about it, and apart from that, until Titus left it, there *was* nowhere else. Many of the characters in *Titus Alone* have been banished from society or, like Muzzlehatch, the zoo-keeper, come to renounce and destroy it. Titus shatters a hovering spy-globe to fragments with his own flint-fragment. The dart-shaped planes of the city are like slivers. The book ends with an explosion which destroys the centre of the city's existence.

This fragmentary quality is also evident in the form and style of the book. It can be seen in the fact that the very length of *Titus Alone* is half that of either *Titus Groan* or *Gormenghast*. And in this half size there are 122 chapters as against the 69 of *Titus Groan* and the 80 of *Gormenghast*. The sentences are often brief: often too they are without finite verbs, fragments of syntax. Paragraphs also are usually short. Incremental repetition is common: 'In the gloom of the cedars his heart was happy. Happy in the chill of the tunnel. Happy in the danger of it all. Happy to remember his own childhood ... Happy in spite of ...' (*TA*, p. 31; see also for example pp. 95, 136, 247, 255). The idiom is often jerkily interrogative: 'Who was this youth? What was he? Why was he?

What was it about him? Who were those people he spoke of? This inner world? Those memories? Were they true?' (*TA*, p. 90; see also for example pp. 20, 80, 112, 122, 136, 174, 191, 257). It seems of a piece with this breakdown of language that one character should say: '"One is so at the mercy of words"' (*TA*, p. 47), or Titus, '"I am sick of language"' (*TA*, p. 107; see also p. 145).

The psychology of the book is also fragmentary. The problem is often that the characters are not felt from within, but have feelings imposed on them (see for example *TA*, pp. 92–3, 135, 171, 188). While Titus is being helped by Muzzlehatch and Juno to escape from the police who are pursuing him as a dangerous vagrant, Muzzlehatch, who has saved him on a previous occasion, bids him '"Change clothes ... We can't wait all night for you"': at which

> Something began to burn in Titus's stomach. He could feel the blood draining from his face.
> 'So you can't wait all night for me', he said in a voice he hardly recognized as his own. 'Muzzlehatch, the zoo-man, is in a hurry. But does he know who he is talking to? Do you? (*TA*, p. 61; see also for example pp. 52, 62)

This seems absurd of Titus, but the reader is given no vantage point by the author from which to see it as such. Often Titus's idiom is one of rather shrill rhetoric. The behaviour of the characters is frequently inexplicable or in excess of the facts. It is hard for the reader to accept the instant love of the forty-year-old Juno for Titus. It is hard too to sympathise with his leaving her (*TA*, pp. 100–2). The book as a whole does not square his adventurous urges with his increasing wish to return to Gormenghast, so that he appears to act inconsistently throughout.[8] Again, the behaviour of Cheeta, the scientist's daughter, in response to Titus's refusal of her seems beyond what is called for. It is not clear why Titus lingers so long after being shown the way out of the realm by Muzzlehatch (*TA*, p. 144). As for Muzzlehatch, after the slaughter of his animals he is found resolving first to avenge their deaths, then to follow Titus to Gormenghast, then to commit suicide, and finally again to return and avenge: and there is no attempt to reconcile these shifts (*TA*, pp. 157–9).

In this book the reader is made much more aware of Peake the narrator in separation from the work. Peake is often explicitly didactic and over-violent in his attacks on the scientific world of the novel. Thus, of the green dart that spies on Titus: 'What did it do but act like any other petty snooper, prying upon man and child, sucking information as a bat sucks blood; amoral; mindless; sent out on empty missions, acting as its maker would act, its narrow-headed maker ...' (*TA*, p. 34). Peake here seems to have become largely self-conscious in his relation to his characters. When Veil, the 'mantis-man' of the Under-River world approaches Titus to slay him, Peake interrupts to consider what drives him:

> What is it threads the inflamed brain of the one-time killer? Fear? No, not so much as would fill the socket of a fly's eye. Remorse? He has never heard of it. It is loyalty that fills him, as he lifts his long right arm. Loyalty to the child, the long scab-legged child, who tore the wings off sparrows long ago. Loyalty to his aloneness. Loyalty to his own evil, for only through this evil has he climbed the foul stairways to the lofts of hell. Had he wished to do so, he could never have withdrawn from the conflict, for to do so would have been to have denied Satan the suzerainty of pain. (*TA*, p. 136).

It is hard to see who would expect that either fear or remorse would drive Veil, and who could believe in the melodramatic loyalties that Peake has given him.

Titus Alone lays more stress on people being in groups than the previous two novels. Titus is hardly ever alone in the sense of being left alone: even in jail his cell is invaded by Old Crime, another prisoner. Whether with the cocktail-party society of the city, the peoples of the Under-River, the watchers of the sunset, the workers at the factory or the guests at Cheeta's barbecue, the reader is always made aware of plurality: and this is heightened by the fact that these societies are most frequently portrayed as composed of self-seeking egos. The book is also scattered with lists of plurals: thus, 'immediately the boats and their crews and the cormoranteers and their bottle-necked birds, and the rushes and the muddy bank and the mules and the vehicles and the nets and the spears and the river itself, became ribbed and flecked with flame' (*TA*, p. 17); 'Every head was turned towards the wicked pair; heads furred and heads naked; heads with beaks and heads with horns; heads with scales and heads with plumes' (*TA*, p. 25); 'Malignant faces, speculative faces, empty faces, ingenuous faces – faces of all kinds' (*TA*, p. 35; see also for example pp. 38, 76, 132, 183). The identity of the self is continually under threat; unity is lost in multiplicity: it is not surprising perhaps that Titus's central aim in the book is to preserve himself and his mind intact. And the process of fissiparity that is evident in *Titus Alone* would, it seems likely, have gone further in Peake's projected fourth 'Titus' book, which was planned to be '*Titus* among the

> Snows, Mountains, Islands, Rivers, Archipelagos, Forests, Lagoons, Fires, Floods, Typhoons, Doldrums, Famines, Pestilences, Poverty, Affluence, Debt, Society, Soldiers, Thieves, Actors, Painters, Psychiatrists, Labourers, Eccentrics, Lepers, Lotus Eaters, Monsters, Hypocrites, Madmen, Bankers, Angels, Devils, Mendicants, Vagrants, Pirates, Mermaids, Dreamers, Decadents, Athletes, Invalids, Blood-Sportsmen, Shapes, Echoes, Textures, Sounds, Tones, Colours, Scents.'[9]

Throughout *Titus Groan*, *Gormenghast* and *Titus Alone* there is variously portrayed a loss of contact between mind and matter. The explanation for this in *Titus Groan* seems to be a fascination for minute details of being at the expense of larger units. Peake isolates Gormenghast from the world and his characters from one another so that he can give full scope to the portrayal of their 'this-ness': the result is an intense concentration on the local to the point where it can take on a life of its own. Nevertheless this is not damaging in *Titus Groan*, for part of the theme of that book is the tension between rebellious individuals and the larger organism that is the castle: and the victory goes finally to the latter.[10] In *Gormenghast* and *Titus Alone* a different kind of dislocation of mind and material has occurred, for in these books Peake is no longer simply celebrating the character of the castle (though he tries to do so in the section involving the academic community in *Gormenghast*), but is moving away from it, with Titus rejecting his ancestral home and departing in search of other realms.

Explanation for this might run as follows. Where *Titus Groan* delighted in 'being', the subsequent books are concerned with 'becoming' and change. Where hardly any overt motives for action are canvassed in the former book, the latter two are full of them. For Peake was at his best in *Titus Groan*. In 'leaving' Gormenghast as he felt drawn to do he also left his inspiration and all that evoked wonder for him. He is thrown more and more back on the aridities of bare mind, searching for adequate motives and justifications for actions with which he does not fully sympathise or is not in touch: increasingly his characters are not felt from inside but have their behaviour largely imposed on them. By *Titus Alone* the process has expressed itself in almost total fragmentation and separation of the author from his created world. To some extent it all comes down to a matter of perspective: in *Titus Groan* Peake is very close to the object, where in the next two books he is increasingly remote from it: and each position is reflected in an imbalance of the relationship of material and mind. But it is also a matter of why Peake felt the need to write *Gormenghast* and *Titus Alone* in the first place: and to that the answer seems to be that he wanted, like many other writers of fantasy, to put overt 'sense' into his story, and to link it, didactically and otherwise, to the 'real' world without letting it speak for itself.

8 Anaemic Fantasy: Morris, Dunsany, Eddison, Beagle

In this chapter the concern will be with a range of writers of fantasy who variously fail to make the wonder they celebrate vital: their work is often delightful, beautiful or exciting, but in the end it lacks the fibre of reality. Here wonder at the nature of created things goes too far and defeats itself.

When in William Morris's late romance *The Wood Beyond the World* (1895) the hero Walter meets a maiden on his wanderings in the wooded country, and each falls in love with the other, the maiden, who has continually shown herself anxious, takes Walter to a hidden bower where she tells him:

'This is what I must needs say to thee now, that thou art come into a land perilous for any one that loveth aught of good; from which, forsooth, I were fain that thou wert gotten away safely, even though I should die of longing for thee. As for myself, my peril is, in a measure, less than thine; I mean the peril of death. But lo, thou, this iron on my foot is token that I am a thrall, and thou knowest in what wise thralls must pay for transgressions. Furthermore, of what I am, and how I came hither, time would fail me to tell; but somewhile, maybe, I shall tell thee. I serve an evil mistress, of whom I may say that scarce I wot if she be a woman or not; but by some creatures is she accounted for a god, and as a god is heried; and surely never god was crueller nor colder than she. Me she hateth sorely; yet if she hated me little or naught, small were the gain to me if it were her pleasure to deal hardly by me. But as things now are, and are like to be, it would not be for her pleasure, but for her pain and loss, to make an end of me, therefore, as I said e'en now, my mere life is not in peril, with her; unless, perchance, some sudden passion get the better of her, and she slay me, and repent of it thereafter. For so it is, that if it be the least evil of her conditions that she is wanton, at least wanton she is to the letter. Many a time hath she cast the net for the catching of some goodly young man; and her latest prey (save it be thou) is the young man whom I named, when first I saw thee, by the name of the King's Son. He is with us yet, and I fear him; for of late hath he wearied of her, though it is but plain truth to say of her, that she is the wonder of all Beauties of the World. He hath wearied of her, I say, and hath cast his eyes upon me, and if I were heedless, he would betray me to the uttermost of the wrath of my mistress. For needs must I say of him, though he be a goodly man, and now fallen into thralldom, that he hath no bowels of compassion; but is a dastard, who for an hour's pleasure would undo me, and thereafter stand by smiling and taking my mistress's pardon with good cheer, while for me would be no pardon. Seest thou, therefore, how it is with me between these two cruel fools?"[1]

As in much of Morris's late style, the mood is indicative and all in one tone: the speaker's emotions do not appear to shift greatly, and the rhythm is correspondingly flat. The language is stylised and archaic: 'I must needs', 'forsooth', 'lo', 'thrall', 'heried': Morris is trying to recreate a sense of the medieval idiom because he wishes to celebrate it in all his fantasy, but the effect is rather one of being distanced from what is said. This is exacerbated by the fact that a great deal of time is being taken to say little more than: 'You are in danger, for this place is evil. I am enslaved by a beautiful witch who delights in tormenting me. She is also an enchantress of men. Her present lover is now tiring of her and would seduce me if he could, knowing that he would be forgiven, though in her rage the witch would probably slay me.' The sentence beginning 'Me she hateth', for instance, says nothing except that to record the witch's hatred is irrelevant to the issue. The words 'peril', 'thrall', 'pleasure', 'pain', 'god', 'wanton', 'wearied' recur. If there is any purpose in this style, its effect is to put the reader into an unreflecting stupor, a reverie of misty words and phrases. The passage is made more indefinite by the way the reader has to proceed some way into a sentence before receiving concrete information, so that his interest is to some extent dissipated before the point is reached: '"This is what I must needs say to thee now"'; '"from which, forsooth"'; '"But lo, thou"'; '"But as things now are, and are like to be"'; '"therefore, as I said e'en now"'; '"For so it is"'; '"For needs must I say of him"'. The sentence, '"Furthermore, of what I am, and how I came hither, time would fail me to tell; but somewhile, maybe, I shall tell thee"', is particularly enervating: first she seems about to tell him her identity, then she says she cannot, then she says she will perhaps say something of it. There are many inversions which render the style inert: '"Of what I am, and how I came hither, time ..."', '"of whom I may say"', '"scarce I wot"', '"by some creatures is she accounted"', '"Me she hateth"', '"small were the gain to me"', '"wanton she is"'. Further there is very little specificity: all there is is a generalised tormented maiden with a vaguely realised witch and a potential seducer. The reader learns almost nothing of the character or appearance of the maid, the witch or the lover save their extreme beauty, or the conventional cruelty or indifference of the last two.

The character of Morris's style is quite different in his early romances (and his early poetry). This is how Florian de Liliis in 'The Hollow Land' (1856) describes the procession of Lady Swanhilda in which his brother Arnald is a page:

And as I gazed out of the window, I saw him [Arnald] walking by the side of her horse, dressed in white and gold very delicately; but as he went it chanced that he stumbled. Now he was one of those that held a golden canopy over the lady's head, so that it now sunk into wrinkles, and the lady had to bow her head full low, and even then the gold brocade caught in one of the long slim gold flowers that were wrought round about the crown she wore. She flushed up in her rage, and her smooth face went suddenly into the carven wrinkles of a wooden water-spout, and she caught at the brocade with her left hand, and pulled it away furiously, so that the warp and woof were twisted out of their places, and many gold threads were left dangling about the crown; but Swanhilda stared about when she rose, then smote my brother across the mouth with her gilded sceptre, and the red blood flowed all about his garments; yet he only turned exceeding pale, and dared say no word, though he was heir to the House of the Lilies: but my small heart swelled with rage, and I vowed revenge, and, as it seems, he did too.[2]

There is far more vital detail and intimacy here. There is the double perspective of events registered and felt both by the participants and the observer. The catching of the cloth in the crown is the sort of untidy thing that might happen in real life, and the picture of the lady's sudden rage at so trivial an infringement of her dignity and her rending the cloth away with such violence that fragments are left dangling from her crown is very vivid. The language is alive, in the way that the syntax lengthens and becomes more complex as the cloth is caught up in the lady's crown; or in the movement of the lady and the canopy downwards followed by 'She flushed up in her rage'; or in the unconscious linkage between the wrinkles of the canopy cloth and of the lady's face; or in the shock of the metaphor, freezing the moment, in 'her smooth face went suddenly into the carven wrinkles of a wooden water-spout'; or in the way the lady, who has been 'she' while the cloth has enwrapped her, becomes 'Swanhilda', now not a lady, as she reappears and rises for revenge. The sense does not simply flow onwards but keeps driving back against itself in 'but' and 'yet': despite having vented some of her rage on the cloth, Swanhilda still slashes at Arnald; despite the blow which draws blood, he remains pale and silent; despite Arnald's silence Florian is enraged and vows revenge, but then says that his brother did so too. It may be that the greater degree of detail in the passage, as in the early romances generally,[3] reflects Morris's Pre-Raphaelitism, but it is not merely the detail but the vitality of the style that gives it power.

In the late romances the characters seem by contrast to have little contact with their environment, save vaguely to see, or sometimes to hear it: they float over the enchanted realms in which they are set. There is small sense of any contact between Ralph and Ursula and the rocky regions they traverse in *The Well at the World's End* (1896): they say the journey is weary, but this weariness is never registered in the description of their experience. The Dry Tree and the venomous pool are only seen, not felt (Book 3, ch. 18). In *The Water of the Wondrous Isles* (1897), wherever the heroine Birdalone goes on her island she leaves no

imprint[4] and the grasses and forests of *The Wood Beyond the World*
seem almost undisturbed. The reader notices, too, that there is
very rarely poor weather, which would give a greater sense of
one's environment, in these works, where in the early tales there
are wind, rain, snow and ice.[5] It seems of a piece with this
absence of felt connection between man and his environment
that there should be few metaphors, which make links between
different orders of being, in the late romances.

These aspects of the style of Morris's late romances are
reflected in the general character of the books. The narratives
are leisurely and repetitive: in *The Water of the Wondrous Isles*
Birdalone's period of servitude to the witch and her slow
memorising of the means by which she will escape the island in
the magic Sending Boat are very drawn-out. By contrast the
early romances are all very short (never more than fifty pages):
Morris's literary development seems to have been one towards
increasing dilation of style throughout his life. In *The Well at the
World's End* the actual quest for the well occupies only a
relatively brief part of the story: the motivation of Ralph is for
long simply one for adventure or whatever befalls him. Similarly
in *The Sundering Flood* (1898) the search for Elfhild only becomes
a dominant motive halfway through the book. As for repetition,
in *The Water of the Wondrous Isles* Birdalone no sooner escapes
from one witch than she finds a group of women in the toils of
another on a different island; later she finds their three lovers,
who set forth to rescue them and whose doing so is reported at
length both by them and by their ladies. And in all the late
romances there is a similar situation and basic plot: a young
woman is held in thrall by another, older woman – the Maid in
The Wood, the Lady of Abundance in *The Well*, Birdalone, and
Atra, Aurea and Viridis in *The Water*, Elfhild (by her aunts) in
The Sundering Flood; and in each case, save only that of Birdalone,
who rescues herself, the lady is set at liberty by a lover. (Even a
penchant for the letter 'w' makes the titles of the first three
romances tend to run together in the mind.)

Nor are these books endowed with themes which inform their
style, shape and length – as, say, are Sidney's *Arcadia* or
Spenser's *Faerie Queene*. There seem to be no strongly felt ideas
behind them. If there is any topic to which they could be said to
recur, it is that of escape or liberation, imaged in the release of
females from imprisonment: such a theme suits well with

Morris's view of art itself as an escape from the unpleasant aspects of real life. (The prison motif is also recurrent in the poetry of *The Defence of Guenevere* (1858): but there there is no escape.) One feature of this concern with liberation is an often prurient interest in women giving themselves sexually to their betrothed or their husbands: in *The Wood* the theme of gradually yielded virginity and in both *The Wood* and *The Water* a stress on stripping and nudity are marked. Possibly Morris intended this as praise of the removal of inhibition, but if so this aspect is lost in the lubricious manner employed: the reader is constantly being introduced to sexually inflamed men and women, half- or wholly-naked maids, threatened ravishments, tortured virgins or beautiful seductresses: the whole of *The Wood* can be seen as a kind of blurred strip-tease. It really seems of little value, for example, to speak of Morris's 'pagan' praise of the earth and generative love in the context of such prurient vignettes[6] as the Maid of *The Wood* being eyed by Walter, or the naked Birdalone being surveyed by her friend the wood maiden, or various female thralls being whipped.[7] No theme of 'right' love governs such scenes as it might in Spenser: they are there only for their own sake. Here indeed is 'fantasy' of a different order.

What also takes away force from Morris's late romances is their failure to admit real pain or loss into their scheme of things. It is not that they end happily – much fantasy does this – but that the heroes and heroines do not appear to suffer much along the way, and are never really at risk. The reader does not see the Maid in *The Wood* being cruelly treated by the witch, and the iron fetter on her leg is more symbolic than real; and the hero Walter has the comfortable experience of being able to dally with the witch herself while the Maid engineers his and her escape. In *The Water* Birdalone's enthralment to the witch on the island is hardly felt at all (save in the form of the threat of chapters XI and XII of Part I). It is Atra, Aurea and Viridis who are shown having a far harder time at the hands of the witch's sister on another island: but then they do not matter so much. In *The Well* Ralph and Ursula, alone of all the multitudes who have come before, are saved from the poison of the pool about the Dry Tree because Ursula notices that a breeze fails to ruffle its surface and they see a crow which drinks from it fall dead. Such pains as are described in these romances are usually the gentle sadnesses of separated lovers – that of Birdalone from Arthur in *The Water*, or of the lovers in *The Sundering Flood*. There is none of the sharp or final agony or bitterness that we find portrayed in Morris's early romances. There, the heroes Arnald and Florian in 'The Hollow Land' are slain and sent to the land of the title for their murder of Queen Swanhilda; 'Lindenborg Pool' is a vision of humanity as loathsome; 'Svend and his Brethren' ends with the violent destruction of a corrupt kingdom after its ruler has left it for ever; Queen Gertha in 'Gertha's Lovers' loses all her lovers in war and then dies herself; 'Golden Wings' ends with the slaughter of the hero before the eyes of his beloved.

The lack of force and reality that has been traced in Morris's late fantasy can still be found where the style of a work has more vivid detail and originality. This can be seen in Lord Dunsany's *The King of Elfland's Daughter* (1924). The story tells how Alveric, Prince of the vale of Erl, enters the Faërian Elfland and brings back as bride Lirazel, the daughter of the Elf-King. They have a son, Orion, but Lirazel soon grows restless for Elfland, and returns there. By the magic of her father, Elfland is so divided from Earth that Alveric cannot find it for all his years of searching until Lirazel, yearning once more for her husband and child, asks and eventually receives from her father the utterance of the last great rune which will make Elfland enter and pervade the mortal world and with it bring Alveric, Orion and herself together once more.

The style of the book is replete with the same use of 'and' and 'but' as conjunctions and with continual dying rhythms, as in Morris.

> And a gleam that was new to the forest appeared on the long strange leaves, and shadows unknown to Elfland slipped out from the monstrous tree-boles, and stole over grasses that had not dreamed of their advent; and the spires of that palace perceiving a wonder, less lovely indeed than they, yet knew that the stranger was magic, and uttered an answering gleam from their sacred windows, that flashed over elvish fells like an inspiration and mingled a flush of rose with the blue of the Elfin Mountains.*

And so on. The effect is to remove identity from what is being

---

* Lord Dunsany (E. J. M. D. Plunkett), *The King of Elfland's Daughter* London and New York: G. P. Putnam's Sons, 1924) pp. 212–13. Page references are to this edition.

described, until much or all sense of specificity is lost in a
soporific bath of desire. But this is not always so much the case.

> Then Alveric pressed on with a new impatience, with the
> north-west wind behind him. And the Earth began to grow
> bare and shingly and dull, without flowers, without shade,
> without colour, with none of those things that there are in
> remembered lands, by which we build pictures of them when
> we are there no more; it was all disenchanted now. Alveric
> saw a golden bird high up, rushing away to the south-east,
> and he followed his flight hoping soon to see the mountains of
> Elfland, which he supposed to be merely concealed by some
> magical mist.
>   But still the autumnal sky was bright and clear, and all the
> horizon plain, and still there came never a gleam of the Elfin
> Mountains. And not from this did he learn that Elfland had
> ebbed. But when he saw on that desolate shingly plain, untorn
> by the north-west wind but blooming fair in the autumn, a
> may tree that he remembered a long while since, all white
> with blossom that once rejoiced a spring day far in his
> childhood, then he knew that Elfland had been there and must
> have receded, although he knew not how far. (pp. 82–3)

Again the sentences are all statements; they are loosely linked;
the rhythms are most fading; and again this blurs identity. As in
Morris there is needless dilation – 'bare and shingly and dull,
without flowers, without shade, without colour'; and a lapse into
vagueness and verbosity in 'with none of those things that there
are in remembered lands, by which we build pictures of them
when we are there no more; it was all disenchanted now'. But the
may tree is singular and fairly memorable, though the account of
its actual appearance is brief compared to the long and again
verbose gloss put upon it. The scene has some vitality because
Dunsany is describing something original: a vision of a landscape from which magic has largely withdrawn, while still
leaving some few scattered tokens of itself.

A similar originality of vision is behind the picture of the troll
Lurulu's experience of the mortal world: in Elfland he knew only
a changeless existence, but here all is continually mobile. Lurulu
has climbed up to a pigeon loft in the village and in so doing has
scared off the birds; but his loneliness is not for long:

Presently there came the roar of the pigeons' returning wings
and the crash of their feet on the slate roof above him, but they
did not yet come in again to their homes. He saw the shadow
of this roof cast on another roof below him, and the restless
shadows of the pigeons along the edge. He observed the grey
lichen covering most of the lower roof, and the neat round
patches of newer yellow lichen on the shapeless mass of the
grey. He heard a duck call out slowly six or seven times. He
heard a man come into a stable below him and lead a horse
away. A hound woke and cried out. Some jackdaws, disturbed
from some tower, passed over high in the air with boisterous
voices. He saw big clouds go hurrying along the tops of far
hills. He heard a wild pigeon call from a neighbouring tree.
Some men went by talking. And after a while he perceived to
his astonishment what he had had no leisure to notice on his
previous visit to Erl, that even the shadows of houses moved;
for he saw that the shadow of the roof under which he sat had
moved a little on the roof below, over the grey and yellow
lichen. Perpetual movement and perpetual change! He contrasted it, in wonder, with the deep calm of his home.
(pp. 192–3)

The reader almost hears the roaring return of the pigeons, and
sees the shadows of the roof and of the moving pigeons. Quite a
strong impression is given of the lichens. And the syntax of the
whole passage, with its short sentences introducing new sights
and sounds, now beginning with 'He', now with the more
independent mode of 'A hound awoke and cried out', gives a
powerful sense of a startled sensibility bombarded with a mass of
diverse new impressions. Particularly effective is the way the
reader is thrown back and forth from 'the far hills' to 'a
neighbouring tree', from looking upwards to looking along, and
from seeing to hearing. And the whole passage is given point
because every item bodies forth the mutability of the Earth:
Dunsany is not here too simply concerned with loving what he
describes, but is making it part of a meaningful pattern.

Dunsany knows he is on to a good thing here – clearly it
emerges from his own experience – and goes on for three more
pages making it rather too much of a good thing. Thus:

Beyond the roofs the tall trees rose up, leafless except for evergreen oaks and some laurels and pines and yews, and the ivy that climbed up trunks, but the buds of the beech were getting ready to burst: and the sunlight glittered and flashed on the buds and leaves, and the ivy and laurel shone. A breeze passed by and some smoke drifted from some near chimney. Far away Lurulu saw a huge grey wall of stone that circled a garden all asleep in the sun; and clear in the sunlight he saw a butterfly sail by, and swoop when it came to the garden. And he saw two peacocks go slowly past. He saw the shadow of the roofs darkening the lower part of the shining trees. He heard a cock crow somewhere, and a hound spoke out again. And then a sudden shower rained on the roofs, and at once the pigeons wanted to come home. (p. 195)

By now Dunsany is having to search about for fresh items. The trees are not very clearly seen or individuated, though they and their buds make the point about time. The breeze and the smoke seem gratuitous. Again there is the technique of moving from near to far as Lurulu sees the garden surrounded by the huge wall – though his ability to see the butterfly enter it is questionable. Then there are peacocks, and then again roof-shadows, and again the hound. Twice the pigeons come back, and twice there is a description of them landing on the roof (pp. 192, 194). And as before, every item makes the same point about temporal motion in Earth.

The habit of repeating the same point with different details can be seen also in the use of simile, as in

Then, like the noise of some city heard amongst birds in woods, like a sob heard amongst children that are all met to rejoice, like laughter amongst a company that weep, like a shrill wind in orchards amongst the early blossom, like a wolf coming over the downs where the sheep are asleep, there came a feeling into the Elf King's mood that one was coming towards them across the fields of Earth. (p. 126)

So much do the items in the list all point one way that the difference in the third analogy is scarcely noticed. Dunsany's book is in many ways a celebration of all that is, but in the end all things come too much together. As with Morris, praise of being effectively results in erosion of being. And actually

Dunsany's story is finally *about* the removal of distinctions: the differences that Lurulu observes between Earth and Elfland are in the end lost, for by the speaking of the great rune, Elfland is brought to encompass nearly all the Earth, and its doing so is described as a tidal wave washing over and enveloping all things (ch. 34). The book ends with a crescendo of the sated, slumbrous rhythms that have suffused it throughout:

> And with the last of his world-disturbing runes sent forth, and his daughter happy once more, the elfin King on his tremendous throne breathed and drew in the calm in which Elfland basks; and all his realms dreamed on in that ageless repose, of which deep green pools in summer can barely guess; and Erl dreamed too with all the rest of Elfland and so passed out of all remembrance of men. (p. 301)

The King of Elfland's Daughter is a beautiful book, and one that moves the reader with longing: but it does not move very deeply, largely because it has not really faced pain and evil. Its emotions are easy, unearned ones: and lacking restraint they flood the book like Elfland itself.

E. R. Eddison's *The Worm Ouroboros* (1922) evades evil in a different manner. The story takes place on an imaginary Mercury, where the evil forces of Witchland war continually with the good of Demonland. In a battle with the magician-king Gorice XII of Witchland outside his stronghold of Carcë, the Demons are defeated and their princes Juss, Spitfire, Goldry Bluszco and Brandoch Daha are captured. By the help of friends within Carcë they escape, but King Gorice conjures a hellish spirit to pursue them at sea, and in the rack that follows Goldry Bluszco is carried off. Through visionary dreams and the help of one Queen Sophonisba of Koshtra Belorn, Juss is able to discover the whereabouts of his brother on the high, isolated and enchanted mountain of Zora Rach nam Psarrion. After many adventures and a journey to the mountain on the back of a hippogriff, Juss recovers Goldry. Finally the princes of Demonland mount an assault of Carcë once more, and this time are so successful that the entire leadership of Witchland is destroyed, King Gorice being carried off to hell in the midst of a conjuration which goes out of control. Yet, returned to Demonland, the princes do not find themselves content, regretting that, because their enemies have been totally destroyed, '"We ... have in the end fought so well we never may fight more"':

> 'We may well cast down our swords as a last offering on Witchland's grave. For now must they rust: seamanship and all high arts of war must wither: and, now that our great enemies are dead and gone, we that were lords of all the world must turn shepherds and hunters, lest we become mere mountebanks and fops.'*

Finding them inconsolable by other means, Queen Sophonisba helps the princes to pray for and have granted a wish whereby their enemies will be restored to life and all things will be as they were four years previously, with the princes seated on their thrones to receive the ambassador of Gorice xi of Witchland; presumably the princes continued for ever in this temporal loop. Here the symbol of the worm ouroboros, the everlasting circle of the snake with its tail in its mouth, is made a part of the story itself.

In this way, nothing is lost, and no pain is final. Time is bereft of its power: the penultimate page of the book quotes Shakespeare's sonnet (no. 18) on deathlessness, 'Shall I compare thee to a Summers day?' which declares, 'thy eternall Sommer shall not fade/Nor loose possession of that faire thou ow'st;/Nor shall Death brag thou wandr'st in his shade.'[8] Goldry is rescued, every wound is repaired, the evil are resuscitated to provide more pleasure for the good. Nor are the evil seen fully as evil. Gorice is cruel and a dealer with evil spirits; his generals, Corsus, Corund and Corinius, are coarse, violent, contentious and lecherous: but they are all involved only in playing the conventional part of villains, of helping evil to live up to its bad name. There is not really, barring a few craggy looks, devilish tomes and a penchant for crabs and woodlice as symbols, all that much in the way of difference between Gorice and his enemies. There is small feeling at the end of the book that, in Queen Sophonisba's words, '"we may rejoice anew that all the lords of Witchland are dead and gone because of whom and their tyranny earth hath groaned and laboured these many years"' (p. 430). Nothing really unpleasant is admitted by the book. The

---

* E. R. Eddison, *The Worm Ouroboros: A Romance* (Cape, 1922) p. 431. Page references are to this edition.

battles, exciting enough to read though they are, are ultimately play battles, and the hostilities are there for hostility's sake and as the arena for prodigious feats of arms (see for example pp. 336–8). King Gorice calls to Juss to desist from the last battle in the unarticulated intuition that if he wins it he will ruin himself by having no-one left to fight (pp. 390–1). Juss describes them all as having '"fought but for fighting's sake"' (p. 431). There is no suggestion, as there is in, say, T. H. White's *The Once and Future King*, that wars cause pain and misery to the participants or to their relatives; no implication that the rulers of a country have aught to do but to consider the extension of their own personal heroism; and no hint that any moral or other issues are at stake in the various contests. The book is without a theme: it is all, delightfully enough, about adventures, from wrestling with Gorice xi to battling with a mantichore or flying on a hippogriff. When the appearance of the mantichores of the mountains about Koshtra Belorn is described to him, Spitfire says: '"These beasts ... were alone enough to draw me thither"' (p. 114). Adventures are a boyish game.

Eddison puts forward a philosophy to justify this approach, though the reader has to wait for his later 'Zimiamvian' novels *Mistress of Mistresses* (1935), *A Fish Dinner at Memison* (1941) and *The Mezentian Gate* (1958) to find it expressed. In the 'Overture' to the first, the narrator, mourning the death of his friend Lessingham, is told by the goddess of beauty Aphrodite, who contains in herself all time and space, that reality and time are circular. A roundel written by Lessingham symbolises this;[9] and the goddess leaves the narrator with the promise that the best and most heroic of men continue to live in 'the fabled land of ZIMIAMVIA'.[10] Zimiamvia, it must be said, is not to be identified with Mercury or with Demonland, but exists on Mercury in the midst of the mountains of Koshtra Belorn and is seen by Juss and Brandoch Daha in *The Worm Ouroboros* (pp. 182–3): nevertheless it is the archetype of what happens on the planet. In Zimiamvia as the goddess shows at the end of the story, 'nothing but death can die and corruption self-corrupted fall like a foul garment to leave perfection bare'.[11] Zimiamvia, it appears, is a kind of Valhalla, where heroism and battle are kept alive for their own sakes and where evil forces exist because they are part of the fabric of reality and of delight in conflict.[12] But its nature pervades all worlds and can be perceived by those of larger vision.

For nothing, to Eddison, is finally ugly or evil: in the 'Letter of Introduction' to *The Mezentian Gate* he writes:

> It may be thought that such dark and predatory personages as the Vicar, or his uncle Lord Emmins Parry, or Emmins's daughter Rosma, are strangely accommodated in these meads of asphodel where Beauty's self, in warm actuality of flesh and blood, reigns as Mistress. But the answer surely is (and it is an old answer) that 'God's adversaries are some way his owne.' This ownness is easier to accept and credit in an ideal world like Zimiamvia than in our training-ground or testing-place where womanish and fearful mankind, individually so often gallant and lovable, in the mass so foolish and unremarkable, mysteriously inhabit, labouring through bog that takes us to the knees, yet sometimes momentarily giving an eye to the lone splendour of the stars. When lions, eagles, and she-wolves are let loose among such weak sheep as for the most part we be, we rightly, for sake of our continuance, attend rather to their claws, maws, and talons than stay to contemplate their magnificences. We forget, in our necessity lest our flesh become their meat, that they too, ideally and *sub specie aeternitatis*, have their places (higher or lower in proportion to their integrity and to the mere consciencelessness and purity of their mischief) in the hierarchy of true values. This world of ours, we may reasonably hold, is no place for them, and they no fit citizens for it; but a tedious life, surely, in the heavenly mansions, and small scope for Omnipotence to stretch its powers, were all such great eminent self-pleasuring tyrants to be banned from 'yonder starry gallery' and lodged in 'the cursed dungeon'.[13]

There is an uneasy mixture in this passage of the feeling that man is bound in reason to feel the world a miserable place with the sense that he is a fool and a wretch for doing so. What, it may be asked, has given Eddison the right to declare what magnificences most men do not see? The passage comes close to demanding of man a larger and more Olympian view, whereby he puts aside his sense of the misery and pain of the world for a sense of its glory and delight: it asks that he rise above the earth, and that he ignore ugliness and pain, which are transient, for beauty, joy and love, which are not. (David Lindsay says the reverse in his *A Voyage to Arcturus* (1920).) For Eddison, accepting Descartes's *Cogito*, 'Consciousness is ... the fundamental reality'; and the fundamental value is that which is desired for its own sake: thus 'the test of any metaphysic is not that it should square with the world as we know it, but that it should square with the ultimate value'.[14] Mundane experience goes against the notion of love and the desirable being finally achievable: 'it affords little evidence of omnipotent love, but much of feeble, transient, foolish, loves: much of powerful hatreds, pain, fear, cruelty'. But from the vantage-point of the divine and universal basis of love and beauty, 'the only solution we can accept is one that shall concede to Evil something less than reality'. From this position, 'this present world is understandable only on the assumption that its reality is not final but partial'.[15] No doubt the Christian would agree, but for him God became incarnate, He took on Himself the sufferings of the world that he might redeem it: eternity and the corruptible were married. Beside the reality and inclusiveness of this vision, the aloof rejections of Eddison seem thin and insubstantial, however much he may believe them himself. It is strange to think of this man writing these things (from a house in a road perhaps with truly Olympian irony called Dark Lane) in the midst of some of the most terrible exhibitions of human brutality that have ever been endured on our planet – the doings of Hitler in the Second World War.

As with *The King of Elfland's Daughter*, the narrative of *The Worm Ouroboros* is very gripping, and it must be said that the sentiments of the reader are closely engaged in Eddison's portrait of the desirable. But the lack of dialectic prevents the book from making a really profound or lasting effect on the mind. In the end evil is only the stimulus for exploits by the good, and contains no threat in itself. Conflict is there for conflict's sake, not as part of any fundamental opposition: the 'worm ouroboros' applies not only to the end of the story being the beginning, but to the fact that the story is essentially self-regarding, concerned only to preserve itself.[16] The cap to this is of course provided at the end, when all the reader's involvement with the struggles described is shown to have been baseless, for nothing is finally at risk and destruction is reversed. The book becomes a kind of bubble cut loose from the earth. In White's *The Once and Future*

King, the love of beautiful things is shot through with the sense that they have gone, and that they are going in the story itself; and even in Tolkien's *The Lord of the Rings*, which arguably is in many ways as evasive as Eddison's work,[17] the Elvish Lothlórien can be felt to be more poignantly lovely because it is doomed to fade. The joys of Lewis's Ransom on Venus in *Perelandra* are so moving because they can only be a glimpse, and he must return to this world. The 'co-inherent' web of reality as portrayed in Charles Williams's novels is glorious, but an understanding of it is only fully to be reached through humility and self-sacrifice which may include death. The works of Morris, Dunsany and Eddison do not concern themselves with our reality, or with much of the fibre of reality at all: they provide make-believe worlds. They lack dialectic, and the responses they ask of the reader are easy ones, all pointing in one direction.

The result is often excess. This is the description of the high presence chamber of the lords of Demonland:

> Its walls and pillars were of snow-white marble, every vein whereof was set with small gems: rubies, corals, garnets, and pink topaz. Seven pillars on either side bore up the shadowy vault of the roof; the roof-tree and the beams were of gold, curiously carved, the roof itself of mother-of-pearl. A side aisle ran behind each row of pillars, and seven paintings on the western side faced seven spacious windows on the east. At the end of the hall upon a dais stood three high seats, the arms of each composed of two hippogriffs wrought in gold, with wings spread, and the legs of the seats the legs of the hippogriffs; but the body of each high seat was a single jewel of monstrous size: the left-hand seat a black opal, asparkle with steel-blue fire, the next a fire-opal, as it were a burning coal, the third seat an alexandrite, purple like wine by night but deep sea-green by day. Ten more pillars stood in semicircle behind the high seats, bearing up above them and the dais a canopy of gold . . .

> But a great wonder of this chamber, and a marvel to behold, was how the capital of every one of the four-and-twenty pillars was hewn from a single precious stone, carved by the hand of some sculptor of long ago into the living form of a monster: here was a harpy with screaming mouth, so wondrously cut in ochre-tinted jade it was a marvel to hear no scream from her: here in wine-yellow topaz a flying fire-drake:

there a cockatrice made of a single ruby: there a star sapphire the colour of moonlight, cut for a cyclops, so that the rays of the star trembled from his single eye: salamanders, mermaids, chimaeras, wild men o' the woods, leviathans, all hewn from faultless gems, thrice the bulk of a big man's body, velvet-dark sapphires, chrysolite, beryl, amethyst, and the yellow zircon that is like transparent gold.

To give light to the presence chamber were seven escarbuncles, great as pumpkins, hung in order down the length of it, and nine fair moonstones standing in order on silver pedestals between the pillars on the dais. These jewels, drinking in the sunshine by day, gave it forth during the hours of darkness in a radiance of pink light and a soft effulgence as of moonbeams. And yet another marvel, the nether side of the canopy over the high seats was encrusted with lapis lazuli, and in that feigned dome of heaven burned the twelve signs of the zodiac, every star a diamond that shone with its own light. (pp. 2–3)

This recalls the *fin-de-siècle* preciosity of Oscar Wilde or J. K. Huysmans. None of the objects described here means anything: the stones for example have none of the symbolic import of those in *The Book of Revelation* nor the sacramental value they might find in the work of George MacDonald. They are there to satisfy the greed of the imagination, and for no other purpose. The basis for this greed is the constant mention of numbers of huge jewels, of figures of exotic beasts and of rich colours. The whole is an image of the kind of value that Eddison puts on the creatures of fantasy themselves. Hippogriffs, harpies, fire-drakes, cockatrices, salamanders, mermaids and so forth are all shaped in precious stones, and are to be coveted in precisely the same way: this can be seen particularly in the last section of the second paragraph, where the two lists, of beasts and gems, parallel and run into one another. And the description goes too far: there are so many jewels and beasts that the reader is overwhelmed by them all, unable to take note of any one in particular. Eddison is neither selective nor emphatic in what he describes: all the items in the list are described as having equal power of fascination; the (repetitive) attempt to make pillars stand out, 'But a great wonder of this chamber, and a marvel to behold', fails to give them more interest than the wonders with which the reader has already been sated. Everything is there for one

purpose, that of fascinating; and everything is uniformly beautiful. Beauty, of course, is native to works of this kind: the evil are
only decoratively black or slobbering. But the fact that each of
the items does just one thing, and all do the same thing, removes
life from the account.

Even when Eddison describes just one object or person he can
lose the picture through multiplicity and failure to focus:

> Benches of green jasper massily built and laden with velvet
> cushions of many colours stood against the palace wall facing
> to the west, and on the bench nearest the Iron Tower a lady
> sat at ease, eating cream wafers and a quince tart served by
> her waiting-women in dishes of pale gold for her morning
> meal. Tall was that lady and slender, and beauty dwelt in her
> as the sunshine dwells in the red floor and gray-green trunks
> of a beech wood in early spring. Her tawny hair was gathered
> in deep folds upon her head and made fast by great silver pins,
> their heads set with anachite diamonds. Her gown was of
> cloth of silver with a knotted cord-work of black silk embroid-
> ery everywhere decked with little moonstones, and over it she
> wore a mantle of figured satin the colour of the wood-pigeon's
> wing, tinselled and overcast with silver threads. White-
> skinned she was, and graceful as an antelope. Her eyes were
> green, with yellow fiery gleams. Daintily she ate the tart and
> wafers, sipping at whiles from a cup of amber, artificially
> carved, white wine cool from the cellars below Carcë; and a
> maiden sitting at her feet played on a seven-stringed lute,
> singing very sweetly this song ... (pp. 75–6)

(The song, preciously enough continuing this clichéd tableau, is
Carew's 'Aske me no more where Jove bestowes ...') The reader
is so swamped by objects in the first sentence of this passage that
he can hardly distinguish the lady as a human being, particularly as the first details to be noted concerning her are that she is
eating cream wafers and a quince tart served from dishes of pale
gold; and there is a revealing ambiguity in the style, whereby it is
momentarily suggested that the lady eats the gold dishes rather
than the food. Most of the description of her for the rest of the
passage concerns her clothing and jewels (even the account of
the light in her eyes suggests gems); and the human aspect of her
beauty is lost by likening it to the sunshine in a spring-time

beech wood. The inversions 'Tall was that lady', and 'White-skinned she was', distance us: it seems significant that both occur when her appearance as a woman is being mentioned. And neither really conveys much sense of her: to say someone is tall while she is seated is a trifle inapt, and the fact that the lady has white skin is hardly startling (here it is part of the larger decorativeness of the scene). Nor is there any suggestion of a personality here. The characterisation in the book is generally perfunctory: there is little distinction among the lords Juss, Spitfire, Goldry Bluszco and Brandoch Daha when we are introduced to them save in terms of the clothes they wear and slight differences of stature (pp. 5–7); they too are precious objects, like all that surrounds them. Everything, including the evil, is precious; everything is to be preserved. This is excess, the author too self-indulgently enamoured of his creation, and the weight and impact of his book suffer accordingly. Thus while the book is enjoyable and exciting, it is not often memorable.

There is one peculiarly impressive scene, however, and that is the account of the struggle with the mantichore on the mountains before Koshtra Belorn. Much of the rest of the book describes incidents and items common to many fantasies: rich palaces, beautiful queens and princesses, fierce and handsome heroes, knightly combat, sieges, devilish conjurations, hippogriffs and so forth, but here Eddison hits on something new. Indeed his whole account of the journey through the mountains is vivid: the description of the inception of a landslide is brilliant (even while it carries on the rather precious flower imagery of the book): 'Suddenly was a noise above them like the crack of a giant whip, and looking up they beheld against the sky a dark mass which opened like a flower and spread into a hundred fragments' (pp. 178–9). With the mantichore the concern is with one beast, where so much of the rest of the book is laden with plurality: one beast, that comes swinging across the rock-face of a cliff as the princes Juss and Brandoch Daha are on a ledge one hundred feet up its sheer black five-hundred feet height:

Swinging from hold to hold across the dizzy precipice, as an ape swingeth from bough to bough, the beast drew near. The shape of it was as a lion, but bigger and taller, the colour a dull red, and it had prickles lancing out behind, as of a porcupine; its face a man's face, if aught so hideous might be conceived of human kind, with staring eyeballs, low wrinkled brow, elephant ears, some wispy mangy likeness of a lion's mane, huge bony chaps, brown blood-stained gubber-tushes grinning betwixt bristly lips. Straight for the ledge it made, and as they braced them to receive it, with a great swing heaved a man's height above them and leaped down upon their ledge from aloft betwixt Juss and Brandoch Daha ere they were well aware of its changed course. (p. 170)

There is no fantastic stereotype here – in contrast to the more romantic chronicle account of the beast earlier (p. 114) – but a real specimen. It is 'a *dull* red' and has 'some wispy mangy likeness of a lion's mane'. The reader visualises its approach very clearly, since he has probably seen apes move at the zoo; and visualises it all the more strongly in that while it is like a monkey in some respects, it is emphatically not one. Composed though the creature is of diverse parts of man, elephant, lion and scorpion, the impression is given that those parts make a single organism: the only stress on its shape being 'as a lion, but bigger and taller' gives an approximate idea of the appearance of the whole creature while making that appearance more vivid through strangeness by revealing that the beast could walk upright. Dialectical vigour is added by the suggestion of both human (the face and the grinning) and bestial attributes. Then the account of the beast's landing amidst the princes is very striking both because unexpected and because the syntax is particularly imitative: the suspensions 'and as they braced', 'with a great swing' give precisely the sense of waiting and of swinging upwards; the omission of the subject of 'heaved' and 'leaped' loses the beast just as it is for the moment 'lost' by those watching it; and the 'leaped down upon their ledge from aloft betwixt Juss and Brandoch Daha ere they were well aware of its changed course' puts the creature on the ledge among them before mentioning their bewilderment, which is thus the more effectively conveyed.

Alone of almost every creature and object in *The Worm Ouroboros*, the mantichore is supremely hideous: and the fight between it and the princes is described in far more ghastly and bloody terms than any other. Brandoch Daha slashes off its lethal tail (and is then knocked off the cliff by it), and Juss rips open its belly so that its bowels fall out; but, lacking his sword,

which breaks against a rock, is forced to grapple close with the
beast to avoid its teeth. While the mantichore uses its claws to
rip up Juss's leg and its weight to crush him, he

> for all his bitter pain and torment, and for all he was well
> nigh stifled by the sore stink of the creature's breath and the
> stink of its blood and puddings blubbering about his face and
> breast, yet by his great strength wrastled with that fell and
> filthy man-eater. And ever he thrust his right hand, armed
> with the hilt and stump of his broken sword, yet deeper into its
> belly until he searched out its heart and did his will upon it,
> slicing the heart asunder like a lemon and severing and
> tearing all the great vessels about the heart until the blood
> gushed about him like a spring. And like a caterpillar the
> beast curled up and straightened out in its death spasms, and
> it rolled and fell from that ledge, a great fall, and lay by
> Brandoch Daha, the foulest beside the fairest of all earthly
> beings, reddening the pure snow with its blood. And the
> spines that grew on the hinder parts of the beast went out and
> in like the sting of a new-dead wasp that goes out and in
> continually. It fell not clean to the snow, as by the care of
> heaven was fallen Brandoch Daha, but smote an edge of rock
> near the bottom, and that strook out its brains. There it lay in
> its blood, gaping to the sky. (p. 171)

It is an extraordinarily vivid and horrible portrait. The frequent
word-pairs – 'pain and torment', 'for all ... for all', 'stifled ...
stink', 'breath and stink', 'blood and puddings', 'fell and filthy',
'hilt and stump', 'severing and tearing' – give a sense of effort
and of the extremity of absorption in the struggle. 'Breath' and
'breast' draw the creature and Juss into even closer intimacy by
their similar sounds. The caterpillar and wasp images are
striking. The two descriptions of the beast's fall, and the way its
spines continue moving give a powerful impression of its
endurance and prepare us for the dwarf Mivarsh's later doubt
as to whether in fact it is dead. The last short sentence enacts
finality. Certainly hideous beasts have their place in fantasy but
this one and its actions are unusually stark. It can only be
described as Eddison's admission for a moment of some of the
very ugliness and realism he has so excluded from the rest of the
book. In its suddenness it recalls the boiling alive and

dismemberment of the cat by the witch Queen Morgause in the second book of T. H. White's *The Once and Future King*, *The Queen of Air and Darkness*: the episode follows hard upon the boyhood idyll of *The Sword in the Stone*, in which the joys of childhood and Merlyn's magic are celebrated, and Arthur comes to learn who he is; the reduction of the cat to its constituent parts of fur, gristle, meat and bone – like the dismemberment of the unicorn by Morgause's sons a few chapters later – can be viewed as the other side of the earlier celebration of being. But as has been seen also, in *The Once and Future King* generally White recognises ugliness, pain and loss far more than Eddison.

Eddison's book has a strong narrative to hold it together (more than can be said of his later Zimiamvian books where action seems often to have turned to contemplation or cumbrous intrigue). But Peter Beagle's *The Last Unicorn* (1968), which portrays the search of the last unicorn in the world for its lost fellows, could also be described as a fantasy in search of a story and of inspiration. The book contains two really memorable images. One is the account of the travelling circus, Mommy Fortuna's Midnight Carnival of exotic beasts, of which the unicorn is for a time made an unwilling member. Most of the wonderful beasts are in fact perfectly ordinary, sad creatures – a dog, an ape, a boa constrictor, a spider, a lion, a crocodile – which with the help of the ready wonder of the audiences of the show have been made by Mommy Fortuna to look like Cerberus, a satyr, the great Serpent of the Midgard, Arachne the spider, a mantichore and a dragon. Two of the creatures are, however, real – the unicorn, and the terrible bronze-winged harpy, which it takes all Mommy Fortuna's magic power to keep from escaping and rending her to pieces. The whole vision of decrepit wonder surrounded by spivs and gawking gulls is unforgettable, not least because so many opposites are present in it – wonder and the commonplace, reality and illusion, the beautiful and the sordid, the terrible and the meek, joy and misery.

> The shadow-dragon opened his mouth and hissed harmless fire to make the gapers gasp and cringe, while Hell's snake-furred watchdog howled triple dooms and devastations down on his betrayers, and the satyr limped leering to the bars and beckoned young girls to impossible delights, right there in public. As for the crocodile, the ape, and the sad dog, they

faded steadily before the marvelous phantoms until they were only shadows themselves, even to the unicorn's undeceived eyes.*

The next morning,

> One by one, the sad beasts of the Midnight Carnival came whimpering, sneezing, and shuddering awake. One had been dreaming of rocks and bugs and tender leaves; another of bounding through high, hot grass; a third of mud and blood. And one had dreamed of a hand scratching the lonely place behind its ears. Only the harpy had not slept, and now she sat staring into the sun without blinking. (p. 32)

The other memorable scene in the book is briefer: it is the view of the castle of King Haggard on its cliff above the sea, where, thanks to the power of Haggard's Red Bull, all the other unicorns of the world have been driven into the sea to become waves, forever driving at the shore with manes of foam, for the perpetual delight of the king. When the unicorn and her companions first see the castle,

> It crept into the sky from the far side of a long, deep valley – thin and twisted, bristling with thorny turrets, dark and jagged as a giant's grin. Molly laughed outright, but the unicorn shivered, for to her the rooked towers seemed to be groping toward her through the dusk. Beyond the castle, the sea glimmered like iron. (p. 82)

Later, when the Red Bull returns to the castle after having been thwarted in its attempt to capture the unicorn to put it with its fellows, 'The horns had become the two sharpest towers of old King Haggard's crazy castle' (p. 107). The many towers of the castle all slant at peculiar angles, and the whole resembles 'one of those odd trees that grow with their roots in the air' (p. 115). The cliff on which the castle stands 'dropped like a knife blade to a thin yellow shore, frayed bare over green and black rocks. Soft, baggy birds squatted on the rocks, snickering, "Saidso, saidso"' (p. 115).

---

* Peter S. Beagle, *The Last Unicorn: A Fantastic Tale* (The Bodley Head, 1968) p. 20. Page references are to this edition.

It is possible to see a single theme running through the book – namely, that of reality versus illusion, and the recovery of magical powers from apparently total decline into decrepitude: through helping the unicorn, Schmendrick the failed magician finds his magical powers enormously increased; and by going to the aid of her fellows, the unicorn sends back into the world much of the wonder and glory it has lost. In other words, the story can to some extent be seen as portraying the search for 'being', 'identity' and wonder which are the essence of fantasy itself. Other episodes, such as Mommy Fortuna's Midnight Carnival or the encounter with the sham outlaws, Captain Cully and his crew (pp. 51–72) would belong here. Yet there is an impression that the author is trying to say too many things for one theme to be clearly present. There is much about the prophecies relating to Haggard and his castle (pp. 86–96), and much too concerning the love of his son Prince Lír for the unicorn when it has been transformed into a woman by Schmendrick, none of which is related to this theme. Even the account of the unicorns is not *closely* related to that of decrepitude – for they are real but imprisoned, where the other figures are run-down and seedy.

Most of the book is not powerfully felt or presented. There may be no potent theme because none has been strongly and lastingly apprehended by the author: it is all in the end a shade theoretic, sustained only by a few flashes of wonder and the odd really striking image. For most of the book one has the impression that Beagle is waiting in the hope that his language and story will catch fire. The description of the meeting with the outlaws (ch. v) is long-winded, clichéd and strained, as too is that of the discourse with the inhabitants of the town of Hagsgate before the approach to Haggard's castle (ch. vii), or the long period of inactivity while the questers are within (punctuated only by the insubstantial and overpitched love-affair between Prince Lír and the woman-unicorn). Several times, for example, there is portrayal of Captain Cully's wish to believe himself a great and legendary outlaw in the face of the petty reality, and after ten pages on the subject the reader is presented with a passage saying all this as though it was novel information (p. 69). It seems symbolic of the book that for much of the time the wizard Schmendrick at the centre of the story has lost all save the most trivial of his powers of magic; or that the unicorn, disguised for most of the story, is seeking the lost wonder of its fellows; or that the essence of the unicorn is elusive beauty; or that one of the basic images of the story, from the cages of Mommy Fortuna to the unicorns locked in the sea, is that of imprisoned glory.[18]

Yet like those who try to catch the unicorn, Beagle must keep trying to trap his inspiration, veering as he does so between intensity and limpness. One can feel the strain behind this descriptive passage:

> So they journeyed together, following the fleeing darkness into a wind that tasted like nails. The rind of the country cracked, and the flesh of it peeled back into gullies and ravines or shriveled into scabby hills. The sky was so high and pale that it disappeared during the day, and the unicorn sometimes thought that the three of them must look as blind and helpless as slugs in the sunlight, with their log or their dank rock tumbled away. But she was a unicorn still, with a unicorn's way of growing more beautiful in evil times and places. Even the breath of the toads that grumbled in the ditches and dead trees stopped when they saw her.
>
> Toads would have been more hospitable than the sullen folk of Haggard's country. Their villages lay bald as bones between knifelike hills where nothing grew, and they themselves had hearts unmistakably as sour as boiled beer. (p. 81)

The wind that 'tasted like nails' is too much of a conceit. The concept of the landscape as flesh peeling back is meant to give an impression of the withered nature of the country round Haggard's domain, yet it only succeeds in calling attention to itself as metaphor; the return to it in the picture of the villages 'bald as bones between knifelike hills' seems a gratuitous piling of conceit upon conceit. The notion of hearts 'unmistakably as sour as boiled beer', as if it were to be taken seriously, simply falls over itself. The idea of the sky being so high and pale that it disappears is successful in conveying vacancy; yet the image of the travellers being like slugs is quite inapt apart from the aspect of their helplessness, and the author goes on to deny its applicability to the unicorn who grows more beautiful in evil places. All the time the reader is aware of the author making efforts to bring off a coup with his imagery.

Another basic weakness of the book is the frequent failure to grasp personality. The unicorn, for instance, does not really exist in the story as a creature of any character. The first external description is the best there is:

> The unicorn lived in a lilac wood, and she lived all alone. She was very old, though she did not know it, and she was no longer the careless colour of sea foam, but rather the colour of snow falling on a moonlit night. But her eyes were still clear and unwearied, and she still moved like a shadow on the sea.
>
> She did not look anything like a horned horse, as unicorns are often pictured, being smaller and cloven-hoofed, and possessing that oldest, wildest grace that horses have never had, that deer have only in shy, thin imitation and goats in dancing mockery. Her neck was long and slender, making her head seem smaller than it was, and the mane that fell almost to the middle of her back was as soft as dandelion fluff and as fine as cirrus. She had pointed ears and thin legs, with feathers of white hair at the ankles; and the long horn above her eyes shone and shivered with its own seashell light even in the deepest midnight. She had killed dragons with it, and healed a king whose poisoned wound would not close, and knocked down ripe chestnuts for bear cubs. (p. 3)

The reader may not be very sure what grace horses have never had that deer have slightly and goats only as mockery, but the rest is quite vivid, particularly the account of her as smaller than a horse, and with cloven hooves. Her various doings with her horn are the kind of lively touch in which Beagle is often proficient: it begins to give some sense of her as a creature. For the rest of the book, however, she is left simply as a fastidious, rather cold animal. It seems significant that almost the first thing Beagle does with her is put her in a circus where there will be a whole collection of other wondrous animals in company with which she may gain an identity peculiarly her own. More significant still, perhaps, is the later magical transformation of her into a woman, the Lady Amalthea, for by these means she is brought to fall in love with Prince Lír and to show human warmth. Even though the relationship fails to convince, the fact that Beagle did this at all suggests that he felt that she was in some way lacking. Without a real grasp of, or relationship with, her as a character, Beagle in the end sentimentalises her:

> She turned a little away from him [Schmendrick], and the sudden starlight of her shoulders made all his talk of magic taste like sand in his throat. Moths and midges and other night insects too small to be anything in particular came and danced slowly around her bright horn, and this did not make her appear foolish, but them most wise and lovely as they celebrated her. (p. 213; see also p. 201)

At the same time Beagle has become morally explicit. The people of Hagsgate are told at the end, '"You may plant your acres again, and raise up your fallen orchards and vineyards, but they will never flourish as they used to, never – until you learn to take joy in them, for no reason"' (p. 210).

The same failure of grip is seen in the other characters, apart from Mommy Fortuna and possibly King Haggard. Molly Grue, the outlaw woman, is a theoretic figure with far too much spiritual insight for her supposed condition. When she sees the unicorn she drops a ludicrous curtsy to it, then approaches it and blames it for not coming to her earlier in her life: '"*Where have you been?*"'; '"How dare you, how dare you come to me now, when I am *this?*"' (pp. 73, 74). Here the unicorn is seen by her as the beauty she never had; but it all sounds rather melodramatic and overpitched. When Schmendrick opposes her coming with him and the unicorn, her face 'closed like a castle against him, trundling out the guns and slings and caldrons of boiling lead'; and when at this the unicorn makes a soft sound, 'the castle of Molly's face lowered the drawbridge and threw wide even its deepest keep' (p. 75): the author is trying to make us find her funny, but the absurd imagery simply loses touch with her. And so she continues with Schmendrick and the unicorn, a shadowy figure tending on a shadowy creature. As for Schmendrick there is a real attempt to portray a character who has grown both vain and despairing, serious and absurd with the weakness of his magic powers (see for example pp. 75–6, 83, 85, 102–6, 150–1): yet the book so continually shows the reader these characteristics, and not very brilliantly, that they lose force. Everyone in the book talks too much and says the same thing several times, as though trying to get it right once and for all: the birds that squat on the beach below Haggard's castle saying '"Saidso, saidso"' over and over again seem to symbolise this. The failure of grasp on material and characters alike seems imaged itself in the way that Schmendrick's usual magic leaves no lasting impression on the minds of its beholders (pp. 49–50).

There is a constant sense of isolation. Like Schmendrick's magic again, the author's imagination works only in solitary bursts. The creatures in Mommy Fortuna's Midnight Carnival are alone in their cages; the people of Hagsgate have avoided coming together to have children; the unicorn is essentially solitary – 'all alone' as the first sentence of the book has it – and is the more alone for being for most of the book the last unicorn. The relationship between the Lady Amalthea and Prince Lír ends when the former becomes a unicorn once more. Thus when the author tries to tell a story, create characters and build relationships he seems to be going against the grain of his own interests: his book thereby becomes largely the product of inaccurate feeling and falls into excess – of emotion, of explanation, of description and of length.[19]

The sources of the anaemic character of the work of Morris, Dunsany, Eddison and Beagle that we have traced are authorial self-indulgence; self-consciousness; uncontrolled love of the wondrous; lack of dialectic and conflict; avoidance of the harsh facts of pain, loss, ugliness and evil; and unacknowledged brevity of inspiration. All these authors, in common with other writers of fantasy, are concerned to celebrate being, but they lack restraint in doing so. This is not to say that the others are always free of these failings (the reader may think, for instance, of Tolkien), but they do not become so dominant as they are in these authors. Nor is it to deny the works considered here merit: Dunsany and Eddison write very gripping narratives imbued with some real flights of imagination. But it is to say that they do not have the tone of realism, or the character of reality, without which fantasy becomes at best shallow and delusive escapism. It is unfortunate for the literary standing of fantasy that the kind of work produced by these writers should so often be taken as characteristic of the genre.

9   Conclusion

The obverse of the praise of the identity of things in fantasy is detestation of whatever restricts or reduces being. In traditional fairy tales, where the theme is more implicit, an enchantment which has turned a prince or princess into some ugly or hostile being, such as a frog or a lion, or has confined someone to a tower or a hundred-year sleep, has to be reversed. In Kingsley's *The Water-Babies*, the result of evil acts is specifically portrayed as a reduction of being: because Tom eats sweets and becomes nasty-tempered, he grows prickles all over himself: because they were self-indulgent, the race of the Doasyoulikes degenerated to apes and finally died out; had Tom not gone on his journey to the Other-end-of-Nowhere, he would have devolved from a water-baby to an eft in a pond.

The shadow in MacDonald's *Phantastes* withers the life of things by turning the wondrous to the apparently commonplace or vulgar. Most of the 'right' deeds of Anodos in that story are the release of people from confinement, into living reality – the white lady from her alabaster block and from her invisibility in the fairy palace, the country from the giants and the congregation of worshippers in the forest from their ignorant servitude. His wrong acts consist of trying to possess or take over being – the child's fairy globe, the white lady repeatedly. A similar repugnance at that which tries to subdue all things to the self is seen in the struggles against magicians portrayed in Charles Williams's novels. C. S. Lewis's White Witch or his Un-man, Tolkien's Sauron, Peake's Steerpike, Beagle's King Haggard, are all evil in trying to enslave the being of others. The central theme of Lewis's *Perelandra* is giving the self willingly into God's hand rather than taking things to the self (symbolised in the contrast between the floating islands and the forbidden Fixed Land). The Ring in Tolkien's *The Lord of the Rings* makes the people who wear it desire to subdue others to their will while it subdues them to its own: Frodo's quest is to dispossess himself of the Ring, destroy the spreading tyranny of Sauron and restore their individual freedoms to the variety of races in Middle-earth. Here as in most fantasy evil is portrayed as the reverse or denial of being, nonentity: Sauron and the Nazgûl are shadows or wraiths. In Ursula Le Guin's 'Earthsea' trilogy the desire of self to aggrandise itself at the expense of others causes evil – whether in the form of the evil shadow of himself that Ged releases in his urge to show himself a powerful mage in *A Wizard of Earthsea*, or in the subjugation of Arha to the service of the Nameless Ones in the dark labyrinth in *The Tombs of Atuan*, or in the desperation of the mage Cob to live forever, even by destroying all other being, in *The Farthest Shore*.

In the opinion of Tolkien, human perception itself can be an evil, in that it enslaves its objects by making them familiar to the point where their identity ceases to be noticed: 'We say we know them. They have become like the things which once attracted us by their glitter, or their colour, or their shape, and we laid hands on them, and then locked them in our hoard, acquired them, and acquiring ceased to look at them.'[1] Fantasy, however, can reverse this by conferring magical life: 'Creative fantasy . . . may open your hoard and let all the locked things fly away like cage-birds. The gems all turn into flowers or flames, and you will be warned that all you had (or knew) was dangerous and potent, not really effectively chained, free and wild; no more yours than they were you.'[2]

Although fantasy delights in things as they are, it is not in itself an unchanging literary kind. While it may not have become more sophisticated over the past century, it has altered in character: for instance, Victorian fantasy is more overtly moral, and tends to deal with the individual, where twentieth-century fantasy (at least since the work of E. R. Eddison) has been more 'epic' in character, viewing the hero in the context of a larger society – whether of Earth, Mercury, Perelandra, Middle-earth, Gormenghast, Watership Down, Gramarye or Earthsea. Nevertheless – and it is curious when one considers how individual is the world of each fantasy – there is a very definite and constant character to fantasy, and in nothing is it perhaps so markedly constant as in its devotion to wonder at created things, and its profound sense that that wonder is above almost everything else a spiritual good not to be lost.

Notes

Unless otherwise stated, place of publication is London.

PREFACE

1. For a full account, see C. N. Manlove, *Modern Fantasy: Five Studies* (Cambridge University Press, 1975) ch. 1.
2. J. R. R. Tolkien, *Tree and Leaf* (Allen and Unwin, 1964) p. 53.
3. C. S. Lewis, *Miracles: A Preliminary Study* (Bles, 1947) pp. 79–81.
4. Charles Williams, 'The Way of Affirmation', *The Image of the City and Other Essays*, ed. Anne Ridler (Oxford University Press, 1958) p. 157.
5. Williams, 'Natural Goodness', *The Image of the City*, p. 78.
6. See on this Manlove, *Modern Fantasy*, pp. 32–8.
7. *Tree and Leaf*, pp. 48–9.

CHAPTER 1: INTRODUCTION

1. Novalis, *Schriften*, ed. P. Kluckhohn and R. Samuel (Stuttgart: Kohlhammer, 1960–68) III, 377 # 620, 438 # 883, 454 # 986. See also p. 449 # 940.
2. Op. cit., p. 136, col. i; cited in Gillian Avery, with Angela Bull, *Nineteenth Century Children: Heroes and Heroines in English Children's Stories 1780–1900* (Hodder and Stoughton, 1965) pp. 41–2.
3. E. L. Griggs (ed.), *The Collected Letters of Samuel Taylor Coleridge*, vol. I (Oxford: Clarendon Press, 1956) pp. 346–8. See also pp. 352–5 for Coleridge's account of the debt of his imagination to fairy tales.
4. For accounts of the development of the fairy tale in England, see Florence V. Barry, *A Century of Children's Books* (Methuen, 1922); F. J. H. Darton, *Children's Books in England*, rev. ed. (Cambridge University Press, 1958); M. F. Thwaite, *From Primer to Pleasure: An Introduction to the History of Children's Books in England, from the Invention of Printed Books to 1900* (Library Association, 1963); Avery, op. cit., chs. 2, 6.
5. Lewis, 'Sometimes Fairy Stories May Say Best What's to be Said' (1956) repr. in Lewis, *Of Other Worlds, Essays and Stories*, ed. W. Hooper (Bles, 1966) pp. 36–7.
6. Margaret Hunt, trans. and ed., *Grimm's Household Tales* (George Bell, Bohn's Standard Library, 1884) II, 181 (tale no. 133).

7. De La Mare, *Told Again* (Oxford: Basil Blackwell, 1927) pp. 97–8.
8. The source of this point is T. S. Eliot's contrast between Shakespeare and Jonson in his 'Ben Jonson' (1919), repr. in his *Elizabethan Dramatists* (Faber, 1962) p. 74.
9. It must be said that in certain cases the Grimms themselves embellished, as for example in the account of how the whole court fell asleep in 'Little Briar-Rose' (Hunt, no. 50). See on this Max Lüthi, *Once Upon a Time: On the Nature of Fairy Tales*, trans. L. Chadeayne and Paul Gottwald, with additions by the author (New York: Frederick Ungar Publishing, 1970) pp. 26–9.
10. Hunt, no. 122.
11. See also the behaviour of the fox in 'The Golden Bird' (Hunt, no. 57).
12. Hunt, no. 64.
13. Hunt, no. 29.
14. On the possible source of this predilection in the early social code of *Jüngsten Recht* or primogeniture, which led to the repression of youngest by elder siblings and thus to popular sympathy for the former, see *Perrault's Popular Tales*, ed. Andrew Lang (Oxford: Clarendon Press, 1888) introd., pp. xcvi–xcviii.
15. Hunt, no. 63.
16. Hunt, no. 88.
17. Hunt, no. 50.
18. This story is not in Hunt. It appears in the first English translation of Grimm, *German Popular Stories*, trans. Edgar Taylor, 2 vols (1823, 1826). There is a note on the tale at vol. ii, 252, 'The usual excrescence is a horn or horns; not as here, "nasus, qualem noluerit ferre rogatus Atlas".'
19. Thackeray owed the idea of a living metal doorknocker to E. T. A. Hoffmann's *The Golden Pot* (1814): see *The Best Tales of Hoffmann*, ed. E. F. Bleiler (New York: Dover Publications, 1967) p. 21.
20. That is, he made the boots magically adjust their size to suit the wearer. In a similar manner he made the newly wakened princess in his 'The Sleeping Beauty' aware that she was a hundred years behind the fashion.
21. *The Rose and the Ring* is in part indebted to Fielding's *Tom Thumb the Great* (1731).
22. See on this Manlove, *Modern Fantasy*.

CHAPTER 2: CHARLES WILLIAMS

1. Williams, *He Came Down from Heaven and The Forgiveness of Sins* (Faber, 1950) p. 121.
2. Ibid., p. 34. This aphorism also appears in Browning's 'Easter Day', sect. iv; it may originate in Plato, *Timaeus*, 53b ff.
3. Williams, *Collected Plays* (Oxford University Press, 1963) p. 31.
4. Williams's ideas may be traced in his *The Descent of the Dove: A Short History of the Holy Spirit in the Church* (Longmans, 1939); *The Figure of Beatrice: A Study in Dante* (Faber, 1943); *He Came Down from Heaven and The Forgiveness of Sins*; and *The Image of the City and Other Essays*. For a comprehensive account of them, see Mary M. Shideler, *The Theology of Romantic Love: A Study in the Writings of Charles Williams* (New York: Harper and Bros., 1962).
5. This phrase is from the dedication to *The Descent of the Dove*.

6. Williams, 'The Cross', *The Image of the City*, p. 138.
7. See e.g. *The Greater Trumps*, pp. 39–40, 61–2, 157–60; *The Place of the Lion*, p. 27; *Descent into Hell*, pp. 16–17; *All Hallows' Eve*, pp. 151–2.
8. Williams, 'Natural Goodness', *The Image of the City*, p. 78.
9. *He Came Down from Heaven*, p. 97.
10. See e.g. *He Came Down from Heaven*, pp. 25, 102–3; *War in Heaven*, p. 137; *Collected Plays*, pp. 160–1.
11. Williams, 'The Figure of Arthur', in *Arthurian Torso: Containing the Posthumous Fragment of The Figure of Arthur by Charles Williams and a Commentary on the Arthurian Poems of Charles Williams by C. S. Lewis* (Oxford University Press, 1948) p. 80.
12. Williams, *Taliessin through Logres* (Oxford University Press, 1938) p. 44.
13. Williams, *Collected Plays*, p. 298; 'John Milton', *The Image of the City*, p. 30.
14. Williams, *Reason and Beauty in the Poetic Mind* (Oxford: Clarendon Press, 1933) pp. 181–2.

CHAPTER 3: URSULA LE GUIN

1. On the use of the word 'mage' rather than 'magician' in the trilogy, see T. A. Shippey, 'The Magic Art and the Evolution of Words: Ursula Le Guin's Earthsea Trilogy', *Mosaic*, x, 2 (Winter, 1977) 147–50.
2. And his mage-tutor Ogion tells Ged that '"Mastery is nine times patience"' (*WE*, p. 28).
3. On acceptance, see also *FS*, pp. 36, 130, 147.
4. Compare Tolkien on 'Recovery' as an essential feature of fantasy, in his *Tree and Leaf*, pp. 51–3.
5. Particularly reminiscent is that in the last: see *The Collected Ghost Stories of M. R. James* (Edward Arnold, 1942) pp. 355–6.
6. See also her 'Science Fiction and Mrs. Brown', in Peter Nicholls (ed.) *Science Fiction at Large* (Gollancz, 1976).
7. Compare Shippey, pp. 154–6, 157–8.
8. See e.g. *WE*, pp. 52–3 (magical and 'natural' boat-handling), 55–6 (magical hide-and-seek), 58–60 and 88 (on the pet otak and its hunting of mice in the grass). Typical is the compound of 'A mage's name is better hidden than a herring in the sea, better guarded than a dragon's den' (p. 83).

CHAPTER 4: E. NESBIT

Abbreviations used (additional to those in text):

BVSL   Nesbit, *Ballads and Verses of the Spiritual Life* (Elkin and Mathews, 1911)
LL1   ——, *Lays and Legends* (Longmans, 1886)
LL2   ——, *Lays and Legends, Second Series* (Longmans, 1892)
MV   ——, *Many Voices, Poems* (Hutchinson, 1922)
PV   ——, *A Pomander of Verse* (J. Lane, 1895)
RR   ——, *The Rainbow and the Rose, Poems* (Longmans, Green, 1905)

1. Op. cit., new ed. (Faber, 1962) p. 148.
2. Op. cit. (Faber, 1945) p. 76.
3. Charles Kingsley, *Madam How and Lady Why, or, First Lessons in Earth Lore for Children*, new ed. (Macmillan, 1879) p. 145.
4. That is, when she was aged between 42 and 55. She had as many publications – if most of them were hack-work – before this period as during it, so that she had a long apprenticeship; though little of it hinted at the imaginative powers in reserve.
5. See e.g. Frank Eyre, *20th Century Children's Books* (Longmans, Green, 1952) p. 12; 'What Makes a Good Book?' *TLS* (23 Nov. 1956) p. 1, col. iii; Marcus Crouch, 'The Nesbit Tradition', *Junior Bookshelf*, xxii, no. 4 (Oct. 1958) 195; Anthea Bell, *E. Nesbit* (The Bodley Head, 1960) pp. 12–13.
6. The 'method' of Anstey's fantasies generally involves the comic impact of the supernatural on everyday life. In *Vice Versa*, the mind of a thoughtless and heartless father is made to change places with that of his son: the father goes in his son's body to the boarding school of which the boy has complained and learns all too painfully that his misery was well-founded; and meanwhile the son ruins his father's business. In *The Tinted Venus* a statue of the goddess Venus comes to life and attempts to win the love of a Victorian hairdresser from his fiancée, first by clumsy guile and later by force. *The Brass Bottle* describes a genie called Fakrash who is accidentally released from a brass bottle by a poor London architect, whose affairs suffer thereafter from the eagerness of the genie to please. Both Nesbit and Anstey expressed their admiration for each other's work (Moore, p. 194). Nevertheless Anstey differs from E. Nesbit in two ways: he does not write from a child's point of view, and he does not use rules and logic in his fantasy.
7. First published in Anstey, *The Talking Horse and Other Tales* (Smith, Elder, 1892); repr. in Anstey, *Paleface and Redskin, and Other Stories for Boys and Girls* (Grant Richards, 1898).
8. E. Nesbit, *Wings and the Child, or, The Building of Magic Cities* (Hodder and Stoughton, 1913) p. 20. See also pp. 3, 74; and letter of 10 Dec. 1913, quoted in Moore, p. 280.
9. It is a strange fact, however, that E. Nesbit often lacked sympathy with her own children: see on this Moore, pp. 43, 146–7, 219–20, 258–62.
10. Moore, pp. 73–7. On E. Nesbit's earlier schools, see Nesbit, 'My School-Days', *The Girl's Own Annual*, xviii (1896–7) 28, 106.
11. For some of these see 'My School-Days', pp. 375, 575, 635–6, 711, 788; Moore, p. 39.
12. See Moore, p. 68; Noel Streatfeild, *Magic and the Magician, E. Nesbit and Her Children's Books* (Ernest Benn, 1958) p. 22.
13. Moore, pp. 105, 111, 114, 126, 147, 156, 237–8, 239; the last describes how at Dymchurch 'E. Nesbit had been known in earlier years to cycle down to the sea front in a billowing garment bearing some resemblance to a tea-gown, and even now she could be seen holding conversation with the Vicar from a seat on her rain-barrel, her long quill cigarette holder between her lips, or walking about arm-in-arm with the humble woman who did her housework.' Nevertheless E. Nesbit followed the *sexual* conventionalism her husband preached: she opposed the Women's Suffrage movement, even

introducing, in the Pretenderette of her *The Magic City* (1910), a direct mockery of it (Moore, pp. 266–7).

14. A daughter *c.* 1889, and a son in 1899 (Moore, pp. 130–1, 184–5).

15. Moore, pp. 114, 126, 147, 150.

16. This despite limitations as a mathematician (Moore, pp. 248–52).

17. See *Wings and the Child*, p. 91 for the first five of these authors; and letter of March 1884, quoted in Moore, p. 106.

18. Moore, pp. 160–1, 163, 175, 193–4, 228, 248. She was one of the first to recognise E. M. Forster's talent.

19. Moore, pp. 143, 211. On her difficulties in inventing plots, see Moore, p. 109.

20. Moore, pp. 240–7. It proved too costly, and ended with the fourth number.

21. See for example her 'precious' *A Pomander of Verse* (1895), or the picture of the dragon curled about the North Pole in her 'The Ice Dragon, or, Do As You Are Told', *BD*, p. 131.

22. Streatfield, op. cit., p. 21.

23. Williams knew at least E. Nesbit's *The Story of the Amulet*: see the entry in his Commonplace Book of 1912–16, quoted in Williams, *The Image of the City and Other Essays*, p. 171.

24. The crows in 'Justnowland' are an exception to this rule: they were once human beings and were warned '"that if we didn't behave well our bodies would grow like our souls. But we didn't think so. And then all in a minute they *did* – and we were crows, and our bodies were as black as our souls. Our souls are quite white now"' (*MW*, p. 193). E. Nesbit may have taken this idea of moral (d)evolution from Kingsley or MacDonald.

25. Op. cit., 2nd ed. (Blackie, 1888) pp. 56, 76.

26. MacDonald, *Orts* (Sampson Low, 1882) pp. 41, 278–9.

27. Similarly with the discovery of the mermaid in a fairground in *Wet Magic* (1913), or the many 'accidents' of the shorter fairy tales.

28. This story is based directly on the method of Anstey's *Vice Versa*; as also is 'The Twopenny Spell' (*OBO*).

29. Op. cit., rev. ed. (Methuen, 1930) pp. 71, 70.

30. E. Nesbit is careful to give a more historical reason which would equally explain the discovery – Mr Tresham's letter to his uncle Lord Monteagle, revealing the plot. But of course the reader is not to *know* that by itself this would have been sufficient to unmask the conspiracy: and Elfrida, who inadvertently 'gave the game away', certainly feels guilty at her betrayal (*The House of Arden* (T. Fisher Unwin, 1908) pp. 206, 212, 212–13).

31. *SA*, pp. 33, 34, 44 (where the reader is told that it weighed 'about three pounds and a quarter'), 128, 175–7, 202, 229, 266.

32. Respectively, 'The Ring and the Lamp' (*OBO*); 'The Charmed Life; or, The Princess and the Lift-Man' (*OBO*); 'Billy the King' (*OBO*); 'Justnowland' (*MW*); 'The Princess and the Hedge-Pig' (*MW*); 'Septimus Septimusson' (*MW*); 'The Cockatoucan' (*NUT*).

33. This is not so much the case in the shorter magic tales, where the emphasis tends to be much more on the almost rococo possibilities of magic rather than on its interaction with real life. The bulk of these stories in fact take place wholly within fairylands.

34. *The Magic City* (Macmillan, 1910) pp. 54–5. Similarly the dragon the

children have to destroy as one of their tasks as saviours of the city is '"the clockwork dragon that had been given ... [to Philip] the Christmas before last"' (p. 121); the waiters at the victory banquet are matches and the food itself is made of wood (pp. 137–42); and the terrible carpet the children have to unravel is '"a little crochet mat I'd made of red wool"' as Lucy explains, and all they have to do is find the end and pull (p. 155).

35. E. M. Forster particularly liked this story of all those in *NUT* (Moore, p. 271).

36. Indeed this junction of time is at once the object of the search and the method of the book. Thus the past is made often as familiar as the present, as, for example, when a Babylonian queen talks with unaffected familiarity (*SA*, pp. 141, 144–59). This 'marriage' can be accomplished in other ways, as in the episodes where Anthea presents a 'Lowther Arcade bangle' to a Stone Age girl; Caesar is taught how guns work by means of cap-pistol; Pharoah is entertained by the 'magic' of striking matches; and the Phoenician captain Pheles steers his ship by night using Robert's shilling compass (*SA*, pp. 83, 251, 270, 277, 338).

37. 'The Will to Live' (*RR*, p. 15). See also 'Tekel' and 'Absolution' (*LL1*, pp. 1–17, 119–33); 'A Tragedy' (*LL2*, pp. 81–3); 'At the Gate', 'The Monk' and 'Earth and Heaven' (*BVSL*, pp. 7–14, 15, 71–8).

38. 'The Will to Live' and 'The Star' (*RR*, pp. 13–15, 89–90).

39. 'Here and There' (*LL2*, pp. 55–6). See also 'August' (*LL1*, pp. 142–4); 'London's Voices' (*BVSL*, pp. 97–8); 'Saturday Song' (*MV*, pp. 33–4). Contrast, however, 'Town and Country' and 'The Choice' (*PV*, pp. 80, 85).

40. See 'Lullaby' (*LL2*, pp. 51–2); 'Magnificat', 'Evening Prayer' (which rejects the notion of a transcendent and 'other' God) and 'The Three Kings' (*BVSL*, pp. 19–20, 21, 30–3); 'Mary of Magdala' (*MV*, pp. 60–1).

41. See 'Lullaby' (*PV*, p. 17); 'Two Lullabies', 'Baby Song' and 'Mother' (*LL2*, pp. 45–8, 49–50, 57); 'Mother Song' and 'Death' (*RR*, pp. 69–70, 137–8); 'The Crown of Life', 'Evening Prayer' and 'Submission' (*BVSL*, pp. 17–18, 21, 101); 'From the Portuguese – II', 'In Trouble' and 'The Mother's Prayer' (*MV*, pp. 68–9, 74–5, 88–91).

42. This was reprinted as 'Inasmuch As Ye Did It Not' in *BVSL*, pp. 102–5 and *MV*, pp. 91–4.

43. Unpublished poem of 1902, quoted in Moore, p. 196.

44. *LL2*, p. 111.

45. Moore, p. 134. See also p. 268, 'she was superstitious to an extreme degree'.

46. E. Nesbit, 'My School-Days', *The Girl's Own Annual*, xviii (1896–7) 314, col. iii.

47. For others see 'My School-Days', pp. 184, 264–5.

48. E. Nesbit's first extant prose composition, written when she was six or seven, was a story set in Rome, about Mira, daughter of Agrippa and Claudia, who discovers a secret meeting of Christians in an underground cavern, the corridor leading to the cavern being lined 'with dead bodies'. The manuscript broke off shortly after this point (Moore, pp. 79–80).

49. *Fear* contains thirteen horror tales, five of which are reprints from the seven in *Grim Tales*. *Man and Maid* and *To the Adventurous* have only scattered tales of terror.

50. This story originated in a visit of E. Nesbit's to the grisly wax-work show in

the Musée Grévin in Paris in 1905 (Moore, p. 236).

51. Both of these stories appeared in *Man and Maid*.

52. Her biographer remarks: 'Her horror stories were probably more disturbing to her than to her readers. They fail to capture the emotions that she is so palpably bent upon arousing, for the same reason that an actor will fail to capture the emotions of his audience when he is so much moved by his part that he loses control of it. The terrors she wrote of were all actively her own. A great many of the stories, for example, concern cataleptic trances and premature burial – a subject which it always distressed her to contemplate; yet she never succeeded in conveying the fear which she is known to have felt herself' (Moore, pp. 236–7).

53. There the fun is often generated by bringing together reality and children's illusions about life.

54. Marcus Crouch, *Treasure Seekers and Borrowers, Children's Books in Britain, 1900–1960* (Library Association, 1962) p. 15.

55. Which makes quite strange her biographer's statement that 'She was seldom either precise or logical in her mode of thinking' (Moore, p. 272).

56. On her would-be imitators, see Marcus Crouch, 'The Nesbit Tradition', *Junior Bookshelf*, xxii (October 1958) 195–8.

CHAPTER 5: GEORGE MACDONALD

1. For the present writer's previous accounts of these works, see Manlove, *Modern Fantasy*, pp. 71–2, 75–9. There they are treated more as expressions of MacDonald's ideas and beliefs than in their own right; and are identified rather more than contrasted.

2. C. L. Dodgson's *Alice* books, though dream-like, are informed with dream-logic as MacDonald's fantasies are not. Dodgson was, it should be said, on terms of close friendship with the MacDonald family.

3. *Phantastes* has many similarities with Novalis's *Heinrich von Ofterdingen* (1802) and with Hoffmann's tale, the latter of which MacDonald had been re-reading in 1856 with great admiration (Greville MacDonald, *George MacDonald and his Wife* (Allen and Unwin, 1924) pp. 259, 297–8).

4. George MacDonald, *Orts* (Sampson Low, 1882) pp. 24, 25. For a critical account of MacDonald's thought on the imagination, see *Modern Fantasy*, pp. 60–71.

5. MacDonald, 'The Fantastic Imagination' (1893), repr. in MacDonald, *A Dish of Orts: Chiefly Papers on the Imagination, and on Shakspere* (Sampson Low, 1893) p. 319.

6. *George MacDonald and His Wife*, p. 548.

7. For these, see particularly MacDonald, 'The Imagination: its Function and Development', *Orts*, pp. 1–42, and 'The Fantastic Imagination', op. cit., pp. 319–22. For some appraisal, see *Modern Fantasy*, pp. 64–71.

8. For a full account, see *George MacDonald and his Wife*; a more critical view is offered in *Modern Fantasy*, pp. 55–60.

9. On the lack of change in MacDonald's vision and thought, see *George MacDonald and his Wife*, p. 403; and, more critically, in relation to the ideas in the novels, Robert L. Wolff, *The Golden Key: A Study of the Major Fiction of*

George MacDonald (New Haven: Yale University Press, 1961) p. 305.

10. For some account of this in relation to *Phantastes*, see *Modern Fantasy*, pp. 75–9.

11. See particularly Carl G. Jung, *Symbols of Transformation* (2nd ed., 1970), *The Archetypes and the Collective Unconscious* (2nd ed., 1969), *Aion: Researches into the Phenomenology of the Self* (1959), *Psychology and Alchemy* (2nd ed., 1968) and *Mysterium Coniunctionis: An Inquiry into the Separation and Synthesis of Psychic Opposites* (1963) – respectively vols 5, 9 Parts i and ii, 12 and 14 of *The Collected Works of C. G. Jung*, trans. R. F. C. Hull, 20 vols (Routledge & Kegan Paul, 1957–79), and cited here as *ST, ACU, AI, PA* and *MC*. On mothers, see *ST*, pp. 207–393 and *ACU*, pp. 75–110; on water, trees and caves, *ST*, pp. 218–22, 274, and *ACU*, p. 135; on mirrors, *PA*, pp. 108, 110, 111; on sun and moon, see esp. *MC*, pp. 92–110, 129–46, 173–83; on the Shadow, *ACU*, pp. 20–2 and *AI*, pp. 8–10; on the anima, *ACU*, pp. 27–30, 54–72 and *AI*, pp. 11–22.

12. On devouring mother see Jung, 'The Dual Mother', *ST*, pp. 306–93. Lilith is portrayed as a child-devourer in the Cabbala – see *The Jewish Encyclopaedia*, ed. Isidore Singer, 12 vols (New York: Funk and Wagnalls, 1901–6), s.v. 'Lilith'; and *The Zohar*, ed. Harry Sperling and Maurice Simon, 5 vols (Soncino Press, 1949) i, 60, 82–3.

13. See E. T. A. Hoffmann, *The Golden Flower Pot*, trans. Thomas Carlyle (1827), repr. in *The Best Tales of Hoffmann*, ed. E. F. Bleiler, pp. 4–5, 31–2.

14. Compare Vane's feeling at the end of *Lilith*, 'It may be … that, when most awake, I am only dreaming the more!' (p. 420).

15. See pp. 27, 35, 37, 55, 59, 164.

16. Some preparations may be made *for* one, such as '*The Chamber of Sir Anodos*' that the hero finds in the fairy palace (p. 76), or Anodos's part in the battle with the giants (pp. 149–50).

17. This to some extent reverses the present writer's earlier view, in *Modern Fantasy*, pp. 75–8, that the two elements are opposed and express a division in MacDonald's creative purpose.

18. See also the epigraph (from Jean Paul Richter) to ch. 28 (p. 125): '"From dreams of bliss shall men awake/One day, but not to weep:/The dreams remain; they only break/The mirror of the sleep."'

19. In September 1895, shortly before the publication of his *The Wonderful Visit* (1895), H. G. Wells wrote to MacDonald remarking the coincidence of their independent use of the notion of travel into or from dimensions beyond the three that we know. Both, however, may have been recalling the speculations of A. Square [pseud. of Edwin A. Abbott], *Flatland: A Romance of Many Dimensions* (1884). Wells went on to say: 'Your polarization and mirror business struck me as neat in the extreme': it may be that this was a partial source for his *The Invisible Man* (1897). (Letter quoted in Greville MacDonald, *Reminiscences of a Specialist* (Allen and Unwin, 1932) pp. 323–4.)

20. On this see also Jung, *PA*, loc. cit., citing Schopenhauer.

21. This expresses MacDonald's benign determinism – on which see *Modern Fantasy*, pp. 60–2.

22. On this see also Jung, *ST*, Part ii, chs 4–6, respectively entitled 'Symbols of the Mother and of Rebirth', 'The Battle for Deliverance from the Mother'

and 'The Dual Mother'. Significantly the next chapter and stage is called 'The Sacrifice' (pp. 394–440) and can clearly be paralleled in Anodos's final sacrificial death – see esp. pp. 414–15 on the 'unconscious compulsion' of the child-state.

23. Cf. Jung, *ACU*, pp. 177–9, 'The Child as Beginning and End'. Jung declares that

the 'child' symbolizes the pre-conscious and the post-conscious essence of man. His pre-conscious essence is the unconscious state of earliest chidhood; his post-conscious essence is an anticipation by analogy of life after death. In this idea the all-embracing nature of psychic wholeness is expressed. Wholeness is never comprised within the compass of the conscious mind – it includes the indefinite and indefinable extent of the unconscious as well (p. 178).

24. This is done by Vane's burying Lilith's now severed evil hand at a certain point in the desert sand of the dried-up watercourse.

25. See MacDonald, ''Σπεα ''Απτερα, *Unspoken Sermons, Second Series* (Longmans, Green, 1885) pp. 21–2.

26. The walls also vanish by moonlight (pp. 160–1).

27. See also p. 158, where on approaching the last forest Anodos finds an unarmed youth 'who had just cut a branch from a yew growing on the skirts of the wood'.

28. *George MacDonald and his Wife*, p. 482; see also pp. 348, 349–51. MacDonald also uses the stair-symbol in his 'The Golden Key' (1867), *The Princess and the Goblin* (1872) and *The Princess and Curdie* (1883).

29. MacDonald, *England's Antiphon* (Macmillan, 1874) p. 56. See also MacDonald, ''Σπεα ''Απτερα, *Unspoken Sermons* (Strahan, 1867) p. 196, 'The whole system of the universe works upon this law – the driving of things upward towards the centre.'

30. MacDonald, ''Σπεα ''Απτερα, *Unspoken Sermons, Third Series* (Longmans Green, 1889) pp. 91–2.

31. For further account of man's God-given true name or signature, see *Unspoken Sermons* (1867) pp. 105–7.

32. Cosmo reflects, ' "how many who love never come nearer than to behold each other as in a mirror; seem to know and yet never know the inward life; never enter the other soul; and part at last, with but the vaguest notion of the universe on the borders of which they have been hovering for years?" ' (p. 99).

33. This may explain why *Phantastes* lends itself more to a Freudian, and *Lilith* to a Jungian reading: see Wolff, op. cit., and Roderick F. McGillis, 'The Fantastic Imagination: The Prose Romances of George MacDonald', University of Reading Ph.D. Thesis (1973), respectively.

34. *Orts*, p. 4. See also MacDonald, *A Book of Strife in the Form of The Diary of an Old Soul* (Allen and Unwin, 1882), July 18, 'not that thou thinkest of, but thinkest me'.

35. Op. cit. (Hurst and Blackett, 1863) vol. III, p. 194.

36. See e.g. pp. 44–5, 71, 72, 78, 127, 129–30, 166.

37. It is difficult to understand R. F. McGillis's claim in his 'George

MacDonald – the *Lilith* Manuscripts', *Scottish Literary Journal*, vol. 4, no. 2 (Dec. 1977) 56, that 'MacDonald clearly intended to avoid ... direct references to God' in order to encourage us 'not to read *Lilith* as a Christian document, as many readers do'.

38. On relative translucency, see pp. 36, 44, 53, 137.
39. Incorporation in rather than rejection of the Shadow by the self is seen as the key to psychic wholeness by Jung: see e.g. *ACU*, pp. 20–2.
40. *Unspoken Sermons, Second Series*, p. 169.

1. A useful account of the nineteenth-century development of the medieval revival is Alice Chandler, *A Dream of Order, The Medieval Ideal in Nineteenth-Century English Literature* (Routledge & Kegan Paul, 1971) – useful apart from the contention that the dream ends with Henry Adams's *Mont-Saint-Michel and Chartres* (1913).
2. See e.g. White, *Gone to Ground* (Collins, 1935) pp. 33–4; *England Have My Bones* (Collins, 1936) p. 225.
3. White, *The Scandalmonger* (Cape, 1952) p. 218.
4. Quoted in W. J. Weatherby, 'The Lion of Alderney', *Manchester Guardian* (20 Apr. 1961) p. 9.
5. 'Parfit Gentil Knyght', *Time*, LXXII (8 Sept. 1958) 65.
6. White, *Farewell Victoria* (Collins, 1933) p. 19.
7. *England Have My Bones*, p. 225.
8. White owed a considerable literary debt to Swift: a particular instance is his development of the history of the Lilliputians in his *Mistress Masham's Repose* (New York: G. P. Putnam's Sons, 1946).
9. See Tolkien, 'On Fairy Stories', *Tree and Leaf*, p. 52.
10. *England Have My Bones*, p. 12.
11. Ibid., pp. 5, 6.
12. Four books – *The Sword in the Stone, The Queen of Air and Darkness, The Ill-Made Knight* and 'The Candle in the Wind' – make up *The Once and Future King*: the first three of these were originally published, respectively, by Collins in 1938 and by G. P. Putnam's Sons in New York in 1939 and 1940; 'The Candle in the Wind' was composed as a play in 1938, but was rejected. The original title of the second book was *The Witch in the Wood*: both this and the original *The Sword in the Stone* were considerably modified to conform with the demands of the epic – the first with episodes taken from an unpublished fifth book, 'The Book of Merlyn' (written in 1940), which White originally proposed until his publisher Collins's refusals discouraged him altogether. Almost from the outset White had intended a total account of Arthur: he first offered the whole five books under the title *The Once and Future King* to Collins in 1941; by 1948 he had dropped the fifth book; and in 1957 he finished his final revision. See Sylvia Townsend Warner, *T. H. White, A Biography* (Cape, 1967) pp. 98, 122, 175–90, 242, 272.
13. White is to be found trying to discover how armour worked, and what it was like to wear it, in a letter of 10 June 1939, written before he embarked

on *The Ill-Made Knight* (quoted in Warner, pp. 126–7).

14. White, *Burke's Steerage, or, The Amateur Gentleman's Introduction to Noble Sports and Pastimes* (Collins, 1938) p. 130. See also *England Have My Bones*, p. 259.
15. *The Scandalmonger*, p. 218.
16. *Farewell Victoria*, p. 19.
17. White, *The Book of Beasts* (Cape, 1954) p. 247.
18. In its concern with how things work, however, its literary kinship is as much, say, with Virgil's *Georgics* as with the *Idylls* of Theocritus.
19. Manlove, *Modern Fantasy*, pp. 180–90.
20. Cowper, 'Yardley Oak', ll. 80–5. See also Cowper's view of change in *The Task*, I, 367ff.
21. White, 'The King', *Loved Helen and Other Poems* (Chatto and Windus, 1929) p. 36.
22. White, *The Goshawk* (Cape, 1951) pp. 82, 83.
23. Letter of 4 Feb. 1940, quoted in David Garnett (ed.), *The White/Garnett Letters* (Cape, 1968) p. 57.
24. *The Goshawk*, pp. 60–1.
25. *Farewell Victoria*, pp. 240–1.
26. See e.g. the manner of the passage describing the construction of a castle, or the accounts both of the Wart's actual transformation into a fish and of his subsequent life under water, in *The Once and Future King*, pp. 37, 41–8. More generally, White's love of detail, his clarity, his passion for outdoor sports, his amateur's enthusiasm and his reverence for tradition and order, are very reminiscent of Kingsley.
27. *England Have My Bones*, p. 79.
28. Warner, pp. 182–3.
29. White said of the original version, 'It is more or less a kind of wish-fulfilment of the things I should have liked to have happened to me when I was a boy' (letter of 14 Jan. 1938, quoted in Warner, p. 98).
30. Letter of 28 June 1939, quoted in Warner, p. 130.
31. For full accounts of all Arthur's strategies and their effects, see *The Once and Future King*, pp. 254–5, 272–3, 450, 455–8, 504, 508, 666–7, and letter of 8 June 1941, quoted in Garner, p. 86.
32. White seems to have found something analogous to such a state in America, during a lecture tour he made there late in 1963, just before his death: this visit is enthusiastically recorded in his *America at Last, The American Journal of T. H. White* (New York: G. P. Putnam's Sons, 1965).
33. *England Have My Bones*, p. 228.
34. Ibid., p. 240.
35. Ibid., p. 239.
36. Compare the account of White's start at writing the Tristram story, under the title of 'The Sad One', in 1959: there King Mark is White himself, and Tristram, the lover of King Mark's wife La Beale Isoud, is a fictional version of a boy called Zed with whom White had fallen in love; on this see Warner, p. 286. Contrast this with White's contemptuous account of Tristram in *The Once and Future King*, pp. 525, 599.
37. This issue is touched on only at pp. 383 and 456, and there very indirectly.
38. White himself was a self-confessed sadist. See Warner, p. 310 and Garnett, p. 8.

39. White did owe much of this to Ray, David Garnett's wife, and particularly to her suggestion that he learn about the creation of female characters by reading the Russian novelists (Garnett, p. 69). See White's letter of 10 Oct. 1939, quoted in Warner, pp. 150–2, grappling with the character of Guenever.

40. One should recall, however, that with this passage he was in substance following Malory – though given his freedom with Malory's interpretations there was no need for him to have done so –

> But nowadayes men cannat love sevennyght but they muste have all their desyres. That love may nat endure by reson, for where they bethe sone accorded and hasty, heete sone keelyth. And ryght so faryth the love nowadayes, sone hote sone colde. Thys ys no stabylyté. But the olde love was nat so. For men and women coude love togydirs seven yerys, and no lycoures lustis was betwyxte them, and than was love, trouthe and faythefulnes. And so in lyke wyse was used such love in kynge Arthurs dayes. (*The Works of Sir Thomas Malory*, ed. E. Vinaver (Oxford University Press, 1954) p. 791).

41. There is no need to look to White's homosexuality here: this is a plain analysis of sexual difference to which many people would assent.

42. In this sense it is fitting that the last book should end 'THE BEGINNING'.

43. Mordred is a type of the annihilating wind, shortly to be considered.

44. Garner, pp. 153–4.

45. Vinaver, *Malory* (Oxford: Clarendon Press, 1929) p. 84.

46. *Hamlet*, iv, vii, 114ff.

47. 'The Candle in the Wind' was not extensively altered from its original dramatic form when converted into prose narrative; but to conclude, as does John K. Crane in his *T. H. White* (New York: Twayne Publishers, 1974) pp. 112–13, that the resultant lack of the backcloth that has been present in the other books makes this one, with its emphasis on a few figures only, slightly incongruous, is to miss the point.

48. Quoted in Warner, p. 117. The geese, and the passage on the wind, were originally set in the unpublished final volume 'The Book of Merlyn' (finally brought out by the University of Texas Press in 1977), where Arthur learns the answer to his and humanity's problems through a discussion with Merlyn and a number of animals, and through two visits, one to the geese, and the other to a nation of ants. It is clear from its recurrence that the 'wind' passage represented a moment of vision, and it is significant that White should have been drawn first to place it at the original pedal point of his epic, amidst the 'happier' discoveries of the close. Exactly the same might be said of his treatment of Arthur's experience of the ants (this episode was also transposed to the first book): the ants are utterly mindless, living without any feeling or individuality in soulless dictatorships; they are a picture for Arthur of how society should not be lived, but they are also for White a vision of the nonentity which drew him even while it repelled.

49. John Moore, quoted in Warner, p. 94.

50. Ibid., p. 93.

51. The nearest folk analogue the present writer has found for this is a Marathi proverb from Bombay, India, cited in Stith Thompson and Jonas Balys,

The Oral Tales of India, Indiana University Publications, Folklore Series, x (Bloomington, Indiana, 1958) M382 (citing as source A. Manwaring, *Marathi Proverbs* (Oxford: Clarendon Press, 1899) p. 211): 'Futile moving to avoid death. Man told by Death he will die where he stands sells everything and moves to another town. He goes for a ride on a mare which runs away with him and throws him on the spot he so dreads, killing him.' White's parents lived in Bombay, though he himself was sent to school in England in 1911, when he was five: it is not impossible that he heard the tale, or a modification of it. It does not appear in the *Arabian Nights* or in the likely medieval and Renaissance collections – the *Gesta Romanorum,* Boccaccio's *Decameron,* Straparola's *Nights,* Basile's *Pentamerone* – nor in Chaucer or Edgar Allan Poe.

52. White, *The Green Bay Tree, or, The Wicked Man Touches Wood* (Songs for Sixpence, No. 3) (Cambridge: Heffer, 1929) ll. 20ff.
53. This is the approach of Rosemary Jackson, *Fantasy: The Literature of Subversion* (Methuen, 1981) esp. ch. 6.

CHAPTER 7: MERVYN PEAKE

1. On this in these authors see Manlove, *Modern Fantasy.*
2. Shakespeare, *Coriolanus,* I, i, 113. The whole of Menenius's fable of the mutinous parts of the body (I, i, 94ff.) and the frequent images of dissociated limbs in this play are an illuminating parallel with the theme in *Titus Groan.*
3. *Modern Fantasy,* pp. 230–47.
4. Ibid., pp. 247–9.
5. Ibid., pp. 253–4.
6. Ibid., p. 256. Compare also the behaviour of Flay when exiled (*TG,* pp. 442–3).
7. For an interesting sidelight on this, in regard to Peake's interest in broken vases, see Colin Greenland, 'The Smashing of the Central Vase', *Mervyn Peake Review,* no. 4 (Spring 1977) 27–9.
8. See *Modern Fantasy,* pp. 249–50.
9. Maeve Gilmore [Mrs Peake], *A World Away: A Memoir of Mervyn Peake* (Gollancz, 1970) p. 106.
10. *Modern Fantasy,* pp. 217–30.

CHAPTER 8: MORRIS, DUNSANY, EDDISON, BEAGLE

1. *The Collected Works of William Morris,* ed. May Morris (Longmans, Green, 1910–15) xvii, 34–5.
2. *Works,* I, 255.
3. See also *Works,* I, pp. 206–8, 215–16, 245–8, 257–8, 322–3.
4. See e.g. *Works,* xx, 23–7.
5. *Works,* I, 207, 245, 257–8.
6. Charlotte H. Oberg, *A Pagan Prophet: William Morris* (Charlottesville: University of Virginia Press, 1978) ch. 7. Robert Currie, 'Had Morris Gone

Soft in the Head?', *Essays in Criticism*, 29 (1979) 350–2, argues that some of this, particularly the frequent portrayal of tyrannical and promiscuous women, stems from Morris's feelings about the relationship between his wife and Dante Gabriel Rossetti.

7. *Works*, xvii, 79, 112–14; xx, 15–18, 240–2.
8. See also the Shakespeare sonnet (no. 116) quoted as epigraph to Eddison's *The Mezentian Gate* (1958).
9. Eddison, *Mistress of Mistresses: A Vision of Zimiamvia* (Faber, 1935) pp. 22–3.
10. Ibid., p. 27.
11. Ibid., p. 448.
12. Eddison, *The Mezentian Gate* (Plaistow: Curwen Press, 1958) p. xii.
13. Ibid., pp. xii–xiii.
14. Eddison, *A Fish Dinner in Memison*, new ed. (Pan/Ballantine, 1972) Letter of Introduction, pp. xix, xxiii–xxiv.
15. Ibid., pp. xxvi, xxvii.
16. See also the closing chapter of *The Mezentian Gate*, entitled 'Omega and Alpha in Sestola'.
17. See Manlove, *Modern Fantasy*, pp. 177–90. Actually, Tolkien's work is quite heavily indebted to Eddison's – on which see *Modern Fantasy*, pp. 157, 285–6.
18. See also the song on being imprisoned in one's skin at pp. 78 and 160.
19. See also Brian Attebery, *The Fantasy Tradition in American Literature: From Irving to Le Guin* (Bloomington, Indiana: Indiana University Press, 1980) pp. 158–9.

CHAPTER 9: CONCLUSION

1. Tolkien, *Tree and Leaf*, p. 52.
2. Ibid., p. 53.

Index